# Mainstreaming Palestine

# MAINSTREAMING PALESTINE

## Cinematic Activism and Solidarity Politics in the United States

**Umayyah Cable**

MINNESOTA

University of Minnesota Press
*Minneapolis*
*London*

The University of Minnesota Press gratefully acknowledges the generous assistance provided for the publication of this book by the University of Michigan Office of Research and College of Literature, Science, and the Arts.



Chapter 3 was previously published in a different form as "An *Uprising* at *The Perfect Moment*: Palestine in the 1990s Culture Wars," *GLQ* 26, no. 2 (April 2020): 243–72.



Published by the University of Minnesota Press
111 Third Avenue South, Suite 290
Minneapolis, MN 55401-2520
http://www.upress.umn.edu

ISBN 978-1-5179-1995-5 (hc)
ISBN 978-1-5179-1996-2 (pb)

Library of Congress record available at https://lccn.loc.gov/2025008148

Printed in the United States of America on acid-free paper



UMP BmB 2025

Dedicated to my mom, Layla
a.k.a. *jabal al-nar*

What we must again see is this issue involving representation, an issue always lurking near the question of Palestine.

—Edward Said, *The Question of Palestine,* 1979

# Contents

# Preface

This book was initially sent out for peer review in September 2023, several weeks ahead of Israel's genocidal (and ongoing as of this writing) attack on Gaza, which accelerated on October 7, 2023. After four agonizing months of watching through the screen of online social media as my people were being annihilated, in January 2024 I received a rejection from a prominent university press. I was ready to quit. What was the point of anything anymore in the face of such horror, in the face of such apathy to horror, and worse yet, in the face of outright support for such horror? During those four months and in the months following rejection, I also watched as the facets of the argument in this book unfolded before my eyes at every turn. This, dear reader, did not help things, as it required resisting the urge to tear the whole manuscript apart to account for the contemporaneous examples of my argument.

No book is perfect. Certainly, there will be those on both the left and the right who will, to put it lightly, disagree with the claims in this book. Indeed, I too am ambivalent about some of those claims. But it is my ethical responsibility as a scholar to listen to, acknowledge, and represent my research findings, no matter my own fraught feelings about them. When I realized the overall argument of this book and its resultant title, I shuddered at the implications. Where, when, and how I grew up, "mainstream" was a dirty word. It was a word that implied, at best, erasure of difference, and at worse, violent conformity. From an early age I was acutely aware of how my Palestinian identity, my gender nonconformity, and my queer sexuality relegated me as an outsider. I did not belong in, nor did I desire to be a part of, the mainstream. The relentless bullying I experienced as a child and adolescent—about my name, about my Palestinianness, and about my gender deviance—reminded me daily that I was not welcome in the mainstream even if I had desired to be part of it.

What I did desire, though, was for the burden of narration to be lifted from me. Every introduction ("What does your name mean?") turned into an interrogation ("Oh, you're Palestinian? Do you hate Jews?"), or a teach-in ("Where is Palestine? Wait, don't you mean Pakistan?"), or an outright attack ("You're a terrorist! You're an anti-semite!"). For this reason, there were vast periods of my youth that I spent as a loner. In my teen years, I filled that lonesomeness with cinema, voraciously watching as many independent and international films as possible (shout-out to the legendary video rental institution formerly in Cambridge, Massachusetts: Hollywood Express, RIP).

Cinema has always been a solace for me, offering comfort amid alienation. I think it has also been a comfort for many of the actors in this book, serving to relieve both that burden and that lonesomeness. It makes total sense to me, then, why cinema has emerged as a mobilizing agent for Palestinian liberation and solidarity activism in the United States. Cinematic activism is not only a method for advancing Palestinian liberation and solidarity politics; it is also a balm for the alienation many have experienced as either Palestinians or supporters of Palestinian liberation. As I write this preface in late summer of 2024, the student intifada movement has swept the United States by storm and been met with horrific, draconian state violence. Despite these attempted repressions, the student intifada persists. I find solace there, too, as students now are doing what felt impossible to me as a student twenty years ago. Despite some of the pitfalls of mainstreaming analyzed in this book, I hope, dear reader, that you will be able to remember that sense of solace that I and so many others have found through engagements with cinematic activism.

*Umayyah Cable*
Ypsilanti, Michigan
August 2024

# Abbreviations

AAUG: Association of Arab American University Graduates
ADC: American Arab Anti-Discrimination Committee
ADL: Anti-Defamation League
AIPAC: American Israel Public Affairs Committee
AMPAS: Academy of Motion Picture Arts and Sciences
BAAQUP: Bay Area Art Queers Unleashing Power
BDS: Boycott, Divestment, and Sanctions
BIPOC: Black, Indigenous, and/or People of Color
BPFF: Boston Palestine Film Festival
FHAO: Facing History and Ourselves
HFPA: Hollywood Foreign Press Association
ICA: Institute of Contemporary Art, Boston
ICJ: International Court of Justice
JDL: Jewish Defense League
LGBTQ+: Lesbian, Gay, Bisexual, Transgender, Queer/Questioning, Plus
MECA: Middle East Children's Alliance
MFA: Museum of Fine Arts, Boston
PBS: Public Broadcasting Service
PFLP: Popular Front for the Liberation of Palestine
PLO: Palestine Liberation Organization
QUIT!: Queers Undermining Israeli Terrorism!
SAG: Screen Actors Guild
SAG-AFTRA: Screen Actors Guild–American Federation of Television and Radio Artists
SWANA: Southwest Asia and North Africa

# Introduction

*Beware the Palestine Solidarity Culture Industry*

On March 10, 2024, five months into Israel's accelerated genocidal onslaught against the Palestinian people of Gaza,[1] English filmmaker Jonathan Glazer ascended the stage at the 96th Academy Awards ceremony in Los Angeles, California, to accept an Oscar for his film *The Zone of Interest* (2023). At once historical drama and psychological thriller, *The Zone of Interest* recasts the story of the Auschwitz concentration camp in German-occupied Poland as not simply a genocidal project, but a project of settler colonialism as well. Standing at the microphone, a sheet of paper trembled in his hand as he read a prewritten speech to a live television audience of 19.5 million US viewers:

> All our choices were made to reflect and confront us in the present, not to say look what they did then, rather look what we do now. Our film shows where dehumanization leads at its worst. It's shaped all of our past and present. Right now we stand here as men who refute their Jewishness and the Holocaust being hijacked by an occupation which has lead to conflict for so many innocent people. Whether the victims of October the [interrupted by applause] . . . Whether the victims of October the 7th in Israel or the ongoing attack on Gaza, all the victims of this dehumanization, how do we resist? Aleksandra Bystroń-Kołodziejczyk, the girl who glows in the film, as she did in life, chose to. I dedicate this to her memory and her resistance.[2]

Unlike Vanessa Redgrave, who was met with boos and hisses upon delivering a speech critical of Zionism at the Oscars in 1978, Glazer was met with applause and cheers. And although Hollywood Zionists later condemned Glazer in an open letter, the supportive reception of

Glazer's speech during the 2024 Oscar ceremony is an indication of how a shift in the discourse on Palestine has taken place within Hollywood and US culture more broadly over the past fifty years.

Shortly after the Academy Awards, Glazer, along with numerous other actors and filmmakers from Europe, the United States, and the Southwest Asia and North Africa (SWANA) region,[3] donated items and experiences for an online silent auction fundraising campaign, Cinema for Gaza, which fundraised for the UK charitable organization Medical Aid for Palestinians. The silent auction featured things such as posters for *The Zone of Interest* signed by Glazer, producer James Wilson, and composer Mica Levi; video conference calls with Susan Sarandon, Tilda Swinton, and Ayo Edebiri; musician Annie Lennox's handwritten lyrics to "Sweet Dreams"; and a poster for the film *Joker* (2019) signed by Joaquin Phoenix, among various other kinds of cinephilic memorabilia and experiences. Some of those experiences also included opportunities to rub elbows with Palestinian filmmakers or own a piece of Palestinian cinephilic memorabilia, such as signed movie posters, a visit on set with Palestinian filmmaker Annemarie Jacir; a personalized masterclass on filming in Palestine with Palestinian filmmaker Najwa Najjar, and a limited edition *Only Murders in the Building*–themed jigsaw puzzle signed by the show's Palestinian American director Cherien Dabis and the show's lead cast members Steve Martin, Martin Short, and Selena Gomez. Altogether, the Cinema for Gaza campaign raised over US$315,000 for Medical Aid for Palestinians, exemplifying what I refer to as *philanthro-spectatorship,* which is one of the key facets of *cinematic activism,* a theoretical and practical framework I explore throughout this book.

I begin with this contemporary Academy Awards anecdote because it encapsulates the tensions, promises, and pitfalls of the process of "mainstreaming" interrogated throughout this book. *Mainstreaming Palestine: Cinematic Activism and Solidarity Politics in the United States* historicizes this decades-long process of "mainstreaming" a discourse on Palestinian liberation and solidarity politics within a US culture dominated by hegemonic Zionism.[4] That mainstreaming, I argue, is the result of fifty years of cinematic activism, a social movement organizational strategy that takes the texts, practices, and social relations of cinema as the focal point for movement mobilization and communication. Through visual, semiotic, and discursive analysis of film, video, print news, and archival material, and participant observation and ethnographic interviews at film festivals, this book employs an interdisciplinary methodology to explore how Palestinian cinema and Palestine solidarity cinema and their dissemination through cinematic activism have produced—literally, figuratively, cinematically, and discursively—Palestinian liberation and solidarity politics in the US public sphere. Through these processes, the topic of Palestine has shifted from one of taboo and unspeakability to inclusion within liberal multiculturalism, and has ultimately begun a process of normalization within the US mainstream.

In the wake of October 7, 2023, as Palestinians in Gaza were disseminating visual evidence of the genocide globally—practically in real time—through social media apps such as Instagram, TikTok, and X (formerly Twitter), the discourse on Palestinian liberation and solidarity politics consumed mainstream US media, popular culture, and electoral politics in unprecedented and enduring ways. Largely driven by students, the rapid uptick in Palestinian liberation and solidarity activism that swept the United States during the 2023–2024 academic year came to be known as the "student intifada."[5] Palestinian liberation and solidarity activism mobilized on an unprecedented mass scale in the United States, literally bringing business as usual to a halt, whether in occupying university administrative buildings, shutting down freeways and major thoroughfares in numerous major US cities, or slashing Starbucks's market value by $11 billion through a consumer boycott.[6]

The surge in popular support for the Palestinian liberation struggle from fall 2023 to the present and its accompanying visibility within mainstream US media is evidence of a shift in US public opinion that was well underway prior to October 7, 2023.[7] This shift in public opinion and media representation is remarkable given how Palestinians and the Palestinian liberation struggle have historically been demonized and negatively portrayed in US popular media such as film, television, and news reportage. Public expressions of sympathy toward Palestinians and willingness to disseminate, let alone even acknowledge, Palestinian liberation politics have, until recently, been considered taboo and even unspeakable within the US public sphere. This unspeakability originates in hegemonic support for the state of Israel, which has historically permeated US culture and institutions in ways that mediate or proscribe the discourse on Palestine, erase Palestinian existence, and discipline and censor Palestinian liberation and solidarity activism—a discursive process I refer to as *compulsory Zionism.* Not so long ago, even mentioning the word "Palestine" in social interactions or within film, media, or fine art would prompt an avalanche of censure, oftentimes resulting in ostracism—a phenomenon referred to by Palestine Legal, the US-based Palestine solidarity movement's civil and constitutional rights watchdog organization, as "the Palestine exception to free speech."[8] Of course, these attempts at censure have persisted even during this rapid increase in Palestinian liberation and solidarity activism in the US public sphere. But as this book shows, there has indeed been a realm in which the discourse on Palestinian liberation and solidarity has consistently been able to subvert such attacks. That realm is cinema.

What is different in the wake of October 7 is the ways in which mainstream news and entertainment media have covered the actions and messaging of the various groups that make up the contemporary Palestinian liberation and solidarity movement within the United States.[9] Through this increased coverage of the movement, mainstream news outlets have started to disseminate key points and political analysis from the movement itself. Take, for example, MSNBC news anchor Ali Velshi's five-minute news spot from December 2023 on the American Israel Public Affairs Committee, in which he details the committee's influence on US domestic and foreign policies primarily through things such as financial contributions to congressional and presidential campaigns, candidate endorsements, and television and internet campaign commercials. Or take this March 2024 example from *The Hollywood Reporter,* one of the leading film and entertainment industry daily magazines, wherein the headline reads: "Free Palestine March Set for Los Angeles Ahead of Oscars: 'No Awards During a Genocide.'" Or this one from *The New York Times*: "Some Oscar Attendees Delayed by Protesters Calling for Cease-Fire in Gaza." Or this one from the UK daily newspaper *The Guardian*: "Oscars Kick Off Behind Schedule as Pro-Palestine Protesters Delay Stars' Arrival." The very fact that the phrases "Free Palestine" and "Pro-Palestine" appear in these headlines or that a mainstream cable news network would feature a critical analysis of the Zionist lobby's influence on US politics is remarkable given the kind of censorship of Palestinian liberation politics within popular news and entertainment media as historicized throughout this book. The mainstream media coverage of both the genocide and the activism in opposition to it offers a contemporaneous example of the shift from taboo to normalization in the discourse on Palestinian liberation politics in US media and popular culture.

I use the word *normalization* intentionally throughout this book. The term primarily refers to the 1979 Egypt-Israel peace treaty, which states "signatories shall establish among themselves relationships normal to states at peace with one another."[10] Within the context of Palestinian liberation and solidarity activism, the term now refers to people, states, and organizations that ignore Israel's political and human rights atrocities and treat it as a "normal" entity rather than as a rogue state. A key facet of the Boycott, Divestment, and Sanctions (BDS) movement is "anti-normalization," which stresses "the importance of refusing to acknowledge the Israeli regime as an entity entitled to normal relations."[11] My use of the term *normalization* with respect to Palestinian liberation and solidarity politics is meant to signify how increased normalization of Palestinians and their liberation struggle coincides with decreases in normalization of Zionism and Israel. Examples of the denormalization of Israel in the wake of October 7 include things like Samsung Next, the innovation branch of the Korean technology and electronics company Samsung, pulling its operations out of Israel, and the suspension of talks and indefinite collapse of a $2 billion deal that would have resulted in the United Arab Emirates' Abu Dhabi National Oil Company and the United Kingdom's British Petroleum buying a 50 percent stake in Israel's biggest natural gas company, NewMed Energy.[12]

This shift is evident in other forms of entertainment media as well. Within the past few years, for example, Netflix—one of the most mainstream sources of entertainment available in the United States—has both created a "Palestinian Stories" streaming category and produced the television series *Mo,* created by Palestinian American comedian Mohammed Amer. In an Instagram post about the significance of a show like *Mo* on a platform as big as Netflix, Palestinian American Emmy-nominated film and television writer, director, and actress Cherien Dabis, who plays Mo's sister on the show, asserted that *Mo* is "making us one step closer to 'rebranding' Palestine!"[13] In her post, Dabis also thanked the show's production company, A24, a prominent independent film and television production and distribution company in the United States (which I discuss in greater detail in chapter 4). Dabis's use of the nomenclature of "branding" is significant here because it speaks to the ways in which film, television, and media have been crucial to the production of solidarity with the Palestinian liberation cause. My conceptualization of the discursive process of mainstreaming is informed by scholars such as Evelyn Alsultany, Roderick Ferguson, Sarah Banet-Weiser, and Roopali Mukherjee, who have theorized and historicized the relationships between social justice activism, representation, consumerism, and the rise of what we now refer to as diversity, equity, and inclusion (DEI).[14] More specifically, mainstreaming is akin to Sarah Banet-Weiser's conceptualization of branding, wherein "a brand exceeds its materiality. More than just the object itself, a brand is the perception—the series of images, themes, morals, values, feelings, and sense of authenticity conjured by the product itself."[15] But mainstreaming has also been driven by an ongoing, decades-long dialectic struggle between Palestine-focused cinematic activism, a social movement strategy that uses film and media production, exhibition, circulation, and spectatorship to advance Palestinian liberation and solidarity politics within US culture, and the hegemonic discourse of compulsory Zionism that seeks to naturalize and privilege Israel's subjugation and erasure of Palestine and Palestinian existence.

I employ an interdisciplinary methodology entailing visual, semiotic, and discursive analysis of film, video, print news, and archival material, along with participant observation and ethnographic interviews at film festivals. This methodology has been critical to charting the dialectical push and pull that has ultimately brought us to this contemporary moment wherein knowledge about the Palestinian liberation struggle has become intelligible to more general US publics and entered the US mainstream cultural and political discourses, for better or worse. Over the last fifty years, a diverse array of people, namely activists, artists, and allies from overlapping Arab American communities, LGBTQ+ communities, and Jewish anti-Zionist communities, along with scholars specializing in Palestine studies and Arab American studies, Palestinian filmmakers and Palestine solidarity filmmakers, and film and media workers alike have together organized to leverage cinema in order to produce knowledge, identify subjects, and articulate objectives of Palestinian liberation politics for

US audiences and media consumers. That organizing has manifested in numerous ways, from one-off film screenings to mobilizing protests and boycotts of cinema institutions that are complicit in Palestinian oppression, and through more institutionalized means such as establishing film-specific organizations for the distribution of Palestinian cultural representation and the establishment of annual Palestine-themed film festivals. These cinematic activists have periodically been met with resistance or censorship on the part of supporters of compulsory Zionism, who aim to undermine, erase, or censor Palestine-focused cinematic activism. In turn, these cinematic activists, who desire to transcend the struggle with Zionism toward a politics of Palestinian liberation, self-determination, and self-representation, respond with new forms of resistance.

There are also pitfalls to this project of cinematic activism. Indeed, cinematic activism has two sides: the texts and practices of cinema-based social movement organizing and political education on the one hand, and the aestheticization and commodification of activism *as* cinema itself, on the other hand. This book therefore will demonstrate how, within a media context largely dictated by global capitalism, the mainstreaming of Palestinian liberation politics has had mixed results: increased visibility, intelligibility, solidarity, but also aestheticization and commodification. The aestheticization of activism and the symbolism of Palestinian liberation (most notably the watermelon, which represents the colors of the Palestinian flag) has itself been commodified and rendered as a form of cinema. Highly stylized videos and advertising campaigns representing, romanticizing, and *selling* that activism and symbolism have become just another product to be consumed within the culture industry. Not unlike how the LGBTQ+ rights movement (which also historically leveraged cinematic activism to advance its cause) was aestheticized and commodified into what is now commonly referred to as "rainbow capitalism," the Palestinian liberation and solidarity movement in the context of global capitalism is currently undergoing a similar and rapid process of aestheticization and commodification. The result, as explained in greater detail in the book's conclusion, is a simulation of solidarity: watermelon capitalism. This commodification is a solemn reminder not to mistake representation for liberation, nor to mistake mainstreaming for justice, but rather to strategize the uses of representation in the ongoing processes of liberation. A practice of cinematic activism, not unlike most other social movement methods, must always negotiate a number of these kinds of intellectual, political, and even ethical tensions.

## Compulsory Zionism and the Political Queerness of Palestine

The study of cinema affords a uniquely rich site for understanding how and why compulsory Zionism is hegemonic in the United States and in turn understanding how and why the expression of Palestinian identity and politics have historically been disciplined in the US context, including attempts to censor Palestinian cinema. Compulsory Zionism is a theoretical concept through which to analyze the confluence of racial, ethnic, and sexual politics that haunt and animate Palestinian liberation and solidarity politics in the United States. The phrase refers to Adrienne Rich's concept of *compulsory heterosexuality,* which sees heterosexuality as compulsory because it constitutes an institution that is "forcibly and subliminally imposed."[16] Erella Shadmi made this link to Rich's work and put forth the phrase *compulsory Zionism* in the 1990s to describe cultural hegemony within Jewish Israeli society of the 1950s and 1960s as "an uncompromising demand, enforced by means of a wide range of methods, to adopt the values, attitudes, and behaviors prescribed by Zionist ideology."[17] Shadmi's critique is also indebted to the work of Ella Shohat, who historicized how Zionism functions to produce a racially disciplined Israeli society that privileges white, European cultural norms over Arab, Mizrahi culture while also repressing Palestinian perspectives.[18] Shadmi thus likened Zionism to heteronormativity. Within such a framing, Arab subjectivity—both Mizrahi and Palestinian—emerges as *politically queer,* in need of either discipline and assimilation or denigration and abjection.

Here the phrase *politically queer* does not serve as a marker of sexual or gender identity, but as a signifier of coalitional leftist politics and a subject position of radical abjection. Cathy Cohen argues that the term *queer* and the politics that follow from it must not be limited to gender and sexual identity categories but must contend with a variety of nonnormative and marginal subject positions that must include a multiplicity of vectors, particularly race and class. Cohen conceptualizes *queer* in intersectional terms in order to hail a form of *politics* designed as a leftist political framework that "makes central the interdependency among multiple systems of domination."[19] Gil Hochberg, in writing on the sexual politics of Palestine and Israel, has used the term *queer* to refer to "a body of politics dedicated to the queering of the political as such . . . and as a verb, questioning normative articulations of the political and the very processes by which we determine the scope of what counts as political."[20] In *Possible Histories: Arab Americans and the Queer Ecology of Peddling,* Charlotte Karem Albrecht points out how American Orientalist ideas about Arab racial categorization and sexuality have historically been informed by Eurocentric notions about the relationship between sexual normativity and whiteness.[21] As such, Palestinian racialization (and Arab racialization more broadly) in the United States is always already queer within the context of US white supremacist culture. In *Queer Terror: Life, Death, and Desire in the Settler Colony,* C. Heike Schotten offers a telling reminder of the biopolitical and necropolitical stakes of queerness as a category of abjection, writing that "queerness functions as a lever of classed, racialized, and nationalized exclusion, with the results that some populations, whether 'queer' or 'queered,' become either dead or disposable, either killable or eligible for targeted killings."[22] In this context, Palestinians, whose lives are "understood as threatening, as 'terrorist,' as requiring reflexive condemnation, destruction, and murder" again inhabit a queer subject position.[23] *Queer,* in other words, stands as both an adjective—marking bodies, issues, desires, and so forth as abject and terrifying—and as a verb, radically reconfiguring the meaning of "political" and the parameters of "politics."

I take up Cohen, Hochberg, Karem Albrecht, and Schotten in their theorizations of queerness as a way to illustrate the positionality of Palestinian liberation politics vis-à-vis compulsory Zionism. To reiterate, when I refer to Palestinian liberation and solidarity politics as politically queer, I do so not to delineate nonnormative sexualities and/or genders but to signify, as Cohen calls for, a subject position of radical alterity and a politics of resisting the dominant norms of compulsory Zionism and all its accompanying heterosexism and homonormativity.

My intervention with regard to "compulsory Zionism" lies through an expansion of the concept's applicability. While Shadmi was concerned with Zionism's effects on Jewish-Israeli society, my application is much broader in terms of understanding how Zionism operates transnationally and on a variety of subjects, both Palestinian and non-Palestinian. I consider Zionism compulsory in the context of the United States in that it constitutes a discourse of support for the state of Israel that has been forcibly and subliminally imposed on a number of representational, institutional, and political levels. This understanding is informed by Nadine Naber, Eman Desouky, and Lina Baroudi, who have outlined how, within the US context, Zionism constitutes "a politically organized racial project that directly and systemically targets Arabs and Arab-Americans."[24] Michael Omi and Howard Winant define a racial project as "an interpretation, representation, or explanation of racial dynamics, and an effort to reorganize and redistribute resources along particular racial lines."[25] As such, I assert that compulsory Zionism is invested in interpreting, representing, and explaining Israel and Palestine in ways that reorganize and redistribute political solidarities and social movement aims along racial and ethnic lines, and that privilege certain racial, ethnic, and sexual minority groups over others.

The concept of compulsory Zionism also helps us to understand the specificity of anti-Palestinian racism. Not simply reducible to a more general notion of anti-Arab racism, anti-Palestinian racism is predicated on the privileging and enforcement of Zionism at all costs. Indeed, the history of the phrase "compulsory Zionism," which pre-dates Shadmi, reveals how the very concept of compulsory Zionism is deeply rooted in European antisemitism and racist desires to eradicate Jewish populations from Europe.[26] The idea of compulsory Zionism has transformed over time from one of antisemitic, white, European racial supremacy, and Jewish eradication, to one of ethnocracy, Zionist supremacy, and Palestinian eradication. Put succinctly, anti-Palestinian racism is the love child of European antisemitism and political Zionism, and it is through compulsory Zionism that anti-Palestinian racism is enacted.

To be clear, this book does not argue that discourse on and representations of Palestine have been absent from the US public sphere or mainstream cultural or political realms. Rather, the issue of Palestine has been hypervisible in the US context, yet largely through the lens of compulsory Zionism and in the shape of negative stereotyping in mainstream US news media and Hollywood cinema. Several scholars have noted the long-standing anti-Palestinian rhetoric and representations that have permeated film and media in the United States.[27] In the aftermath of the 1982 Israeli invasion of Lebanon and the resultant massacre of Palestinian civilians in the Sabra and Shatila refugee camps, US mainstream media began producing slightly less biased representations of the Palestinian condition.[28] Such representations were still shaped by US news producers who, in classic Orientalist fashion, constituted a "corporate institution for dealing with [the Middle East] . . . by making statements about it, authorizing views of it, describing it."[29] Despite the proliferation of more sympathetic views in the 1980s and 1990s, such depictions still emerged from an Orientalist "regime of representation" designed to authorize representations of Palestine.[30]

Compulsory Zionism constitutes a rhetorical structure—oftentimes that of narrative—designed to produce knowledge about Palestine with the intention to manage expectations, opinions, and solidarities with particular material, political, but also emotional effects. In terms of its representation in US cinema, compulsory Zionism is deeply rooted in the American settler-colonial project's identification with Israel through Christian ideology. With its canonical place in Christian and Jewish narratives of deliverance and conquest, the Exodus story, Robert Warrior asserts, has greatly shaped the US origin story. Such narratives "made their way into American's consciousness and ideology," resulting in the construction of "America's self-image as a 'chosen people.'"[31] Taking this point further, Steven Salaita notes that "early settlers conceptualized North America as a New Canaan," indicating that settlers assumed the subjectivity of the biblical Israelites, with North America as their Promised Land. Through this framing, the United States and Israel share an "underlying ideology," one that "encompasses a teleology of divine fulfillment . . . [and] as such, the emergence of Zionism in Europe in the late nineteenth century entered a dialectic with the project of American settlement."[32]

Melani McAlister identifies Hollywood as a primary vector through which such narratives have been ingrained in the American psyche, naturalizing and popularizing the relationships between Christian Zionism and US settler colonialism through cinema. Through films such as *The Ten Commandments* (1956), *Ben-Hur* (1959), and, most importantly, *Exodus* (1960), McAlister asserts that Hollywood has played a strategic role in cultivating American political and spiritual identification with Israel, noting how "in *Exodus,* the Zionist story of Israel also became an American tale . . . as the American frontier had been tamed, so the desert bloomed."[33] As settler-colonial states with a shared religious mythology, in the words of Robert Warrior, "it is these stories of deliverance and conquest that are ready to be picked up and believed by anyone wondering what to do about the people who already live in their promised land."

As these biblical narratives played out on the silver screen of the 1950s and 1960s, the US government's competition with the USSR over political hegemony played out through the highly contentious and unpopular Vietnam War (1955–1975). The newly formed state of Israel's geographic position in relation to Soviet proxy states made it an ideal geopolitical outpost for protecting US interests during the Cold War. With the demonstration of Israel's strength of expansionist will through the vast territorial seizures of the West Bank, Gaza Strip, the Jawlan region of Syria (Golan Heights), and Egypt's Sinai Peninsula in the June War in 1967, the United States found further strategic and symbolic reasons to align itself with Israel. As the United States lost the Vietnam War, the consolidation of the American-Israel "special relationship" took on even greater significance. As McAlister argues, films such as *Black Sunday* (1977) enabled American audiences to exorcise their Vietnam War demons and vicariously reclaim a sense of victory through identification with Israel's militaristic and political prowess. In these ways, film has been a primary site for the naturalization of American identification with Israel and the normalization of compulsory Zionism in US popular culture.

## Cinematic Activism Framework

Over the past fifty years, the social movement strategy of cinematic activism has effectively moved Palestinian liberation and solidarity politics away from the margins and into the mainstream of US culture. The push to include sympathetic representations and self-representations of Palestine, Palestinians, and Palestinian liberation politics within US mass media and popular culture—*mainstreaming*—has been an ongoing process for several decades. I use the word *mainstream* as shorthand to encompass this process. The word also hails several related concepts through which scholars have theorized cultural processes and power relations, including cultural hegemony, popular culture, the public sphere, capitalism (both cultural and economic), the culture industry, and discourse, to name a few. In short, *mainstream* stands for a popular cultural realm in which issues, topics, and trends are normalized and readily recognizable by a general public. *Mainstreaming* therefore refers not only to a process by which issues and topics that had previously circulated at the field's discursive edges are expedited—either intentionally or by happenstance—toward more central or prominent positions, but also how those issues and topics become more intelligible to a wider public (or audience, as it were). In the context of the Palestinian liberation and solidarity movement, mainstreaming has meant pushing anticolonial, left-leaning representations of the Palestinian cause farther into a more central US public sphere in ways that make the topic of Palestine far more intelligible, and thereby bringing greater and more diverse groups of people into solidarity with the Palestinian liberation struggle.

As a framework, cinematic activism helps to identify the mechanisms of mainstreaming, or *how* the process of mainstreaming is undertaken. "Cinema" in the context of the United States is afforded a particular kind of privilege and protection, in that it is considered an elevated, even sophisticated form of cultural production. That cultural production, in turn, enjoys a special relationship to constitutionally protected freedom of expression. What is therefore significant about cinematic activism is that, unlike many other forms of Palestinian speech and activism related to liberation and solidarity, cinematic activism has succeeded, in multiple ways, at subverting the discipline and censorship of compulsory Zionism. At its most basic level, the cinematic activism framework situates how film production and distribution practices are organized to attract spectators and amass an audience in solidarity with the Palestinian liberation cause. The texts of cinematic activism are not solely relegated to "film." Rather, I understand the premise of cinematic activism as taking the multidimensional meaning of "cinema"—as text, as space, as event, and as social relation—as a starting point for organizing a set of practices for the movement, whether the media text is a film or not. Cinema, therefore, is the inspiration for both organizing *and* transforming spectators into an audience, and audiences into activists. In the case of cinematic activism for Palestinian liberation, that audience is imagined as a community of Palestinian liberation and solidarity activists and would-be activists, and those texts and practices are ultimately working in the service of disseminating information about and representing Palestine in ways that challenge or seek to overcome compulsory Zionism. But the act of spectatorship is not passive, and so my focus on spectatorship is also a focus on reception: how spectators make meaning of the texts they consume.

Cinematic activism cannot exist without a text as a central organizing element, that thing that exists at the center of cinema culture, that thing that is altogether sensual, temporal, and emotional, that thing we call a movie. The term *movie* is most often associated with feature-length narrative films. However, the film and media texts examined in this book are not strictly limited to movies but rather encompass a variety of filmic and multimedia texts, such as audiovisual formats like filmstrips, feature-length documentaries, experimental video art, editorial public television broadcasts, and Hollywood awards ceremony television broadcasts. In the context of this book, *production* refers to not only the conceptualization and making of those filmic and multimedia texts but also the social and institutional mechanisms through which to distribute them.

While I do indeed offer close readings of the film and media texts discussed in this book, this project is primarily concerned with distribution. Ramon Lobato reminds us that in the twenty-first century, "formal theatrical exhibition is no longer the epicenter of cinema culture," and that examining film and media distribution "from below" is critical to understanding and recognizing some of cinema's most radical social and political effects.[34] The field of cinema studies has historically taken a "top-down" approach to the study of distribution through an overwhelming focus on the formal channels through which media is delivered to the masses: theater chains, DVDs and streaming services, broadcasts, and other formal institutions through which films circulate. In the spirit of Lobato's commitment to understanding how the "shadow economies" produce informal distribution networks "from below," I use the term *distribution* to describe both the avenues of circulation and the things (films, multimedia, but also ideas and directives) being delivered to spectators. Distribution here refers to the formal and informal ways that Palestinian cinema and solidarity cinema must circumnavigate the roadblocks of compulsory

Zionism and successfully circulate in innovative ways, from formal exhibition in theaters, museums, and television broadcasts to grassroots organized screenings in people's houses, in church basements, at conferences, and on college campuses.

Unlike the passivity of "circulation" and the institutional valence of "exhibition," the term *distribution* accommodates both the formal and informal processes by which film, media, and ideas move around, find spectators, and create audiences, while foregrounding the agency necessary to take on the power structures that prevent that dissemination in the first place. Again in the words of Lobato, "questions of distribution," after all, "are nothing if not political. If we understand politics as a struggle for power and resources, then distribution is politics at its purest."[35] Within the field of political philosophy, "distribution" is a concept deeply tied to questions of justice, particularly regarding the allocation of wealth and resources. The Palestine solidarity cinema discussed in chapters 1 and 2 of this book invoke this idea of "distributive justice" as their main theses by articulating how the financial relationship between the US government, the ethnic cleansing of Palestine, and Israeli settler colonization is one characterized overwhelmingly by distributive *injustice.* In this sense, distribution refers not only to the dissemination of film and multimedia texts but also to the ideas, ideologies, and politics associated with and represented in those texts.

As Issam Nassar, Stephen Sheehi, and Salim Tamari remind us in *Camera Palaestina: Photography and Displaced Histories of Palestine,* the concept of "distribution" is by no means devoid of colonial violence. In interrogating Jacques Rancière's concept of "distribution," Sheehi points out that the original French word, *partage,* translates as both "sharing" and "partition," the latter of which is a word, idea, and practice laden with a history of colonial violence in the Palestinian context.[36] Indeed, the process of mainstreaming discussed in this book is an example par excellence of Rancière's concept of "the distribution of the sensible," succinctly defined as "the system of divisions and boundaries that define, among other things, what is visible and audible within a particular aesthetic-political regime."[37] This fraught meaning of distribution is important to understanding the ways in which the body of spectators engaging with Palestine-focused cinematic activism is constituted and at times divided.

To whom and where are these productions distributed? Spectatorship, the activity of consuming cinema, is central to cinematic activism. Without spectatorship the filmic texts and their ideas and politics languish in a vacuum. Spectatorship is not a passive practice; rather, it is a first step in the assemblage of an imagined community. It is the site of consciousness raising, and it is the process of receiving that which is being distributed: in this case, Palestinian liberation and solidarity politics. What spectators do upon that reception, what meaning they make of those politics, is of particular import to my understanding of cinematic activism. My thinking here is informed by what Hollis Griffin, in writing on the contentious debate about trigger warnings for media texts in classrooms, refers to as "activated spectatorship," or the ways in which spectators are at once primed to expect difficult affects while also emboldened as agentic subjects.[38] That is all to say, spectatorship is leverageable, by which I mean that it can be mobilized to produce not just meanings but also material or financial effects. For example, outdoor film screenings were often held in the evenings in the student intifada encampments on university campuses across North America during the 2023–2024 academic year, serving both educational and recreational purposes to help buoy students as they worked to maintain the encampments. But nowhere is this spectatorial mobilization more evident than in the numerous fundraising campaigns for Gaza circulating throughout social media in spring 2024, such as the aforementioned Cinema for Gaza campaign, which exemplifies how "cinephilia is channeled into activism."[39] This kind of material and financial mobilization of spectatorship is examined in greater detail in chapter 5 and the conclusion, where I refer to it as *philanthro-spectatorship.*

The spectators studied within this book are diverse and at times incongruous. Many of them are already simpatico with Palestinian liberation and solidarity politics, whether as Palestinians themselves; Black, Indigenous, and/or People of Color (BIPOC) activists; those of SWANA identity; as Jewish anti-Zionists; or as other allies who are already well versed in the arguments and politics of the cause. Indeed, it is from this simpatico premise that the grassroots organizing analyzed in chapters 1 and 5 begins. But there are also hostile spectators, such as the enraged Public Broadcasting Service (PBS) viewers and journalists discussed in chapter 2, or the film critics and journalists discussed in chapters 2 and 3. And then there are antispectators, such as the anonymous domestic terrorist in chapter 2 who attempted to thwart the exhibition of *Occupied Palestine* with a bomb threat, or the members of the Jewish Defense League in chapter 4 who terrorized theatergoers and protested outside of the Academy Awards ceremony in 1978. Antispectators, however, are not always hostile spectators, such as the Palestinian liberation and solidarity activists who staged public protests outside of film festivals trafficking in compulsory Zionism, as discussed in chapter 5, or more recently, the aforementioned protesters from *The Hollywood Reporter* headline, who in March 2024 shut down traffic around the Dolby Theatre in Los Angeles, causing a thirty-minute delay to the start of the Academy Awards ceremony. And then there is a vast group of would-be spectators, those for whom the distribution of Palestinian cinema, solidarity cinema, and liberation and solidarity politics is thwarted by people and institutions in positions of power, either because those spectators are *presumed* to be hostile, or worse, because they are presumed to be too uninformed or too uneducated to be allowed viewership, as is discussed in chapters 2 and 3. It is this *presumption* of hostility or ignorance that served as justification for the management and control of distribution, which at times has been tantamount to censorship.

Palestinian spectators play a critical role in Palestine-focused cinematic activism in that it is through their reception of Palestinian cinema and solidarity cinema that the meaning making of cinematic activism for Palestine is experienced. I understand "Palestinian spectator" here in terms of Sheehi's interpretation of Rancière's work on "the emancipated spectator," as "the Palestinian subject as Palestinian spectator."[40] In the context of the United States, Palestinians in diaspora are some of the primary consumers of the films in question, and their relation to the content of the film is both as spectator and subject; their experience of this cinematic activism is therefore one of simultaneously seeing and being seen. In this sense, the Palestinian spectator-subject inhabits a position and experiences an aesthetic of what Edward Said refers to as "contrapuntal," or that contradictory state of being simultaneously exiled and included.[41] The kind of representation of Palestinianness within the film or media text of cinematic activism therefore has substantial implications not only for the meaning of "Palestinian liberation" but also for the articulation of who or what is considered Palestinian and therefore included in or excluded from that liberatory project.

The facets of the cinematic activism framework outlined above correspond to various Palestinian liberation and solidarity movement goals. On a more granular level, production and distribution are largely concerned with representing Palestine, Palestinians, and the Palestinian liberation cause from Palestinian perspectives. That representation in turn becomes the centrifugal force around which a substantial segment of Palestinian liberation and solidarity activism has organized, through such things as infotainment film screenings hosted by activist groups, protests at film festivals and other high-publicity events, and the establishment of annual Palestine-themed film festivals. That organizing, in turn, not only increases visibility but also functions to institutionalize the Palestinian liberation and solidarity movement in the United States, especially through the establishment of Palestine-themed film festivals within elite US cultural institutions. This process of representation, organizing, and institutionalization facilitates additional movement goals related to spectatorship, namely, spectator political education with the hope of changing public opinion, and directives to act (or donate) in accordance with a wider array of movement goals, such as fundraising, organizing to protect free speech and academic freedom, and adhering to the stipulations of the BDS movement.

## Palestinian Cinema and Palestine Solidarity Cinema

I trace the origins of Palestine-focused cinematic activism in the US context to the founding of the Association of Arab American University Graduates in 1967. The AAUG was initially formed in response to the events of the June War and subsequent Israeli military occupation of the West Bank, Gaza Strip, Sinai Peninsula, and Jawlan region (Golan Heights). Yet that same need to respond to these events originated both in the horror of watching such events unfold and in seeing the emergence of a sudden and pervasive rise of anti-Palestinian racism (and anti-Arab racism more broadly) in US news reportage and entertainment media. In the words of former AAUG president Rashid Bashshur, the AAUG's activities were intended to serve as a corrective to the "daily assaults on our culture, our people, and our countries of origin in the mass media and in the public discourse" in the context of the United States.[42] In this sense, concerns over media representation and an express intention to intervene in and change news and entertainment media discourses have been foundational to organized Arab American activism.

The efforts of the AAUG laid the groundwork for much of the cinematic activism examples laid out in this book, whether literally in the organization's own media projects as discussed in chapter 1, and in the organization's relationship to particular films and people such as David Koff's *Occupied Palestine* as discussed in chapter 2, or figuratively in terms of the organization's influence within the Arab American communities that would go on to mobilize Palestine-themed film festivals as discussed in chapter 5, or in the formal and rhetorical qualities of the cinematic activism texts circulating throughout today's online social media, as discussed in the conclusion.

Before proceeding, it is necessary to establish some basic facts about the history of Palestinian cinema. Nurith Gertz and George Khleifi historicize Palestinian cinema into a set of four periods: the first period (1935–1948); the second period (1948–1967); the third period, which is also referred to as the revolutionary period (1968–1982); and the fourth period (1980 to present). For the purposes of this book, the most important things to know about this periodization scheme is that the overwhelming majority of third period films consist of documentaries, formal and experimental alike, while the fourth period marks a radical shift toward narrative films and an emphasis on auteurism. It is important to note here that what scholars and filmmakers refer to as "Palestinian cinema" of the third period (1968–1982) was a global phenomenon in that the films of this era were all produced in exile, and that Palestinian cinema was not solely conceived in terms of ethnic or nationalist identity and authorship. Put another way, the Palestinian cinematic movement of the third period was inherently diverse in terms of ethnic, racial, sectarian, and national identities, meaning that the moniker of "Palestinian cinema" also encompassed films made by filmmakers who were not necessarily of Palestinian heritage or identity. While this was not necessarily a point of contention during the revolutionary period, the 1980s marks a moment of transition from the third to the fourth period of Palestinian cinema, a move marked by the transition toward narrative filmmaking and a greater emphasis on auteurism as Palestinian narrative cinema began circulating throughout the A-level film festivals of Europe and competing in global cinema's political economy. To this day, global cinema's political economy is still largely structured by the concept of "national cinema." Within such a context, the Palestinian cinematic movement underwent an important transition in the 1980s in terms of periodization in that Palestinian cinema's global reception as a national cinema consolidated the relationship between "Palestinian cinema" as a category and "Palestinian cinema" as the product of Palestinian national and ethnic identity. The moniker of "Palestinian cinema" therefore came to represent Palestinian authorship and identity.

Throughout the researching and writing of this book, I repeatedly encountered both explicit and implicit comments, suggestions, complaints, and conflicts around the categorization of Palestinian cinema, what counts as a Palestinian film, and who counts as a Palestinian filmmaker. At the same time, I encountered the lumping together of works by non-Palestinian filmmakers and other cultural producers into the category of "Palestinian." I see the inclusion of non-Palestinian cultural producers under the umbrella of the category of "Palestinian" as a byproduct of mainstreaming, which has the unfortunate effect of producing a discursive and representational occupation of Palestinian cultural production and identity. To better navigate this particular pitfall of mainstreaming, I propose a distinction between "Palestinian cinema" and "Palestine solidarity cinema," understood in terms of filmic/filmmaker identity and film genre, respectively. This delineation between Palestinian cinema and Palestine solidarity cinema is not necessarily perfect, and indeed as outlined in chapters 1 and 2, the borders between Palestinian cinema and Palestine solidarity cinema are sometimes overlapping and unclear, whether unwittingly or intentionally. My attempt to define this distinction between Palestinian cinema and solidarity cinema is informed by Palestinian scholar and scholar of Palestinian cinema Nadia Yaqub, who takes a "Palestinian-centered approach" to the study of Palestinian films.[43] Such an approach also requires careful attention to questions of authorship and narration, so much so that it was necessary for me to delineate between Palestinian cinema (as authored by Palestinians) and Palestine solidarity cinema (as narrating Palestine and often authored by allies).

In the interest of greater specificity, I therefore define "Palestinian cinema" as a body of ethnic cinema produced and authored by people of Palestinian heritage, and "Palestine films" as a genre of solidarity films that takes Palestine—Palestinian suffering, the Palestinian liberation struggle, and/or critiques of Zionism or the state of Israel—as their subject. As a genre, Palestine films can be narrative, documentary, animated, or experimental. They can be authored by either Palestinian filmmakers or non-Palestinian filmmakers. Indeed, the vast majority of Palestinian filmmakers traffic in Palestine films. This distinction is also important for understanding why I do not use the phrase "Palestinian cinematic activism" throughout this book and instead use "cinematic activism for Palestine" or "Palestine-focused cinematic activism." To blanket refer to all Palestine-focused cinematic activism *as Palestinian* is to suddenly include a whole lot of people performing that activism under the moniker (and by extension identity) of Palestinian. This is problematic for a number of reasons, not least of which has to do with the issue of transracialism, wherein non-Palestinians who experience the suppression or ostracism of the "Palestine exception," come to embody (and sometimes even identify with) the Palestinian subject position, and consequently come to represent Palestinianness or are identified by others as Palestinian.

Terri Ginsberg conceives of "Palestine solidarity films" less in terms of category and more in terms of an analytic, so as "not to categorize them typologically, as an anatomy, but to understand them as aesthetic-discursive moments in a global political development that is widely misrecognized, misrepresented, and misunderstood."[44] However, by thinking about Palestine solidarity cinema in terms of a category like genre, we can begin to understand how the nature and meaning of "solidarity" is sometimes obscured in ways that, at times, impede Palestinian self-representation and the goals of Palestinian liberation politics. The concept of genre itself is useful for thinking about how to categorize the diverse array of sympathetic media texts about Palestine and Palestinians that can loosely be grouped under the moniker of "Palestine films." But any consideration of genre also necessitates an interrogation of how that genre is comprised, including consideration of things such as narrative, form, plot, characters, and authorship. The purpose of a genre is to categorize a diverse array of media texts through their shared and easily recognizable characteristics. Much in the same way that a film such as *Batman* can be understood as representing the genre of action film because it adheres to the particular formal, narrative, and plot conventions associated with action films, anti-Zionist films such as *Jaffa: The Orange's Clockwork* (2009), *Israelism* (2023), and even to a certain extent liberal Zionist films such as *Waltz with Bashir* (2008) and *Munich* (2005) can also be understood as belonging to the genre of Palestine films.

It is within the diversity and conflict amid these media texts that the struggle for Palestinian self-determination is waged, as questions of rhetorical structure and subgenre begin to tell a deeper story of the stakes and investments of this type of media. The genre of Palestine films is not automatically exempt from the rhetoric of compulsory Zionism. Indeed, when we consider the genre through a decolonial lens, we can begin to see where the rhetoric of compulsory Zionism sometimes frames Palestine solidarity cinema. Another way we can understand how Palestine solidarity cinema constitutes a genre is through the concept of form, which in its simplest terms can be understood as "the creation and satisfaction of desire."[45] Form is the production of a spectator's expectation. A spectator may not always approach a media text with a particular expectation, but it is nonetheless a media text's job to produce a particular expectation. The very production of that expectation results in a spectator's desire for that expectation to be fulfilled, to be satisfied by adhering to the formal conventions of the genre, including narrative, plot, and character. In many ways, Palestine films are all about bad form, in that they produce an expectation and desire for decolonial representation of Palestine but often fail to fulfill those expectations.

## Compulsory Zionism and Cinematic Activism in Dialectic Struggle

The extent to which enforcers of compulsory Zionism have responded to certain facets of Palestine-focused cinematic activism is only matched by their strange absence with regard to other facets of Palestine-focused cinematic activism. For example, the public controversies surrounding Palestine films and Palestinian cinema in chapters 2 and 3 do not hamper the institutionalization of the Boston Palestine Film Festival at the Museum of Fine Arts as discussed in chapter 5. Likewise, although spectacle and controversy are part and parcel of the

Academy Awards ceremony, the tenor of Glazer's Palestine solidarity speech and its reception at the Oscars in 2024 represents a marked change since Vanessa Redgrave's Oscars speech in 1978, as discussed in chapter 4. Still, enforcers of compulsory Zionism continue to respond in increasingly hostile ways to the growing presence and successes of cinematic activism for Palestine, whether in the Anti-Defamation League (ADL) and the Israeli government's attempts to have the film *Farha* removed from Netflix, or the US Congress's sudden attempt to ban the social media app TikTok (the latter occurring just before the leak of a secret audio recording of ADL CEO Jonathan Greenblatt urgently bemoaning that the Zionist movement in the United States has a "TikTok problem").[46] These are merely a few contemporary examples of the long-standing methods for censoring and silencing Palestinian self-representation and solidarity politics in the United States, from the insistence on "balance" and the forcing of Palestinian voices in dialogue with Zionist rhetoric to outright threats of and acts of violence against Palestinians and solidarity activists. These censorship methods do not emerge from a vacuum; rather, they are symptomatic of a larger cultural context of compulsory Zionism within the United States.

The pathological forcing of Palestinian voices into conversation and debate with Zionists and about Zionism epitomizes how compulsory Zionism functions as a rhetorical structure by continually reproducing a narrative cohered around a partisan dyad, complete with a plot that revolves around conflict between a protagonist (Israel) and an antagonist (Palestine). There are abundant critiques of this dualism and the harms it produces, especially in terms of its ability to represent the power differentials of the colonial playing field as seemingly level.

## Tensions Inherent to Mainstreaming

While cinematic activism has been successful in bringing Palestinian liberation and solidarity politics to the mainstream, this discourse has not been sanitized of controversy. On the contrary, as the saying goes, all publicity is good publicity, and especially with regard to Palestine, entrance to and circulation within the mainstream is frequently resultant from controversy or framed as spectacle. As noted earlier, my use of "mainstream" throughout this book refers to a large-scale discursive field with boundaries delimiting what is considered intelligible, permissible, acceptable, worthy, attractive, or legitimate to the largest common denominator, otherwise known as "the public." To that end, "mainstreaming" is a process by which an issue becomes more visible, intelligible, and popularized.

*Mainstreaming Palestine* also considers how the topic of Palestine—specifically in terms of Palestinian cinema, but also with regard to Palestine solidarity politics more broadly—has moved from marginal to mainstream within the political economy of cinema in the United States. Hollywood is both an industry and an institution. As an industry, it is a commercial business endeavor in that it manufactures the film arts at an industrial level with the goal of maximizing profit. As an institution, which I mean in a figurative sense, it is constituted by a set of long-standing organizations that have shaped the norms around the production and consumption of those film arts. "Controlling the way people make and watch films," argues James McMahon, "is an institutional face of capitalist power," and "capitalist power is about the ability of business concerns to set the terms that mould the future of cinema."[47] Put another way, Hollywood's methods for controlling how we produce and consume cinema tell us a great deal about the institutional power the industry has within our society. When that power is finely attuned toward profit maximization, it not only shapes our experiences of cinema but also tightly controls cinema's aesthetic, economic, and political possibilities.

The logic of capitalization requires reduction of risk. The film industry is one that is notoriously rife with risk, which is why risk reduction is one of Hollywood's most pressing "business concerns" in shaping "the future of cinema," to borrow McMahon's words. This logic of capitalization produces what McMahon refers to as an "order of cinema," which imposes limitations on what cinema can and cannot do, as well as what types of projects are green-lighted or blacklisted in the interest of capital.[48] Here, "capital" is not necessarily limited to crass financials; it is "a quantitative, symbolic expression of organized power over society" and a measure of an industry's ability to "strategically sabotage social relations for the purposes of pecuniary gain."[49] While McMahon's political economic analysis is concerned with how the business interests of Hollywood's major studios control creativity throughout the industry, applying his conceptualization to Hollywood awards shows, as I do in chapter 4, illuminates how Hollywood's ritualistic ceremonies of recognition and legitimization inform perceptions of risk, are leveraged in the service of risk management, and therefore influence social power relations within both the industry and the institution.

In the context of cinema's global economy, there are both productive and problematic outcomes at stake within this process of mainstreaming. The more productive outcomes discussed in this book include the wider dissemination of Arab American activist literature and Palestinian cultural productions (from film and media texts to academic scholarship), increased visibility of Palestinian and Palestinian American cultural politics and cultural identities, generating a greater awareness of the Palestinian condition and struggle from a distinctly decolonial and anti-imperialist perspective, marshaling a diverse range of people into solidarity with the Palestinian liberation cause, and mobilizing those allies into various kinds of political and cultural activism.

The problematic outcomes discussed in this book are not necessarily unique to the issue of Palestine and therefore identify issues endemic to many social movements operating within neoliberal capitalist societies. Some of the more problematic outcomes discussed here speak to the cynicism that lurks around solidarity politics, especially when film and media are involved, including the performance of Palestine solidarity to gain a certain kind of cultural cachet; the deradicalization of Palestine solidarity politics; the marginalization of diasporic Palestinians (especially those who identify as LGBTQ+ or women) within the US-based Palestine solidarity movement and cinematic activism; various cults of personality; the co-option of Palestinian cultural politics for other aims, including personal gain, career advancement, and cultural capitalism; the commodification of Palestine in the service of capitalist profit; and the rise of a "professional Palestinian" social media influencer class within the Palestinian liberation and solidarity movement. That is all to say, a downside of mainstreaming Palestine is the potential reduction of cinematic activism for Palestine to just another spectacle in what Theodor Adorno and Max Horkheimer call "the culture industry." That spectacle, as Guy Debord articulates, is not a singular, objectified image or even a "collection of images, but a social relation among people mediated by images."[50]

Debordian concerns about spectacle are especially pertinent in thinking about the institutionalization of cinematic activism for

Palestine. Social relations under capitalism are not simply mediated by images; they are also mediated by institutions. Institutions that traffic in images—such as the Museum of Modern Art, Metropolitan Museum of Art, and Brooklyn Museum in New York, and the Yerba Buena Center for the Arts in San Francisco—have been under increased scrutiny of late and indeed have been the target of myriad cinematic and art activism campaigns due to their financial ties to destructive and exploitative industries, from weapons manufacturing to pharmaceuticals. More specific to Palestine, the institutionalization of cinematic activism for Palestine in places such as the Museum of Fine Arts in Boston also means placing Palestinian liberation and solidarity politics in uneasy relation to the fine art industry and museum world's historic legacies and ongoing maintenance of settler colonialism, institutionalized racism, sexism, and myriad other -isms.

Another downside of mainstreaming is the separation of Palestinian liberation politics from the very media texts and practices that seek to promote the greater cause of Palestinian liberation. This separation is at times intentional, omitting the explicit endorsement of particular political objectives and directives (such as BDS) as a form of strategic naivete,[51] trusting aesthetic representation to sufficiently perform the work of political advocacy. The Boston Palestine Film Festival, as analyzed in chapter 5, employs this form of strategic naivete, and it is one of the things that has enabled its success and longevity in the face of the compulsory Zionism of US politics and institutions.

Other times that separation is performed through an excessive aestheticization of Palestine wherein the "cinematic" consumes the "activism" to the point of divorcing the content from the cause. This is the case with numerous social media accounts dedicated to producing content about Palestinian liberation and solidarity activism, wherein the activism itself becomes the focus of the content. And sometimes that separation enables, whether intentionally or accidentally, the co-option of the very category of "Palestinian," reducing it to a genre of cultural production wherein Palestinian identity is either absent or, worse, appropriated by non-Palestinian cultural producers. This was certainly the case in the reception of David Koff's documentary film from 1980, *Occupied Palestine,* and it remains the case today through the proliferation of non-Palestinian social media accounts and brands selling Palestinian symbolism and Palestine-themed consumer products. This muddying of the waters regarding the category of "Palestinian" has immense consequences for Palestinian identity by enabling the inclusion of content and authors that focus on Palestine as part of the "Palestinian" category, while at the same time Palestinian cultural producers whose work strays from the normative scripts on Palestinian liberation are both casually and forcibly excised from the category of "Palestinian cinema."[52] To put it another way, we must not allow film, media, or literature's *content* to be the primary determining factor for inclusion within the category of "Palestinian," because doing so enables the appropriation of Palestinian identity for cynical aims, including the enforcement of compulsory Zionism.

## Methodology and Structure

This book employs a cultural studies methodology to analyze changes over time to the US-based discourse on Palestinian liberation and solidarity politics as produced through cinematic activism. As an interdisciplinary approach to research that is largely concerned with power and representation, cultural studies enables and emboldens the use of diverse materials and analytical approaches. Since "cultural studies" is inherently a broad, interdisciplinary methodological category, it is ethically important for me to name and explain the intellectual and analytical traditions that have shaped my thinking about these materials and my approach to reading them. As such, I name the methodology employed in this book as one of *decolonial visual critique* to mean two distinct yet imbricated ways of understanding and analyzing visual media texts. By "decolonial," I mean that my inquiry privileges the Indigenous (Palestinian) perspective, knowledge, and subjectivity, and takes seriously the relationships between self-representation and self-determination. At the same time, "visual critique" in many ways deemphasizes visual—that is to say, textual—analysis and instead emphasizes the machinations of the visual text within its particular historical, social, and economic contexts: its production, its modes of circulation and exhibition, and its reception by various audiences. Such an approach therefore necessitates a political economic analysis. Informed by Marxism, political theory, and cinema studies, political economic analysis of cinema entails understanding multiple, interrelated components in the circuitry of social power relations under capitalism: the political, the economic, the national, the transnational, capital, and culture.[53] Rather than focusing on semiotic or aesthetic analysis of filmic texts, political economic analysis of cinema is primarily concerned with how film production, distribution, and consumption are managed with respect to larger economic and political structures, such as capitalism and the nation-state, respectively.

In this sense, I understand decolonial visual critique as a Marxist approach to the study of what Mishuana Goeman refers to as "visual sovereignty." In writing on Native self-representations that utilize the aesthetics of Indian stereotypes, Goeman asserts that "Native performances imagine different sets of power relations between Native people and settlers by presenting us with complicated visions that, rather than distance themselves from pop culture and its wooden Indian figures, cannibalize it, producing a visual sovereignty that deals with the hegemonic structures of settler societies."[54] To that end, a decolonial visual studies methodology of decolonial visual critique takes seriously not simply Palestinian self-representation in the absence of a self-determined nation-state, but also the role, labor, and place of Palestinian people, their voices, knowledge, and experiences in the production and dissemination of Palestinian representation within a global political economy structured by capitalism and by colonialism.

The research represented here is both archival and ethnographic. I marshaled evidence from a wide and sometimes unwieldy set of materials, ranging from film and multimedia, print news articles and opinion editorials, television broadcasts, the archived files of grassroots organizations and personal papers, and participant observation and qualitative interviews. This approach was necessary both to chart out changes over time and honor the labor leading up to the contemporary moment, and to understand and appreciate the work of cinematic activism as it occurs in the here and now. The resultant product is a fusion of cultural history, critical ethnography, and cultural theory.

The book is structured in five chapters. Each chapter addresses a set of filmic or media texts and analyzes them within the context of the organization or institution that produced or distributed them. Since many of the films and media I focus on in the book prompted backlash and controversy over their distribution in the United States, many chapters also incorporate an analysis of the mainstream news media discourse on the controversies surrounding those media texts.

In addition to being organized chronologically, the chapters chart the development of what I identify as the genre of Palestine films and their circulation through different kinds of exhibition spaces. This structure in turn shows how shifts in technology, alongside changing distribution and spectatorial practices, propelled Palestinian cinema and solidarity cinema further into the US public sphere. The first two chapters focus on the 1970s and 1980s and are concerned primarily with educational media, such as filmstrips and documentary films, and their exhibition in smaller, intimate, more private spaces, such as living rooms, classrooms, and church basements. Chapters 3 and 4 focus on the 1990s and 2000s to 2020s, respectively, and examine the shift toward narrative cinema, experimental video art, and autobiographical documentary filmmaking, and in turn follow the movement of Palestinian cinema into more highly publicized institutional spaces such as museums, theaters, and Hollywood awards ceremonies. Last, chapter 5 focuses on the post-9/11 period to the present and examines more explicit efforts to "mainstream" Palestine solidarity media through the establishment of Palestine-themed film festivals within some of the most powerful cultural institutions in the United States.

The book concludes by highlighting the advances in form, content, reach, and reception of Palestinian cinema, solidarity cinema, and Palestine-focused cinematic activism that have been made since the early forms of cinematic activism discussed in chapter 1. The conclusion therefore engages a brief discussion of the role of new media—the internet and online social media networks—in the proliferation of Palestinian liberation and solidarity politics in the twenty-first century. Yet this conclusion also cautions against overdetermining the effectiveness of cinematic activism for Palestine, especially as it manifests via social media, by raising questions about how the commodification of Palestinian liberation and solidarity politics through social media influencer accounts and streaming platforms like Netflix threatens to reduce Palestinian liberation and solidarity politics to a Baudrillardian simulacra of solidarity.

Just like in the 1970s where this book begins, cinematic activism for Palestine in the contemporary moment remains largely grassroots; however, its distribution has become mainstream. What I mean here is that in the contexts of media convergence and neoliberal multiculturalism, the internet and its numerous social media platforms like Instagram and TikTok have enabled a mass scale of distribution and spectatorship unimaginable at the turn of the twenty-first century, let alone in the 1970s where this book begins. I believe that the unprecedented mobilization and action of the Palestinian liberation and solidarity movement underway in the United States in the wake of October 7 was made possible through the use of cinematic activism to grow and advance the movement. Indeed, much of the aesthetic, style, and narrative of social media content about the genocide and the solidarity and liberation activism in defense of Palestine mimics that of the films and media examined in this book. Today's social media activism on Palestine—which I discuss in the conclusion—is both an example and a product of the longer lineage of cinematic activism charted in this book.

Since the 1960s, cinema has been a critical tool for the communication and dissemination of the Palestinian liberation struggle. In the context of the United States, cinema has not only communicated the Palestinian liberation struggle; it has also functioned to organize and mobilize the Palestinian solidarity movement. And like the cinematic activism examples examined in this book, the contemporary cinematic activism of online social media is also the target of Zionist suppression and censorship. It is too easy to attribute the unprecedented post–October 7 Palestinian liberation and solidarity activism to the livestreaming of genocide on social media without acknowledging how the foundations of this movement have been gradually laid over the last several decades through grassroots—and eventually mainstream—cinematic activism.

Palestinian cinema, the genre of Palestine films, and their distribution through the praxis of cinematic activism together exemplify a successful stratagem through which the topic of Palestinian liberation has entered the US public sphere. In turn, cinematic activism has entered the mainstream in ways far more resistant to the kind of immediate censorship and suppression that is conjured within academe and politics. As such, this book offers an archive of the exception to the Palestine exception to free speech, demonstrating how and where the discourse on Palestinian liberation prevails.

# 1 Producing Education, Distributing Solidarity

## *The Association of Arab American University Graduates' Educational Filmstrips of the 1970s*

The filmstrip *Palestine Is the Issue* begins with a set of images that would have been familiar to US spectators of the 1970s: Commercial airline passenger planes, photographed from a distance, stand out of place in the vast, bleached expanse of a landing strip in the Jordanian desert. Small figures stand in the shadow of a plane's wings. A Palestinian flag flies just below the plane's tail. A psychedelic symphony of string and horn instruments plays over the still images. The music is simultaneously familiar yet not immediately recognizable. Indeed, it is a thirteen-second sample of "A Day in the Life," the final track on The Beatles' experimental album *Sgt. Pepper's Lonely Hearts Club Band.* The lo-fi recording gives the music a degraded sound quality, and when paired with the images on screen, this sampled cacophony gives the impression of a jet engine accelerating for takeoff. The strings build to a frenzied crescendo until the horns suddenly bring it all to an abrupt and dramatic close just before the narration begins: "In September 1970, four luxury passenger jets made emergency landings in the Jordanian desert. For the first time, the world at large paid heed to the Palestinians. It took this series of airline hijackings to make the Western world ask: 'Who *are* the Palestinians? Why are they angry?'"

The filmstrip *Palestine Is the Issue* opens with news photographs of the hijacking of four commercial airline passenger planes by the Popular Front for the Liberation of Palestine (PFLP) in 1970. By the time this filmstrip began circulating in the United States in 1974, the stereotype of the Palestinian as terrorist-hijacker had become hegemonic in US culture through the contextless repetition of this kind of imagery on the news and in entertainment media. *Palestine Is the Issue* utilizes this ripped-from-the-headlines sensationalism as a dramatic hook to draw spectators into the narrative before flipping the script: "Let us now look at the root causes of Palestinian anger, for these are the roots of the Arab-Israeli conflict that threatens to embroil us all." From the start, the narrator implicates the spectator, suggesting that it is in their personal interest to understand what is going on "over there" and how such circumstances are related to their lives "over here."

If we consider the representation of Palestinian liberation and solidarity politics in the United States within a mainstreaming matrix (from taboo and unspeakable, to liberal and neoliberal multicultural inclusion, to normalization), then the 1970s represent the earliest developmental stage in that matrix: the time of taboo and unspeakability. Between 1974 and 1976, the Association of Arab American University Graduates (AAUG) produced two educational filmstrips intended for screenings in academic, activist, and ecumenical contexts with the intention of breaking the silence. At forty-five and sixty minutes in length, respectively, *Palestine Is the Issue* (1975) and *Palestinians: Holding On* (1976) were technologically typical of filmstrips of the time. Not actually moving picture films, educational filmstrips of this era were more akin to narrativized still-image slideshows. A visual narrative of still images printed vertically on 35-millimeter positive film was accompanied by an audiocassette that provided a voiceover narration and soundtrack (Figure 1). The use of filmstrips as progressive educational tools had gained popularity in North America in the postwar era, and they were especially popular in the 1960s and 1970s as media studies scholars such as Marshall McLuhan promoted audiovisual media's role in shaping an ideology of global democratic citizenship.[1] The AAUG filmstrips implicitly invoked that discourse with their intentions to (1) educate a general US public about dispossession of Palestine and Israeli settler colonialism from the Palestinian perspective, (2) implicate US spectators in the Palestinian people's fate, and (3) therefore instigate their audiences to support the Palestinian liberation cause.

Regardless of whether the AAUG filmstrips succeed or failed in these aims, in this chapter I argue that the story of their origin, production, and distribution is illustrative of how media has been central

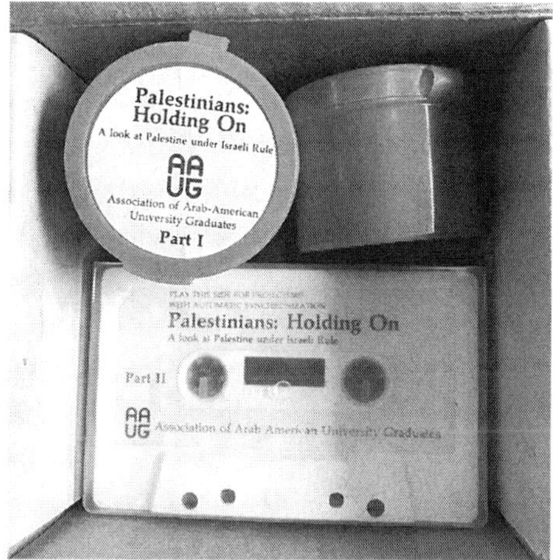


Figure 1. *Left:* The first four frames of the AAUG filmstrip *Palestine Is the Issue* (1975). *Above:* The filmstrip *Palestinians: Holding On* (1976) in its storage canisters and accompanying audio cassette tape. Filmstrips copyright the Association of Arab American University Graduates. Photos by the author.

to Arab American activism around the issue of Palestine since the origins of the Arab American leftist movement. While a substantive body of work exists on the mainstream US media's role in producing anti-Palestinian stereotypes and pro-Israel bias in US culture,[2] there have been fewer academic studies of Arab American media activism.[3] And while an equally substantive body of work has emerged in recent decades focused on Palestinian art and cinema's revolutionary politics, discourses, and aesthetics,[4] little attention has been given to the role of grassroots cinematic activism around the question of Palestine in the context of North America. This chapter, therefore, takes the AAUG filmstrips as an example of how Arab American alternative media production and distribution has constituted a critical method for cultivation and circulation of Palestinian liberation and solidarity politics in the United States. The story of the AAUG's foray into media production and distribution begins in a moment of unspeakability and offers a starting point for recovering the history of Arab American media activism and the broader Palestine solidarity activism movement's grassroots uses of media to challenge compulsory Zionism in the United States, educate general US audiences about Palestine, and cultivate Palestine solidarity politics among different identity-based and cause-based groups in the United States and Canada.

Today, still and moving images are an integral part of Palestinian liberation and solidarity activism in the United States, and such images circulate throughout the United States to a degree that would have been unimaginable when these filmstrips were produced in the 1970s. From culture jamming and street art to film festivals and online social media campaigns, Palestine-focused cinematic and media activism is far more visible and accessible in today's media atmosphere. Indeed, the use of new media—by which I mean content that is primarily available digitally and through the internet or social media apps—has proven to be an important method to grow the Palestine solidarity movement and challenge the dominant discourse on Palestine in the United States (a point I return to in the conclusion of this book). Despite the dearth of scholarship on the AAUG's media projects,[5] agents and institutions of compulsory Zionism recognized early on how the AAUG's foray into cinematic activism posed a threat to the compulsory Zionism of US culture. For example, in its 1983 report, *Pro-Arab Propaganda in America,* the Anti-Defamation League (ADL) referred to the AAUG as "a kind of pro-PLO (Palestine Liberation Organization) brain trust" and named the organization one of the five most prominent anti-Israel Arab propaganda organizations operating in the United States.[6] The report went on to specifically identify the filmstrip *Palestine Is the Issue* and its criticism of US policies in the Southwest Asia and North Africa (SWANA) region as part of a larger "campaign aimed at discrediting Israel in the eyes of the American Public."[7] A similar report published by the American Israel Public Affairs Committee (AIPAC) in 1984, *The AIPAC College Guide: Exposing the Anti-Israel Campaign on Campus,* identified groups such as the Organization of Arab Students (OAS) and their work to hold film screenings at college campuses across the country as part of that larger campaign to discredit Israel.[8] While the AIPAC report notes that the activities of groups such as OAS have "not succeeded in forming alliances with most mainstream American student groups," they have indeed "succeeded, to a substantial degree, in defining the parameters within which much of the campus debate about Israel and the Middle East takes place."[9] The ADL and AIPAC references to the uses of film and media suggests that the AAUG's filmstrips and early cinematic activism campaigns were critical to *redefining* the parameters of campus debates over Palestine and Israel. Indeed, as I discuss in chapters 2 and 3, the ADL and AIPAC's attempts to repress Palestinian cinema and Palestine films later in the 1980s and 1990s furthermore indexes the import of that cinematic activism in the larger struggle to further change the discourse and cultivate Palestine solidarity politics in the United States.

As I will enumerate later in this chapter, the AAUG filmstrips were screened most often by student groups on college campuses, largely because they were the most affordable option among the array of multimedia products available for rent from the AAUG. This chapter seeks to recover the AAUG's history as an alternative media production and distribution channel and demonstrates how Arab American activists and allies conceived of film and multimedia—and executed its production and distribution—as an integral method for combatting compulsory Zionism. The AAUG's early foray into cinematic activism for Palestine was not only central to the expansion of grassroots Palestine solidarity activism in the United States in the 1970s and 1980s but also laid the groundwork for contemporary Palestinian liberation and solidarity activism strategies.

## The Association of Arab American University Graduates

The formation of the AAUG is often heralded as the advent of Arab American political activism.[10] In June 1967 Palestinian political scientist Ibrahim Abu-Lughod began his new teaching position at Northwestern University in Evanston, Illinois. That same month, Israel invaded and occupied the Palestinian territories of the West Bank and Gaza, along with the Jawlan region (Golan Heights) of Syria and the Sinai Peninsula of Egypt. The US media reportage of the war reflected staunch American political support for the Israeli state along with pervasive anti-Arab bias.[11] It was from this moment of crisis, in the fall of 1967, that Abu-Lughod and fellow Arab and Arab American academics across the country began to mobilize the AAUG.

The AAUG was conceived as a pedagogical social movement that would work to dismantle racist, anti-Arab stereotypes and misconceptions that saturated US political rhetoric, media, and popular culture at the time.[12] It sought to accomplish this through teaching, public intellectualism, and academic scholarship. At the time of the organization's founding, activism around Palestine largely meant undertaking the task of educating people about Palestine. The AAUG is widely recognized for its production of an extensive body of academic literature on Palestine, which included monographs, edited volumes, informational papers, and pamphlets for use in academic as well as ecumenical contexts. Most notably, the organization published a series of edited volumes on Arab American communities and politics, as well as a newsletter. Although it was not an AAUG-branded product, two of the organization's founders, Ibrahim Abu-Lughod and Edward Said, founded the academic journal *Arab Studies Quarterly*. Since Palestine was one of the AAUG's central concerns in its early advocacy of Arab American cultural politics, much of this literature necessitated an engagement with and critique of Zionism as being hegemonically imbedded within US academe. The AAUG is less recognized, however, for its production and distribution of audiovisual materials. Indeed, one of the original motivations for the organization's formation was a concern over Palestine's lack of visibility and outright misrepresentation in US print and televisual news reportage.[13] The organization's leaders of the time recognized that if the AAUG's purpose was to challenge and correct the negative representations of Arabs, Arab Americans, and the Palestinian question in US higher education and mainstream media, then it needed to produce self-representations on both registers.

The AAUG was nonetheless deeply invested in the processes and practices of academic knowledge production and publishing, an investment that meant that the organization had to reckon with accusations of elitism from among the larger Arab American community. The AAUG membership did indeed consist predominantly of academics working in the humanities and social science fields of political science, anthropology, literature, and sociology, as well as nonacademics working in professional fields such as law, medicine, and engineering. But many prominent AAUG members, especially Ibrahim Abu-Lughod and Edward Said, stridently believed in the uses of cultural production not only as educational tools but also, within the context of colonialist representational hegemony, as expressions of Arab self-determination.[14] When the AAUG first undertook the filmstrip project in 1974, of the AAUG's seven-hundred-strong membership,[15] only eleven members worked professionally in fields related to art, media, and visual culture production.[16] However, the organization's foray in filmstrips, a medium that was expressly praised and promoted for its potential to democratize knowledge acquisition, suggests that the AAUG's leadership took the accusations of elitism seriously enough to consider alternative methods for the dissemination of its academic discourses. As I will discuss later in this chapter, the AAUG's efforts to collect and distribute an array of audiovisual materials later in the 1980s, consisting mainly of documentaries and short video public service announcements, indicates that the filmstrips were the start of the AAUG's larger attempts to democratize knowledge about Palestine through the distribution of alternative media. Making Arab American cultural politics more *visible* necessitated making Arab American cultural politics *visual,* and so the AAUG undertook the task of marshaling visual evidence and producing multimedia material to be used for the organization's educational and political aims. Filmstrip production was one channel through which the AAUG attempted to achieve this aim, condensing the organization's academic discourse on Palestine into a concise audiovisual narrative that would have been more accessible to a general American audience.

At the time of AAUG's emergence in the late 1960s and early 1970s, the leap between having an interest in using media for educational purposes and producing media was no small feat, especially considering the technological and budgetary constraints of working with film. For example, during the early Cold War period, a twenty-minute 16 mm moving picture film typically cost $15,000 to $20,000 to produce.[17] Video technology had been around since the 1950s, but consumer and "prosumer" (low-end professional grade) video technology was not readily available at the time the AAUG conceived of these filmstrips. Betamax and VHS "home video" technology entered the consumer markets in 1975 and 1976, respectively, but would not become popularized until the 1980s.[18] The filmstrip format thus offered the AAUG a far more economical way to produce, archive, and distribute alternative, independent audiovisual informational resources.

The AAUG's organizing, and its specific intentions and labor around using audiovisual materials to achieve its goals, was critical to making other Arab American activist formations and practices possible. Several organizations, including the American Arab Anti-Discrimination

Committee (ADC), emerged out of the AAUG organizing.[19] Chief among those offshoots, the ADC has, from its founding in 1980, taken the relationships between representation, the media, and civil liberties as a central focus of its organizing mission.[20] Despite ADC's genealogical relation to the AAUG, the latter's role in supporting and disseminating Palestine-focused media activism has largely gone unrecognized. Tracking the origin story of how the AAUG's filmstrips came to be reveals how the production and distribution of alternative media has been integral to cultivating allies in solidarity with Palestine and growing the Arab American leftist movement.

Studies of Arab American intellectual history and activism have only mentioned the AAUG filmstrips in passing. One reason for this is because the filmstrips themselves have remained largely inaccessible due to outdated technology. Finding a functioning projector is an epic project in its own right. During my time as a Mellon Postdoctoral Fellow at Northwestern University, I had the institutional support that was necessary to pursue such an endeavor. I visited the Eastern Michigan University Archive, which houses a vast special collection of AAUG material. I waited patiently and investigated the AAUG organizational materials over the course of several days as the audiovisual technician lovingly tinkered with two ancient projectors, until he was eventually able to coax one back to life and projected the filmstrips onto a basement wall so that I could screen them. Though these filmstrips are not readily available to us in this moment, that does not mean that they lacked influence in the past or did not influence how cinematic activism is conducted today.

Charting the historical trajectory of Arab American cinematic activism is critical to contextualizing the expansion of grassroots Palestine solidarity activism in the United States. The AAUG's early multimedia projects such as the filmstrips, although modest in scale, set the stage for far greater cinematic activism projects. Through its mail order rental program, the organization enabled the circulation of David Koff's blacklisted film, *Occupied Palestine*, furnished expert speakers for local network news and public television programs, and helped to fund and support Palestinian filmmakers, such as Mai Masri (whose work is discussed in chapter 3) by acting as a conduit through which they could apply for grants. In addition, many of the organization's former leaders and members were responsible for the production of *Arabic Hour,* the all-volunteer public access television show produced in the Boston area and broadcast on local public access stations across the country.

The nomination of Palestinian cinema for Oscar and Golden Globe awards, or the mobilization of Palestine-themed film festivals in the post-9/11 era may seem a far cry from the AAUG filmstrip production. Yet the very presence of Palestine-themed film festivals in institutions such as the Museum of Fine Arts in Boston and the Gene Siskel Film Center in Chicago, not to mention the live broadcast of Palestinian filmmakers winning prestigious Hollywood awards to an audience of tens of millions of television viewers, indicates how far the parameters of the discourse on Palestine in the United States have shifted since the earliest years of AAUG activism.

I chose to centralize and historicize cinematic activism, starting with the AAUG's otherwise obscure media products, because academia and media have emerged as two of the most prominent terrains of struggle upon which the discourse on Palestine in the United States has been silenced, shaped, challenged, and reshaped. More specifically, if media is how we understand how the discourse on Palestine has been silenced and misrepresented in the United States, I am therefore arguing that we must study media as an essential terrain for both repression and resistance. As my analysis of the AAUG filmstrips demonstrates, Arab American cinematic activism has created alternative educational spaces that challenge how we think about where, when, and how Arab American studies takes place. Furthermore, analyzing the filmstrips' form, content, and circulation not only reveals how they constitute a distillation and transliteration of the AAUG academic discourse on Palestine but also challenges our whole conception of public intellectualism. The filmstrips serve as an early example of how Arab American studies actively sought to bridge academic discourses, public intellectualism, and activism through the production and circulation of alternative media.

When the AAUG filmstrips began circulating in the mid-1970s, the media stereotype of the Palestinian as terrorist-hijacker cast a steep shadow over Palestine solidarity activism in the United States. However, as the historical arc of this book demonstrates, by harnessing the power of representation and leveraging institutional mechanisms, the grassroots practices of Arab American cinematic activism have been integral to bringing Palestine solidarity politics out of that shadow and, at times, into the spotlight of US culture and politics.

Today, much of new media activism around Palestine is reminiscent of the AAUG's filmstrip aesthetic and political goals. Digital photography, digital video, and visual infographics and their circulation online have become increasingly powerful tools in raising awareness and mobilizing people to action. For example, the independent nonprofit organization Visualizing Palestine produces infographics that are designed with visual literacy in mind. The organization takes large amounts of academic and NGO data about Palestine and makes it accessible to general audiences through a distinctly stylized visual infographic format. In another example, the Boycott, Divestment, and Sanctions (BDS) movement produced a digital video explaining Israel's colonial history and the contemporary conditions under Israeli occupation. But the BDS movement's video is not merely a history lesson; it is a call to action, stating: "When those in power refuse to act to stop this injustice, we need a global citizen's response to stand alongside Palestinians in their struggle for freedom, justice, and equality." Akin to AAUG's filmstrip tactics, spectators of the BDS movement video are hailed as global citizens, but this time with a specific directive.

That said, while the AAUG's media projects were ahead of their time—the organization excelled in its audiovisual representation of Palestine at a time when very few media resources from the Palestinian perspective were readily available in the United States—the filmstrips fell short in their lack of specific directives that would help spectators answer their call for action. Although a collaborative effort between Palestinians and Americans, the filmstrips are not necessarily clear examples of Palestinian self-representation. Still, the project was designed to cultivate solidarity across national and ethnic lines and, in their very creation, the filmstrips did just that. While the AAUG is often critiqued as "elitist," "insular," "utopian," and, ultimately, a failed project,[21] the cinematic activism undertaken by AAUG members in the 1970s and 1980s opened new channels by which to educate, implicate, and instigate general US audiences into solidarity with the Palestinian liberation cause. With the creation of two low-budget filmstrips, the AAUG transformed the way Arab American activists and allies disseminated information about Palestine and conducted their grassroots activism and laid the groundwork for contemporary Palestine-focused cinematic activism. The chapter that follows this one more closely examines which channels, literally, became sites of contest over the question of Palestine during the 1980s.

## Historical Context of Ethnic Media and Palestinian Cinema During the 1970s

The period between the late 1960s through the 1970s was a highly productive time for the Palestinian cinematic movement and the production of Palestine films. The PLO had essentially institutionalized cinematic activism starting in 1968 through the establishment of various film units across the coalition's various factions. These film units produced a plethora of films articulating and depicting the Palestinian struggle as a national liberation movement against colonialism and imperialism, pursued through armed revolution, and motivated by love.[22] These films, typically in Arabic and English and with subtitles, were distributed worldwide in order to disseminate Palestinian self-representations and advance the Palestinian liberation cause. The Palestinian struggle also had the support of other, well-established Third Cinema–style film production projects in the United States and Europe. For example, in 1973 California Newsreel produced a documentary film titled *Revolution Until Victory: We Are the Palestinian People.* As was the intention of Third Cinema, these solidarity films were likely screened to particular audiences that were already simpatico with the leftist liberation ideologies promoted therein.

The 1970s fall squarely within what Nurith Gertz and George Khleifi have referred to as the third period of Palestinian cinema and what Nadia Yaqub historicizes as the revolutionary period of Palestinian cinema. The Palestinian cinematic movement of this era was, to varying degrees, affiliated with and supported by the PLO and its various factions, such as the PFLP that was responsible for the airplane hijackings described at the beginning of this chapter.[23] The films produced in affiliation with the PLO were made in the style and with the intention of Third Cinema, meaning that they were shaped by the ideologies of Third World liberation—Marxism, Leninism, Maoism, and Trotskyism—and as such designed to address spectators as comrades in shared struggle. This is reflected in Palestinian revolutionary cinema's extensive focus on the figure of the *fida'i,* the Palestinian resistance fighter, and their training for armed revolution.

Given the robust body of Palestinian revolutionary cinema and solidarity cinema at the time, why then did the AAUG opt to produce its own media instead of using existing films from the Palestinian cinematic movement? Simply put, the Palestinian cinematic movement's 1970s affiliations with groups such as the PFLP, which the US government, politicians, and mainstream news and entertainment media characterized as "terrorists," was not the right kind of optic for the AAUG's public relations. However, a more nuanced answer to this question is that the AAUG's media projects functioned in part as public relations materials for the organization itself, that the AAUG used its media productions to educate spectators in the hopes of generating Palestine solidarity politics, and that through the dissemination of its academic content to wider, nonacademic audiences, the filmstrips also served to establish the AAUG itself as an authority on the topic of Palestine and Zionism. Given the academic focus of the organization, the liberal tradition of "academic freedom" insulated these productions from the ever-searching sensors (and censors) of compulsory Zionism.

The AAUG's media activism of the 1970s was distinct from the Palestinian cinematic movement of the time on multiple practical and ideological levels. The organization's media projects were more akin to the larger project of "ethnic media" production in the United States in the 1960s and 1970s, which functioned to preserve and transmit ethnic culture and identity by maintaining language and promoting ethnic pride, to establish a minority news agenda, to announce community events and cover minority social activities (including minority business advertising), to promote the group's political and social interests and motivate them to be socially and politically active, to serve as collective expressions of anger at injustices, and to provide comfort and respite from negative images in general market media.[24]

The category of ethnic media, however, is not synonymous with "radical media," and indeed the history of ethnic media in the United States largely tells a story of assimilation, social control, and symbolic empowerment. The AAUG's media production necessarily should be understood within this historical context. This context helps us understand the political stakes and nature of the AAUG as an organization, but more importantly how the organization's cinematic activism set the tone for the longer trajectory of the Palestine-focused cinematic activism historicized throughout this book. At first glance one might assume that the AAUG produced radical media in that it focused largely on the question of Palestine and critiques of Zionism. But for the most part, the AAUG's cinematic activism adhered to norms and aims of other ethnic media activism of the same time period in that it was intended in part as a way to leverage respectability politics (hence the emphasis on "university graduates" in the organization's title) in order to mobilize the Arab American community through mechanisms of symbolic empowerment.

Therefore, the AAUG's decision to produce its own material is informed by the kind of spectator the organization sought to address—and indeed the content of that material reflects this as well. Unlike the Palestinian revolutionary period films or other Third Cinema productions in solidarity with the Palestinian cause, the AAUG filmstrips did not presume a preexisting solidarity among the spectators of its media. In fact, the AAUG's media was designed to appeal to spectators not as comrades in shared struggle but as potential patrons to be persuaded to support the Palestinian cause. Indeed, the filmstrips' content, which focuses extensively on the function of US tax dollars in the Zionist occupation of Palestine, is an appeal to spectators to pursue a liberal approach centered on electoral politics of reform rather than abolition of the Zionist occupation of Palestine. The implied message is that if spectators are outraged by the use of their tax dollars to harm Palestinians, then they should lobby their representatives in Congress who can potentially change the situation. The intended audience for AAUG media material, therefore, was an audience who not only believed in liberal democratic processes of the US government but also was privileged to be considered a primary constituent of that government. Put another way, I contend that the intended audience was predominantly white, liberal, and upper-middle class.

Although considered radical at the time, the AAUG was not a revolutionary organization. It was a liberal organization that operated according to respectability politics and that largely adhered to the norms of US academia. The organization was heavily criticized as bourgeois and elitist for its "racial uplift" representation of Arab Americans as "university graduates." Indeed, with the organization's prerequisite of college education and its collection of dues, the AAUG was more akin to an academic association than a social or activist organization, which is reflected in the AAUG's membership predominantly consisting of those working in academe and fields such as law and medicine. And while the AAUG's academic discourses were considered radical within the context of the United States, in many ways the AAUG's work, and especially its media productions, offers an early example of how the topic of Palestine began to be normalized in the context of the United States. In choosing not to screen or distribute films associated with the PLO, the AAUG made the deliberate decision to separate itself from the Palestinian revolutionary movement and craft a more palatable, less radical image of Palestinian liberation politics and solidarity in the hopes that its media texts would be more readily circulated throughout the United States and be screened by more mainstream audiences.

## Filmstrip Origin Story: Producing Education

In the early 1970s, a white American couple in Illinois was coming to consciousness on the issue of Palestine. Jeanne and Allen Carr resided in Evanston, home to Northwestern University, where AAUG founding president Ibrahim Abu-Lughod taught political science. Jeanne Carr was a professional copywriter with a voracious passion for crossword puzzles. Her husband, Allen, worked as a professional art director and photographer. In the late 1960s Jeanne began acquiring British newspapers to expand and diversify her crossword puzzle talents, and it was through this practice that she first noticed the vast differences between British and US reportage on Palestine and Israel. Jeanne was so concerned by the discrepancies in reportage between the US and British press that she wrote numerous letters to the editor of the *Chicago Tribune* calling the paper out for its complicity with a one-sided Zionist narrative and demanding reportage to more fairly represent the Palestinian perspective. So determined was Jeanne Carr that she even wrote letters under various pseudonyms, most likely to circumnavigate the paper's stonewalling of her letters, but also perhaps to amplify the urgency of the criticism or make it appear as though a larger number of readers opposed the *Tribune*'s bias.[25]

Abu-Lughod and his wife Janet Abu-Lughod noticed Jeanne Carr's letters and, seeing as they were all residents of Evanston, took a chance by looking up the Carrs in the phone book and reaching out to them. This was the beginning of a deep, lifelong friendship between the two families, and it was also the start of a creative and academic collaboration that would result in the filmstrips. With the Carrs' interest in media analysis and expertise in visual art direction, photography, and copywriting, and the Abu-Lughods' academic knowledge of the politics and history of Palestine and Israel, the couples joined forces to script and produce the filmstrips for the AAUG, which ultimately lead to the organization's foray into a mail-order film rental program and independent distribution platform.

The filmstrips do not necessarily fit neatly into the category of Palestinian cinema, but do adhere to the genre of Palestine films. They were produced out of a spirit of collaboration, and their audio, visual, and narrative aesthetics, although modest, were designed with an eye and an ear toward popular culture, as exemplified by this chapter's opening description of the sampling of The Beatles' "A Day in the Life." Ibrahim and Janet, along with AAUG member H. S. Haddad, provided research and consultation, Jeanne drafted the scripts, and Allen played a large role in amassing an archive of primary and secondary visual source material. The Carrs traveled with the Abu-Lughods to Palestine twice between 1974 and 1976 to gather visual evidence and record audio interviews with Palestinians living under occupation. A photographer by training, on these trips Allen took 35mm still photographs—both black-and-white negatives and color positive slides.[26] With the ability to pass as a mere tourist if stopped and questioned by the Israeli military, he recorded interviews with Palestinians living under occupation on a handheld audio cassette tape and with a relatively small, 35mm still camera, surreptitiously documented life under occupation. The pop culture influence of the filmstrips' aesthetic is most noticeable through their soundtracks, also produced collaboratively. Carr's voiceover narration is accompanied by an unorthodox score, wherein sections of famous Palestinian liberation and classical folk songs are interspersed with dreamy, Pink Floyd–inspired psychedelic rock courtesy of Second Wind, the high school garage band helmed by Will Johnson, then boyfriend of the Abu-Lughods' daughter Deena.[27]

The nontheatrical nature of the filmstrips could easily classify them as "useful cinema," though they are, in terms of production at least, more akin to Third Cinema, or more so, a blend of useful and Third Cinemas. Haidee Wasson and Charles R. Acland consider useful cinema to be largely cohered as "films and technologies that perform tasks and serve as instruments in an ongoing struggle for aesthetic, social, and political capital." While this emphasis on "capital" may seem ill fitting here, the framework of useful cinema is strategic because of its emphasis on institutions. "The concept of useful cinema," write Wasson and Acland, "identifies a disposition, an outlook, and an approach toward a medium on the part of institutions and institutional agents. In this way, useful cinema has as much to do with the maintenance and longevity of institutions seemingly unrelated to cinema as it does with cinema per se."[28] This latter point will become especially relevant toward the end of this chapter in my discussion of the AAUG's decline and eventual demise.

In contrast, writing about the history of Palestinian cinema, Nadia Yaqub argues that from its earliest formations, Palestinian cinema has been exemplary of a Third Cinema practice in being "inextricably bound to a political revolutionary movement and committed to radical change in the funding, production, conceptualization, distribution, and viewing of films as practiced within the global, commercially motivated reach of Hollywood."[29] How, then, can such seemingly opposing frameworks for understanding cinema—one invested in institutionalization and capital, the other in the radical resistance to capitalism and its attendant institutions—come together to help account for the AAUG's media activism? Answering that question necessitates a closer examination of the filmstrips' production, intention, distribution, and reception as the product of both a struggling organization *and* a revolutionary liberation struggle.

The filmstrips' aesthetic does indeed reflect the economic constraints under which they were produced, but it also reveals the creatively collaborative backstory of how the filmstrips were designed with pop culture appeal in mind in order to draw wider audiences into solidarity with the Palestinian liberation cause. As argued by Yaqub, the revolutionary ethos of Palestinian Third Cinema relied on collaboration, flexibility, and mutability in order to "ensure the type of active political engagement with film that was necessary to its efficacy."[30] However, Third Cinema practitioners of the era did not intend for a film to *sway* its audience, but rather expected spectators to bring a liberatory subjectivity to the fore in their reception of, participation in, and production of revolutionary films.[31] This is indeed where the Third Cinema framework fits less efficiently with regard to *Palestine Is the Issue,* in that the AAUG intended its products—multimedia and otherwise—to not only represent the AAUG as *the* authority on Palestine but also that the consumption of such authoritative texts would indeed persuade audiences and usher them into solidarity with the Palestinian cause.[32]

## Narrativizing the *Issue*

Billed as "a crash course in the Middle East conflict from the British Mandate to present," the aim of *Palestine Is the Issue* (*Issue* from here on) was to educate US audiences by providing "a comprehensive introduction to the Palestine questions from the rise of Political Zionism in the 19th century to the bombing of Palestinian refugee camps in 1974."[33] The filmstrip puts forth an audiovisual multimedia argument outlining how and why political Zionism constitutes a European settler-colonial project, the leaders of which had, from its inception, intended to achieve such aims by ethnically cleansing historic Palestine of its indigenous Arab inhabitants. The filmstrip supports that argument through a methodology of close reading of source material and a practice of visual citation. An amalgamation of maps, newspaper articles, infographics, archival photographs, and Allen Carr's documentary photographs are sequenced with primary source documents, such as slides of Theodore Herzl's book *The Jewish State* and the Balfour Declaration along with typeset quotations from the published works of Herzl, Israeli military commander Yigal Allon, Chaim Weizmann, and Joseph Weitz, all as Allen's voiceover lays out a narrative of key historical events and power dynamics that shaped the events of 1947–1948.

The format, method, and content of *Issue* should sound familiar to anyone versed in Said's scholarship. As a production of an academic organization, the argument in *Issue* reflects the academic critiques of Zionism that began emerging at that time. Scholar Maxime Rodinson made a similar argument in his *Israel: A Settler Colonial State?* (1973), and AAUG scholar Edward Said deployed a methodology akin to that found in the filmstrip in his publications and conference talks during the 1970s, the culmination of which resulted in the publication of

*The Question of Palestine* in 1979, which includes Said's groundbreaking essay "Zionism from the Standpoint of Its Victims."[34] As Sarah Gualtieri argues, it is important here to enumerate the significance of the AAUG as an incubator for Said's transformative and influential scholarship not merely on Palestine, but also in the development of Arab American studies and postcolonial studies as academic fields. Gualtieri argues that closer examination of the AAUG's largely understudied archival material yields a newfound acknowledgment of the import and influence of transnational Arab American studies in the development of the "emancipatory project attentive to power, resistance, and liberation" most often associated with Said's scholarly legacy.[35]

The AAUG's filmstrips were, in their conception and production, the product of the AAUG's academic discourses on Palestine, Israel, and European and American imperialisms. *Issue*'s particular narrative arc and visual argument reflect both the methodologies and arguments of AAUG scholars, most notably Edward Said, Elaine Hagopian, Ibrahim Abu-Lughod, H. S. Haddad, and Michael Suleiman. Since Ibrahim Abu-Lughod served as lead research consultant for the filmstrips, he was in a position to promote certain discourses over others and shape the arguments to be presented within them. At the time of their production, Edward Said had not yet radically changed the course of intellectual thought. *Orientalism* would not be published until 1978 and *The Question of Palestine* not until 1979, but through his conference papers and peer-reviewed articles, Said was gaining attention as a would-be gamechanger. I contend that Abu-Lughod, as Said's close friend and mentor, sought to embed the AAUG's academic discourse and in particular Said's burgeoning academic arguments within the filmstrips as a way to both prime the US public for Said's forthcoming scholarship and test the waters for the kind of Arab American public intellectualism Said would eventually become known for. It is therefore critical to credit the AAUG's filmstrips as not merely an alternative method through which this academic discourse was distributed to a wider, nonacademic audience, but as an incubator for that burgeoning "emancipatory project."

Within this educational mission, *Issue* had additional goals: to implicate spectators in the conditions presented on screen and to instigate them into calling for "a clear revision of U. S. Policy in the Middle

East."[36] *Issue*'s narrative is structured to always tie the events of Palestine's dispossession back to their financial sponsor: the US government. The filmstrip's repeated citation of newspaper reportage on the billions of dollars in financial and military aid Israel receives from the United States every year, often accompanied by references to the US media's biased reporting of major events, implicates US taxpayers and media consumers in the conditions of violence and destruction depicted on screen. For example, Carr describes, in graphic detail, the Irgun paramilitary gang's massacre of Palestinian civilians in the village of Deir Yassin on April 9, 1948. Grainy photographs of dead women and children are followed by a slide of *Time* magazine's brief paragraph reporting on the atrocity. The dissonance between *Time*'s and the filmstrip's representations of the Deir Yassin Massacre is significant because it amplifies how the AAUG utilized mainstream media representations as a foil through which to demonstrate pro-Israel bias in US news reportage and simultaneously fortify the filmstrip's credibility. In other words, the filmstrip verifies its own historical narrative by drawing on readily recognizable news media sources that US spectators would have considered reputable. More so, the juxtaposition of *Time*'s cursory reportage of the atrocity alongside graphic images of dead Palestinian women and children suggests to the viewer that US mainstream media condones and indeed normalizes such violence through its insufficient coverage of Palestinian suffering. The viewer is implicated in Israel's state violence on an ethical level as passive consumers of objectified suffering.

*Issue* continues to implicate its audience in these atrocities by further illuminating the US government's relationship to Israel and its role in financing the oppression of the Palestinian people with US tax dollars. Slides depicting archival and contemporary images of fertile agricultural land, the ruins of demolished Palestinian villages, maps, and myriad infographics are interspersed with graphic photographs of dead and maimed children and elderly women. After a particularly graphic series of images, Carr's narration again returns to US culpability: "But America turns a deaf ear. The United States' solution to the Palestinian problem is more arms for Israel." The second portion of *Issue* becomes increasingly graphic, with photographs and anecdotes about some of Israel's most atrocious acts of violence against

Palestinian refugees discussed in direct relation to use of US tax dollars to fund Israel's military occupation and settler colonization of Palestine.

The AAUG filmstrips not only served to educate spectators about the history and context of Palestine and Israel but also, as was the goal of the educational filmstrip genre, were designed to implicate spectators in the hopes of producing outrage and, ultimately, instigating them to action. Indeed, the medium of the filmstrip itself was promoted as a means by which to manifest McLuhan's utopian vision of a global democratic society.[37] Film as a tool for education gained popularity during World War II, when informational films were used in US and Canadian classrooms to mobilize support for the war effort.[38] After the foundation of the Film Council of America in 1946, a nonprofit organization devoted to promoting, producing, and distributing educational audiovisual material, film was normalized as an educational tool and heralded as a medium through which to cultivate an ideology of global citizenship.[39] Indeed, *Issue* offers an example of how filmstrips of the 1960s and 1970s were conceived as pathways to McLuhan's dream of a democratic "global village."[40] Much like the larger industry of educational filmstrips, *Issue* hailed its spectators as world citizens within a global imagined community responsible for the betterment of a global democratic society.

In his study of postwar educational film in North America of the 1940s and 1950s, Charles R. Acland cites a Canadian Broadcasting Corporation radio program called "Speaking of Films," which expressly promoted the role of educational film in addressing pressing social issues. In this radio program, film was touted as necessary to create "the rarest of all types of citizens . . . world citizens, discovering that the world does not end at their city limits, nor their country's borders. That what happens in a village in Hungary or Greece or Palestine sooner or later affects every one of them. These films are dispelling the bonds of ignorance and prejudice."[41] Acland's example is significant because it indicates that North American filmstrip audiences were already accustomed to the global citizenship discourse disseminated through filmstrips, and that such a discourse already explicitly identified (albeit without detail) the topic of Palestine as important for the production of such an informed, conscientious global citizenry. The narrative presented in *Issue* relies on this preexisting global citizenship discourse as the impetus upon which its spectators should act.

## Grassroots Distribution, Sympathetic Audiences

The AAUG employed a variety of mutable strategies to promote and distribute the filmstrips, which were in regular circulation from 1974 through the late 1980s. During this time, the filmstrips circulated through the AAUG's regional chapters as part of the organization's larger grassroots public relations strategy, but they were also loaned out to a variety of constituencies (such as student organizations, college faculty, and liberation theologists) through a rental program instituted in 1979. The AAUG's Public Affairs Committee (PAC) was a committee of members and leaders charged with handling public relations and media outreach for the organization. A 1976 report from the PAC to the AAUG president outlined the committees' undertakings with regard to mainstream national and local news media, which included tasking members with monitoring their local news broadcasts and assembling a speaker's bureau to place AAUG pundits in high profile media spots. However, the PAC cochairs recognized the limitations of the committee and promoted the responsibility of AAUG's media activism as something to be undertaken by all members: "We cannot hope to react to every and each distortion wherever found. I would like to count on every AAUG member to respond to public affairs events in each member's home area."[42] A 1977 letter to the membership from the PAC implored members to "take the initiative to present our views to our fellow Americans" primarily through active engagements with mainstream media. Members were encouraged to draft letters to the editors of their local papers, and monitor their local news programs and call in to stations to offer comment or correct inaccuracies, in an effort to hold the press accountable for its role in perpetuating anti-Arab racism and misinformation about Palestine and the SWANA region. However, the PAC recognized that this was a tall order for regular members to carry out, and that it was not enough for AAUG members to simply write letters to the editor or monitor the news. In order to counteract misinformation in mainstream media, the AAUG had to furnish a counternarrative in the form of media itself.

Which is why the PAC eventually adopted a grassroots strategy for circulating and screening the AAUG filmstrips. Regional chapters were given copies of each filmstrip and encouraged members to screen them in small groups—in their private homes, to friends and neighbors—and to lend them to church groups and others "who are well meaning and uninformed" and "anyone else you can think of."[43] In addition to instructions from their local chapters, the AAUG membership also received a missive from the PAC in 1977 that endorsed filmstrip screenings as the official strategy of the year and promoted them as a "painless and eloquent way to say it all." The PAC conceived of the strategy as entirely grassroots in nature: "If all 1400 members do this, we can reach over 5,000 people this year alone."[44] This plea to the membership indicates how the AAUG leveraged its alternative media production and distribution practices to endow its members with a responsibility to educate people in the United States about Palestine without burdening individuals with the task of narrativizing the history of Palestine and Zionism all on their own. Instead, through the use of in-house produced audiovisual material, the AAUG gave members the tools necessary to perform the heavy lifting in order to educate the US public about Palestine.

Initially, the AAUG had hoped to provide the filmstrips gratis to a variety of organizations. A 1976 report on the AAUG's projects and programs described the filmstrips as "one of the most effective AAUG educational materials on the Palestinian question."[45] Noting that "many groups wish to obtain these filmstrips for showing to their constituencies," the report proposed the reproduction of one hundred copies of each filmstrip to be distributed free of charge to interested organizations. It is difficult to account for whether one hundred copies of each filmstrip were indeed distributed gratis to sympathetic organizations, yet what is certain is that the AAUG national office furnished regional chapters nationwide with the filmstrips and tasked them with the responsibility of organizing screenings.

The filmstrips' greatest potential for impact lay in their affordable reproducibility and ease of transport and circulation. While AAUG chapters did indeed hold private screenings as per the PAC's recommendations, chapters also lent the filmstrips to various individuals, organizations, and anyone else sympathetic to the Palestinian liberation cause. In one such example from 1976, PAC cochair Bernice

Espy Hicks reported to the executive board that *Issue* had been lent out to a former member of the American Committee for Justice in the Middle East, who had hosted a screening and "loaned it to three or four other gatherings."[46] Espy Hicks continued her missive by noting that she was in communication about potential classroom screenings with a "sympathetic professor" at the United States Air Force Academy, someone who "is able to get things heard and seen, and has been very cooperative."[47]

From 1975 until 1978 the AAUG lacked a consistent policy with regard to distribution, circulation, and pricing, and those inconsistencies contributed to some confusion and the occasional missed opportunity. In addition to relying on regional chapters to screen the filmstrips free of charge, the AAUG made *Palestine Is the Issue* and *Palestinians: Holding On* available for purchase for $100 and $125 each, respectively, and AAUG members could purchase the filmstrips for half price. The question remained as to why individuals or organizations would pay such an exorbitant price for something they could acquire for free from a local chapter. To be sure, by 1978, various individuals and organizations were reaching out to the AAUG to acquire the filmstrips, but confusion about cost and circulation policy sometimes impeded access and the organization's pedagogical aim. For example, when the Instructional Materials Services coordinator for the Livonia Public Schools in Michigan requested to rent the filmstrips in 1978, he received a letter in return informing him that it was the AAUG's policy to sell, not rent, the materials.[48] This exchange indicates how the unclear and inconsistent distribution policy resulted in missed opportunities that ultimately undermined the goal of producing the materials in the first place. This request indeed prompted the AAUG board of directors to reconsider the amorphous film distribution policy. In the wake of this exchange, the AAUG executive board recognized the vast potential inherent in making the filmstrips available to a wider audience through a rental system. By the start of 1979, the AAUG instituted an official rental policy with a far more financially friendly price point of $50, which included a $20 security deposit to be returned upon receipt of the filmstrip and accompanying audio cassette.[49] By the early 1980s, the filmstrip purchase price had dropped to $50 and the rental price had dropped to $5, making it far more financially feasible for student groups and faculty to request the materials, thereby dramatically increasing their circulation.[50] Between 1982 and 1984, the filmstrips were rented by student groups and faculty at colleges and universities in the United States and Canada such as the International Student Association at Eastern Washington University; the Dalhousie Student Union at Dalhousie University in Nova Scotia, Canada; the Arab Studies Center at Georgetown University; Students for a Free Palestine at Illinois State University in Normal; the Committee for Palestinian Rights at Williams College in Williamstown, Massachusetts; and various student groups and faculty at institutions such as Cornell College in Iowa, Kansas State University, the University of Florida, Youngstown State University in Ohio, Delta College in Michigan, Purdue University in Indiana, and the University of Alabama in Huntsville.

In addition to university student groups and faculty members, churches and faith-based organizations were also interested in the AAUG filmstrips. In one such example from 1979, a representative of the Board of Global Ministries of the United Methodist Church, David H. Blackburn, wrote to the AAUG requesting to rent a filmstrip.[51] Blackburn served as the Interpretive Resource Chairman for the nondenominational World Christian Mission conference. Held annually in the San Francisco Bay Area, the conference drew approximately five hundred participants each year who attended for the express purpose of studying a particular theme with the intention to lead study groups with their home congregations. As Interpretative Resource Chairman, Blackburn's role was "to share with them [attendees] the best possible resources that they may use with the congregations throughout the year."[52] Within Blackburn's rental request existed a fruitful opportunity to widely disseminate the AAUG's academic discourse through ecumenical teachings about liberation theology. Blackburn screened *Palestine Is the Issue* twice that summer, once at the World Christian Mission conference in Northern California, and then again for an audience of 150 at the International Missions Conference in British Columbia. In his letter returning the materials, he noted: "In both instances, the viewers were very much impressed and were interested in knowing about obtaining the use of a copy" of the filmstrips from the AAUG.[53]

The new rental policy not only created greater potential for the filmstrips to be screened to a wider audience, it also laid the groundwork for the AAUG to establish a more robust audiovisual material rental program. The organization had emerged as an authority on Palestine and had positioned itself as a vendor of multimedia material. With the success of generating interest in and circulating the AAUG's in-house produced filmstrips, the organization was then poised in the 1980s to take the leap into a more dynamic mail-order film rental program. The circulation of the filmstrips significantly increased in the aftermath of the Israeli invasion of Southern Lebanon and the Sabra and Shatila Massacre in 1982, as more Palestine solidarity groups began forming at universities and through churches across the United States and Canada.[54] At the critical juncture of 1982, the question posed at the beginning of *Palestine Is the Issue,* "Who are the Palestinians? Why are they angry?," gained new relevancy. Americans of conscience, shocked by the outright aggression and violence perpetrated by Israel in 1982, sought alternative information about Palestine and Israel, and the AAUG stood ready to furnish that information through audiovisual material.

## AAUG Acquires *Occupied Palestine*

If the AAUG's interest in producing and distributing media stemmed from a necessity to educate the US public, then part of attaining that greater pedagogical aim meant challenging subtle and overt forms of censorship and defending civil liberties such as freedom of speech. As will be discussed in greater detail in chapter 2, the 1980s were rife with controversy over—and sometimes violence aimed at—Palestine-focused film and media activism. The AAUG's institution of a mail order rental system occurred just as a high-profile controversy over the censorship of Palestine solidarity politics and freedom of speech gained visibility in the United States. In the face of such controversy—and coinciding with the 1982 Israeli invasion of southern Lebanon and massacre of Palestinian civilians in the Sabra and Shatila refugee camps—the AAUG made a major investment to expand and diversify its media offerings and to support artists and activists in the struggle to protect civil liberties in the United States, such as freedom of speech, by acquiring the documentary film *Occupied Palestine* (1981) for circulation through the rental program.[55]

Directed by Jewish-American independent filmmaker David Koff and produced by Academy Award–winning British actress Vanessa

Redgrave, *Occupied Palestine* was dogged by controversy and threats of violence since its premiere in 1981. In 1978 the Jewish Defense League (JDL), the right-wing Zionist faction that the Southern Poverty Law Center classifies as a terrorist organization, bombed an empty theater in Beverly Hills that had been slated to screen Redgrave's earlier film *The Palestinian* (1977), and the premiere of *Occupied Palestine* in San Francisco in 1981 was interrupted by a bomb threat. Given this history, distributors and exhibitors were reluctant to pick up *Occupied Palestine,* and the film was essentially censored from US theatrical release, which I discuss in greater detail in chapter 2. *Occupied Palestine* was also dogged by criticism surrounding Redgrave herself, who had garnered ire in the 1970s for her outspoken support of the Palestinian liberation cause and her rejection of Zionism, which I address in detail in chapter 4. In 1977, she produced *The Palestinian,* a documentary film focused on the PLO. The following year, Redgrave was nominated for and won the Academy Award for Best Supporting Actress for her role in *Julia* (1977), Fred Zinnemann's Holocaust drama based on Lillian Hellman's 1973 book *Pentimento: A Book of Portraits.* Because of Redgrave's production of *The Palestinian,* she became the subject of much controversy during Hollywood's 1978 award season. In April 1978, the JDL picketed the Academy Awards ceremony in protest of Redgrave's nomination. During her acceptance speech, Redgrave elicited a range of gasps, boos, and applause from the awards show audience as she unflinchingly condemned "Zionist hoodlums" and their attempts to intimidate her and others in their efforts to resist fascism and antisemitism.

In early 1982, the Boston Symphony Orchestra (BSO) booked Redgrave to narrate Igor Stravinsky's opera-oratorio *Oedipus Rex.* Upon receiving an outpouring of criticism from patrons, pressure from Zionist institutions such as the ADL, and threats of "violence and bloodshed" if Redgrave performed, the BSO enforced compulsory Zionism when it terminated Redgrave's contract and canceled the scheduled performances.[56] In turn, Redgrave sued the BSO for breach of contract and violation of her right to free speech.[57]

It was at this moment of conflict that the AAUG made a major investment to align its aims to resist censorship of the Palestinian issue in the US public sphere with its burgeoning project to produce and distribute alternative media about Palestine. The organization endeavored to support Redgrave by helping offset the cost of her legal fees in exchange for a print of *Occupied Palestine* and rights to exhibit and distribute it. The AAUG's mail order rental system ultimately became one of the few venues through which to acquire this hotly contested film during the early 1980s. I analyze additional controversies surrounding *Occupied Palestine* in greater detail in chapter 2; however, I will elaborate here on how the AAUG acquired and distributed the film in the service of grassroots Arab American cinematic activism.

The AAUG's main office was located in a Boston suburb, and, in many ways, the BSO-Redgrave controversy made visible the kind of struggle Boston-area members and AAUG leadership faced in their local activism around Palestine. The Boston area has long been a major locus of struggle over the representation of Palestine.[58] Former AAUG president and then Simmons College sociology professor Elaine Hagopian recalls the pervasive fear she and others experienced due to their activism and public engagement in the Boston area. Hagopian, who was born and raised in a Syrian immigrant community in the Boston suburb of Cambridge during the 1930s and 1940s, received so many threatening phone calls and even a note written on her apartment door that for years she slept with a hammer by her bed.[59] In light of this kind of personal harassment of individuals, the Redgrave controversy afforded a critical opportunity to air Arab American struggles over freedom of speech—in the United States and Palestine alike—out in the public sphere.

In May 1982, the New England Chapter of the AAUG sent a fundraising letter to its membership asking for contributions to help Redgrave "win her legal battle with the BSO, and to raise the necessary funds so that we can show her latest film: 'Occupied Palestine' to the Boston community."[60] The AAUG paid Redgrave $15,000 (the equivalent of $40,000 today) in exchange for a print of the film and the rights to exhibit and distribute it.[61] *Occupied Palestine* was available for a rental fee of $250, which included a $100 deposit refunded upon return of the film.[62] Despite the steep price, the film was in high demand among AAUG members, yet due to technical difficulties, its availability as a rental lasted for only one year, from August 1982 to September 1983. After its exhibition at the AAUG annual convention in Montreal in October 1982, the film went on to screen primarily at universities, in cities across the United States, including Bloomington, Ind.; Lexington, Ky.; Boulder, Colo.; University Park, Pa.; Washington, D.C.; Boston; New York City; the San Francisco Bay Area; and in Ottawa and Montreal, Canada.[63]

The film's rental career was short lived, in part because the rental system itself was prone to too many variables. Between the film's compressed rental schedule and the AAUG's inability to enforce compliance with things such as due dates, the film's timely delivery to its next location was wholly reliant on the honor system and faith in its courier. The piecemeal tendency of the rental system created opportune conditions for failure. Such failures held negative implications not only for the AAUG as a national organization but also for local organizers of screenings who had banked on the promise of a high-caliber film as a means by which to cultivate legitimacy and fend off critics. In one such example, the film's transportation between the United States and Canada proved to be especially challenging. In March 1983, the print's whereabouts were temporarily unknown as the courier, Purolator, lost track of it during transit from California to Quebec. The film had been scheduled to screen in Montreal on March 21, and, having launched an extensive advertising campaign for the event, screening organizer Samaa El-Ibyari anticipated an audience of three hundred people.[64] Despite coordinating with the courier by phone in the several days leading up to the event, the film did not arrive in time for its scheduled screening, and El-Ibyari "had to resort to digging out a much inferior, and outdated, film from their archives."[65] In her complaint to the AAUG, El-Ibyari remarked that the organization, and by extension Arabs in Canada in general, had their "credibility undermined by this situation."[66]

In addition to logistical problems, improper handling of and technical difficulties with the film itself caused tension within the AAUG. In another example, the executive committee of the New York chapter penned an angry letter to AAUG's then president Naseer Aruri in August 1983 regarding the technical difficulties they faced in their attempt to screen the film:

> We were surprised when we screened the film (and found the reels to be in improper sequence) that the film was in extremely poor

> condition, poorly spliced with ordinary scotch tape [*sic*], full of cuts and tears, and we broke two projectors while screening it. . . . Needless to say, in spite of all our efforts to salvage the situation, the film caused us great embarrassment during the program by breaking down. Also the first three or four minutes were literally lost.[67]

Although the New York chapter's unfortunate experience with the AAUG's print of *Occupied Palestine* suggests a general lack of quality control within the rental program, it also indicates how the organization was at a crossroads in the 1980s. The rental program began taking off during a period of growing pains for the organization, and the improper management of the media resources exemplified a need for the AAUG to either reorganize its priorities or more fully institutionalize a media program within the organization. Making *Occupied Palestine* available for rent afforded the opportunity to disseminate otherwise unavailable films about Palestine in an aesthetically sophisticated way that surpassed the filmstrips in terms of production quality and narrativization. However, if audiovisual materials were intended to provide easily accessible information to a wider audience, the exorbitant rental cost of *Occupied Palestine* limited that access to people and organizations with socioeconomic means—and even then, organizations faced technical difficulties that hampered their ability to screen the film. In part due to the high rental cost of *Occupied Palestine,* interest in the filmstrips actually increased substantially in the early 1980s, particularly among student groups organizing on college campuses with limited or no resources. With the AAUG now in possession of *Occupied Palestine,* as well as several other short and feature-length films on videotape, such as the short 1982 documentary *Why* produced by the Palestine Red Crescent Society, the British Broadcasting Corporation's 1982 documentary *Fighting for Survival,* and the short independent documentary *Report from South Lebanon* produced by Icarus Films, the organization reduced the filmstrip rental costs to $5.

Although film screenings carried the potential to alleviate Arab American activists from the burden of representation that AAUG members faced in their organizing efforts, incidents such as those described above reveal that adopting media in Palestine activism also amplified the stakes of that representational burden. Relying on media to relay the message alleviated the pressure placed on individuals tasked with narrativizing Palestinian history and created an illusion of objectivity through the use of a third party. For this reason, the use of media was especially helpful for overcoming the kind of reactionary rejection of alternative information about Palestine that stemmed from systemic anti-Arab racism directed at individuals. The AAUG's emphasis on the grassroots dissemination of cinematic activism was taken up, in part, as a method for bypassing accusations of bias by relying on the media itself to do the heavy lifting. This created the potential for major gains in grassroots mobilizing, but it also left local organizations and individuals vulnerable to criticism in the event of logistical or technical failure.

## What Could Have Been: The Arab Media Center and the Dissolution of the AAUG

During the early 1980s a proposal was put forward to the executive board several years in a row for the creation of an Arab Media Center (AMC), to be housed in the AAUG's headquarters located in Belmont, Massachusetts.[68] Envisioned as an audiovisual resource, distribution, and production center to "greatly expand the Association's ability to inform Americans about the Arab world," the AMC was conceived to "develop and exploit the enormous potential of various forms of media: films and filmstrips, slide shows, video cassettes for television and classroom use, tapes for radio, and photographs. Through these means, we can reach sectors of American society on a much wider and more effective scale than before."[69] The proposal highlighted the exponential growth of electronic media and US society's increasing reliance on it for news and information. It further outlined the vast potential inherent in the burgeoning cable television sector, "a rapidly growing area which is in acute need of programs. The Arab Media Center will be geared to produce and distribute programming that can help fill this need."[70]

Indeed, such a project was already in the works, albeit on a much smaller scale. In response to the cursory US news reportage on the 1982 Israeli invasion of Lebanon, several Boston-area AAUG members and leaders established *Arabic Hour,* a weekly community access television show that remains in production to this day. Through what Noah Habeeb calls "the 'for them, by us,' model" of grassroots community media activism, *Arabic Hour* was conceived, not unlike the AAUG itself, as a method through which to communicate an Arab American perspective on political and social issues of the SWANA region and its diaspora, with a strong focus on the question of Palestine.[71] Founded by Michael Haidar and Elias Aoude, *Arabic Hour* regularly featured AAUG members such as Elaine Hagopian and Naseer Aruri. The AAUG was therefore central to the show's production, with Hagopian in particular serving for many years as one of the show's primary hosts.[72]

The AAUG was never able to manifest the AMC. The proposed budget for the AMC's first year alone was over half a million dollars, with an additional $1.2 million needed to sustain the project into a second year. The AAUG had already been offering financial support to a myriad of media projects proposed to the board, some of which, such as the West Bank Video Project, received AAUG funding but never came to fruition. The resource-constrained organization was not in a position to fund a large-scale project like AMC, despite clear evidence indicating its necessity and immense potential for success. Ultimately, factionalism within the AAUG combined with the lack of a definitive strategic plan contributed to the organization's demise. Here again, as Wasson and Acland note, "even as institutions may extol the virtues of technological innovation and progressive change, at one level such actions help preserve and reproduce that institution. Film has long been used in this seemingly paradoxical sense: to both promote change and to resist it."[73] Research in organizational science has shown that institutions that withstand change and remain operational are those that adapt to their changing environments.[74] One cannot help but wonder what could have become of the AAUG had it embraced a certain kind of flexibility, a willingness to adapt, to reinvent, and ultimately invested what little it had toward the establishment of something new, something different, something like the AMC.

Despite the official dissolution of the AAUG in the 2000s, this history of its media activities indicates how prescient the organization was in terms of understanding and utilizing cinema and media in order to distribute Arab American academic and political critique.

Recovering the history of the AAUG's cinematic activism illuminates how the Arab American community and allies worked on a grassroots level to produce and distribute representations of Palestine that would challenge the compulsory Zionism of US news reportage, cinema, and popular media. As will be discussed in the next chapter, although Arab American activists and organizations were not always *visible* or credited for their role in facilitating cinematic activism for Palestine, they were often at work behind the scenes.

# 2 From Grassroots to Mass Media

## *Occupied Palestine* and Solidarity Cinema in the 1980s

Prior to being acquired by the AAUG, *Occupied Palestine* made its US theatrical premiere on October 21, 1981, at the Castro Theatre as part of the San Francisco International Film Festival (SFIFF). Twenty-five minutes into the packed-house screening, the theater received an anonymous bomb threat. The film's roughly one thousand spectators were evacuated, and the San Francisco Police Department conducted a sweep of the premises but found no bomb.[1] Although the bomb threat posed a frightening disruption, it did not deter the film's spectators. Once the police gave the all-clear, the audience again packed the theater and resumed the "passion-stirring" screening, complete with bouts of frequent and rhythmic applause from whom the *Variety* film reviewer present that evening assumed were Palestinian spectators.[2] That same *Variety* reviewer also witnessed a confrontation between filmmaker David Koff and another film critic who "bombarded" Koff for "rabble-rousing." Overall, the screening was a contentious and boisterous event.

This chapter tracks the process of mainstreaming Palestinian liberation and solidarity politics from taboo and unspeakable to liberal multicultural inclusion. Through continued analysis of David Koff's *Occupied Palestine,* this chapter examines the movement of the AAUG's cinematic activism for Palestine from grassroots exhibition and distribution to mass media broadcast on Public Broadcasting Service (PBS), a process that is especially insightful for understanding the transition from taboo to inclusion. At the same time, the 1980s marks a radical shift within the Palestinian cinematic movement, wherein Palestinian cinema begins to move away from the predominantly documentary films of the third period and moves toward narrative cinema. That move toward narrative cinema is also accompanied by the wider circulation and reception of Palestinian films within the political economy of global cinema as "national cinema." As such, questions of filmmaker identity, authorship, and film categorization became increasingly important after this shift, so much so that the discourse on what is or is not a Palestinian film has evolved today into contestations over film categorization and filmmaker identity.[3] Within this context, the reception of *Occupied Palestine* during this transitional period sheds important light on some of the pitfalls inherent in the process of mainstreaming, specifically regarding how Palestine films and Palestinian national cinema are sometimes collapsed when received in a US context structured by compulsory Zionism.

At the time of its release at the SFIFF in 1981, *Occupied Palestine* depicted a radically different representation of Palestine and Israel than what US audiences were accustomed to seeing through mainstream mass media such as print news, broadcast news, or Hollywood films.[4] *Occupied Palestine* was Jewish American filmmaker David Koff's fifth film. His previous works included the Academy Award–nominated feature-length documentary *People of the Wind* (1976) about the Iranian Babadi tribe's annual migration across the Zagros Mountains in search of fresh livestock pasture, the critically acclaimed documentary *Mau Mau* (1970) about an indigenous Kenyan resistance movement against British colonialism, and *Blacks Britannica* (1978), a documentary commissioned by WGBH, Boston's PBS affiliate station, which focused on African, West Indian, and South Asian Britons' experiences of racism and discrimination in the United Kingdom. In sum, Koff was an established documentarian and well known as an activist filmmaker whose works directly address issues of racism, colonialism, and globalization. I therefore treat *Occupied Palestine* as a premier example of how "Palestine films" constitute a genre.

*Occupied Palestine* was shot on location in 1980 in the Palestinian territory of the West Bank, which was at the time, and continues to be, illegally occupied by the Israeli military and civilian settlers since 1967. The film was intended, in the words of Koff, to "break some of the ice of the monolithic slant" in US public opinion and support of Israel as produced through mainstream news and entertainment media's representations of Palestine and Israel.[5] Sympathetic representations of the Palestinian struggle and Palestine solidarity cinema existed long before Koff's film.[6] What makes *Occupied Palestine* interesting is its prescience within the history of the circulation and reception of Palestine films in the US context. The film pre-dates two major geopolitical events that are considered to be turning points in the representation of, discourse on, and reception of the topic of Palestine within mainstream US media: the 1982 Israeli invasion of Lebanon and the start of the First Intifada in 1987. Through his film, Koff set out to disrupt the regime of representation structured by compulsory Zionism and deployed to justify US cultural and political support for the state of Israel and the continued dispossession of Palestine.[7]

The specter of violence at the Castro that October evening in 1981 indicated that *Occupied Palestine* had touched a nerve. That nerve was attached to a greater system of what I discuss throughout this book as compulsory Zionism, which structures and defines the parameters of discourse on Palestine in the United States and renders Palestinian existence invisible and impossible. The *Occupied Palestine* premiere reveals the violent lengths to which enforcers of compulsory Zionism are willing to go to maintain hegemony when faced with a counter-hegemonic narrative. However, the discourse *within* the film and the film's *reception* in mainstream news media reveal that compulsory Zionism, like all forms of cultural hegemony, does not only operate in spectacular or coercive ways, but is also reproduced in subtle ways around (and even within) Palestine films and their attendant cinematic activism. For example, as controversies over Koff's documentary carried on throughout the 1980s, the print news discourse surrounding the film muddied the categorical waters between Palestinian cinema and Palestine films. Although he self-identified as white, Jewish, and American, Koff was both championed and decried as a *Palestinian* filmmaker in mainstream news media.

As mentioned in the book's introduction, the Palestinian cinematic movement of the third period (1968–1982) was an inherently diverse and collective project, and questions of Palestinian identity and authorship were not as contentious as they would later become in the twenty-first century. But the early 1980s marks a moment of transition from the third to the fourth period, and with that transition came the consolidation of the category of Palestinian cinema with Palestinian identity and authorship. Given this context, the mis/representation of

*Occupied Palestine* as a Palestinian film thereby functioned to displace Palestinian filmmakers (and Arab cinematic activists more broadly) from the field of their own cultural production and, more importantly, amplifies how the categorization of Palestinian cinema in this moment became sutured to the legibility and legitimacy of Palestinian identity. The mainstream US news discourse on *Occupied Palestine* as a Palestinian film is just one example of how compulsory Zionism operates in the United States in order to discursively displace, occupy, and erase Palestinian (and also more generally Arab and Arab American) identity. This chapter therefore has three aims: to delineate "Palestine film" as a genre, to articulate how *Occupied Palestine* can be considered a remake of the AAUG filmstrips, and to identify how compulsory Zionism informs the reception of Palestine films in the US context.

## Overlapping Media Publics: The Castro Theatre as Site of Convergence

Before further delving into analysis of *Occupied Palestine,* it is important to historicize the film's premiere within the larger, overlapping contexts of leftist social movement histories, film culture, and Arab immigrant history in the United States, particularly within the context of the San Francisco Bay Area. The following section addresses how the film's premiere at the Castro Theatre reveals how the exhibition of Palestinian cinema and Palestine films has historically afforded a space of convergence wherein conservative attacks on multiple US and transnational social and political justice movements become legible. At the time of *Occupied Palestine's* release, the San Francisco Bay Area maintained a reputation as a region where identity-based and cause-based social and political justice movements thrived within a broader counterculture of artists and intellectuals invested in leftist activism. Beginning in the 1960s, the Black Power movement and the Black Panther Party, the Third World Liberation movement and the fight for ethnic studies, the Free Speech Movement, the antiwar movement, and the Gay Liberation movement all had roots in the Bay Area. The 1960s were also a time of increased Arab immigration to the United States. The McCarran-Walter Act of 1952 and the Immigration Act of 1965, which removed quotas and prioritized skilled workers, refugees, and family reunification, were both influential in facilitating Arab immigration to the United States.[8]

In her ethnographic study of Arab American activism in the San Francisco Bay Area, Nadine Naber discusses how and why California, and the Bay Area in particular, became such a major site for Arab immigrant communities in the United States. In her interviews with "old-timers," those who came during the 1950s, 1960s, and 1970s, Naber identifies larger geopolitical factors that informed Arab migration to the United States. Events such as the Nakba ("the catastrophe" in Arabic) and subsequent creation of the state of Israel in 1948; the Naksa ("the setback" in Arabic), or Israel's invasion and occupation of the remaining Palestinian territories in 1967; and the outbreak of the Lebanese Civil War in 1975 resulted in widespread displacement and an increased number of Palestinian refugees within the Southwest Asia and North Africa (SWANA) region. As these events were unfolding, Arab migrants who previously had come to the United States temporarily for education or work ended up staying as de facto refugees due to their inability to safely return or, as was the case with Palestinians, because they were barred from returning home. Others came as the direct result of war and occupation and gravitated to the Bay Area because they already knew people there.[9] California also emerged as a site of historical and cultural import during this increase in Arab migration in the 1950s through 1990s. Since the 1960s, California has long since been a locus for student activism and counterculture, and by the 1990s California had emerged as one of the most racially diverse states in the United States, becoming one of a small number of states with a nonwhite majority.[10] Relatedly, in *Arab Routes,* Gualtieri traces Arab migration pathways to California that upend the East-Coast-centric migration narratives that dominate the field of Arab immigrant history. Gualtieri shows that early twentieth-century Arab migration to California often took a southern route, with multiple and lengthy stops in Latin America, producing a strong sense of Arab Latinidad among those migrants.[11] For these myriad geopolitical and social reasons, California now has the largest Arab American population in the United States, most of which is concentrated in and around the San Francisco and Los Angeles areas.[12]

The overlapping cultural identities of Arab immigrants on the West Coast in many ways mirrors the region's overlapping cultural and social histories. These overlaps are perhaps best exemplified through the history of the Castro Theatre as a site of overlapping media publics.[13] As one of San Francisco's oldest and most famous cinemas, the Castro holds a significant place in multiple, overlapping social histories, including Arab American immigrant history, architectural history, and LGBTQ+ film cultural history. The Castro's first incarnation was in 1907 as The Liberty, when Abraham Nasser turned his grocery store on the corner of Collingwood and Eighteenth Streets into a nickelodeon by projecting moving pictures onto one of the storefront's blank walls.[14] Nasser was an immigrant from the Mount Lebanon region of the Ottoman province of Greater Syria, which is now the state of Lebanon. By 1920, Nasser's three sons had grown their father's burgeoning nickelodeon into a thriving cinema business. The Nasser brothers owned three theaters: two in the Mission District and one on Castro Street in the neighborhood that was then called Eureka Valley. In order to accommodate their growing business, the Nasser brothers applied for a loan from Humboldt Bank to expand the Castro Street location. Once they secured the loan, the banker referred the Nassers to his younger brother, Timothy Pflueger, an aspiring architect who was not yet licensed at the time the Nassers approached him for the project. As soon as Pflueger passed his California licensure exam, he began the designs for the Castro Theatre. This was Pflueger's first theater project, and it was the beginning of what would become Pflueger's long and illustrious career as one of California's premier art deco theater designers (Figure 2).[15] Over one hundred years later, the Nasser family still owns the Castro Theatre and remains a prominent Arab American family in the Bay Area.

One would think that a screening of Koff's film would be "safe" in a region with such vibrant countercultures, a socially conscious arts and intellectual life, and a relatively large Arab American community. It is with no lack of irony, though, that a film that sought to humanize the Palestinians, who have for so long been dehumanized through mainstream media's construction of the terrorist stereotype, would in turn become the target of a domestic terrorism threat. The *Occupied Palestine* premiere was not the first nor the last time that Arab American communities would be threatened with such violence. A series of domestic terror attacks were perpetrated against Palestinian American civil rights activists and Arab-American civil rights organizations

Figure 2. *Top:* Exterior of the Castro Theatre, San Francisco, CA, circa June 1927. Photographer unknown. Courtesy of Jack Tillmany and OpenSFHistory / wnp5.50467. *Bottom:* Interior of the Castro Theatre, San Francisco, CA, circa June 1927. Photographer unknown. From the Jack Tillmany Collection / Courtesy of a private collector and OpenSFHistory / wnp67.0015.

during the 1970s and 1980s. For example, in 1972 a member of the Jewish Defense League (JDL) was convicted of bombing the Los Angeles home of a Palestinian American activist, and in 1978 another JDL member was convicted of bombing the (empty) theater where Vanessa Redgrave's pro-Palestinian documentary film *The Palestinian* was scheduled to screen the following day. Later, in 1985, the American Arab Anti-Discrimination Committee (ADC) was the target of several attacks: ADC's West Coast director, Alex Odeh, was killed by a bomb planted at the regional office in Santa Ana, California; the national office in Washington, D.C., was ransacked and set ablaze; and a bomb that had been planted at the New England regional office in Boston injured two police officers who attempted to defuse it.[16] In short, for Arab American activists and allies, the 1970s and 1980s were marked by a pervasive and legitimate fear of violence.

Arab Americans were not the only civil rights activists in California or elsewhere to be targeted by domestic terrorism during this same period. In San Francisco in 1977, civil rights activist Harvey Milk—the first openly gay person elected to a public office in California—and Mayor George Moscone were assassinated at City Hall. That same year, the San Francisco International Lesbian and Gay Film Festival was established during the rise of the gay liberation movement. Later renamed Frameline: San Francisco International LGBTQ+ Film Festival (from here on simply referred to as Frameline), the festival was born of an activist ethos that was galvanized in the wake of the Milk and Moscone assassinations, and has since not only rapidly grown into an iconic institution within the Bay Area LGBTQ+ community but is also renowned internationally as a model for identity- and cause-based activist film festival organizing.[17] In June 1981, three years after the assassination of Harvey Milk and only four months before *Occupied Palestine*'s premiere at the SFIFF, Frameline established the Castro Theatre as its permanent annual venue.[18]

These linkages between Arab American immigrant history, the gay liberation movement and its international influence on film festival culture, and the art-historical import of the Castro Theatre's architectural design imbued the threat posed to *Occupied Palestine* that October evening with even greater significance. When taken within this historical context, the threat posed to the spectators, filmmaker, festival organizers, and cultural politics represented through *Occupied Palestine*'s exhibition becomes legible as a danger to multiple marginalized groups and social movements that not only utilize the space of the Castro Theatre but also together constitute a set of overlapping media publics. The bomb threat that evening, therefore, was not merely an attempt to silence an expression of Palestinian liberation and solidarity politics. Compulsory Zionism, which the bomb threat was attempting to enforce, endangered a renowned cultural landmark of great significance to the Arab American community, the LGBTQ+

community, California art history, and the numerous other cause-based and identity-based film festivals that utilize the theater. Put another way, the threat against Palestinian liberation, solidarity politics, and Arab Americans became a threat to multiple, diverse media publics. As will be explored in chapter 3, these overlapping issues would come to a head in the early 1990s when lesbian and gay artists and activists and Palestinian filmmakers would be placed in allied relation to one another in their shared struggles over censorship, state violence, and self-determination.

## Palestinian Cinema and Palestine Films as Genre

One aim of this chapter is to distinguish between Palestinian cinema as a category of national or ethnic cultural production and Palestine film as a genre. What is at stake in such a delineation? And are these distinctions mutually exclusive? While the majority of Palestinian cinema certainly can and does fit within the Palestine film genre, to say that *all* Palestinian-authored films are also always Palestine films is limiting. To do so confines Palestinian cinema to a set of narrative conventions, formal expectations, and indeed audiences, which are inseparable from what is referred to in the US context as "the conflict," thereby entrapping Palestinian cinema in Fredric Jameson's prison of the national allegory.[19] Such a conflation destabilizes the "place" of Palestinian filmmakers (especially those whose films may not address the question of Palestine overtly or didactically) within the category of "Palestinian cinema," making them vulnerable not only to unfair criticisms of their work but also to outright exclusion from the larger field of the Palestinian cinematic movement. Likewise, to conflate Palestine films with national cinema is to unwittingly create a loophole for the colonization of the category of Palestinian cinema. An extreme exploitation of that loophole creates the possibility of Zionist filmmakers' ability to claim the identity of "Palestinian filmmaker" and occupy the field of "Palestinian cinema." This chapter addresses the more subtle ways such a loophole can be manipulated, as was the case with the anti-Zionist film *Occupied Palestine* and its reception within the US context as a Palestinian film.

Deciphering between Palestinian cinema and Palestine films also endows spectators with the possibility of more nuanced engagements with Palestinian and Palestine-related films. Just as Palestine films alleviate the burden of representing and explaining "the conflict" from individual Palestinian shoulders, in similar ways, the distinction between national/ethnic cinema and solidarity cinema has the potential to alleviate a kind of burden of edification for spectators. Such a distinction allows audiences, institutions, and industries to spectate, exhibit, and circulate Palestinian cinema *without* the sense of overt ideological expectations or directives, as is discussed in greater detail in chapters 3 and 5. There are certainly covert political consequences in promoting a depoliticized consumption of Palestinian cinema, not least of which includes the commodification of Palestinian representation and the reduction of Palestinian liberation and solidarity to simulacra. But I want to keep space available for Palestinian filmmakers—especially those in diaspora, those who are LGBTQ+, those who are of mixed race or ethnicity, those who for whatever reason do not conform to the aesthetics and social conventions of the politics of cultural authenticity—to be able to tell stories, make art, and exist in the world as Palestinians *and* cultural producers without the crushing weight that the expectation to narrate places on their creative energies or forecloses opportunities. Put another way, to distinguish between Palestinian cinema and Palestine films affords another kind of visual sovereignty, by which I mean the freedom to be Palestinian, to represent as a Palestinian, and to represent Palestine (or not) in ways that are absent of (perhaps even liberated from) references to Zionism, Israel, occupation, and apartheid.

That said, it is for similar reasons that I am ambivalent about referring to Palestinian cinema as "national cinema," because doing so imposes a constrained criteria for who or what constitutes "Palestine" in accordance with Eurocentric nation-state norms. As a moniker of the global film industry, the nomenclature of "national cinema" is problematic in its own right, especially in the context of increasingly globalized and transnational film production and circulation industries. In the context of the United States, designating a film as representative of a "national cinema" is largely reserved for non-English-language films and their legibility and marketability within the US entertainment market, as well as their eligibility for nomination in Eurocentric awards ceremonies. Within this latter context, "national cinema" is also contingent on the existence of a United Nations–recognized nation-state, which poses significant obstacles in terms of recognition, categorization, marketing, and circulation of films made by diasporic, transnational, and/or ethnic minority filmmakers who happen to be working from within a nation-state context that may not align with their national, ethnic, or cultural identity (discussed further in chapter 4). I am therefore in favor of thinking about Palestinian cinema more in terms of what Hamid Naficy has described as "accented cinema." Naficy deciphers the aesthetics of accented cinema in terms of how identity, homeland, and belonging are imagined among exilic, diasporic, and ethnic filmmakers. Unlike national cinema, which is inherently sutured to the geopolitical construct of the nation-state, accented cinema acknowledges and celebrates the deterritorialized nature of exilic and diasporic filmmaking, the affective dimensions of that deterritorialization, the refusal of notions of cultural purity or authenticity, attention to authorship, preoccupation with borders (geographic, geopolitical, social, cultural, etc.), and, perhaps most importantly, a simultaneous criticism and cooptation of any and all film styles, whether national, classic Hollywood, or that of a particular film movement.[20] Various attempts to codify Palestinian cinema in terms of national cinema have invariably left people and places out of the picture and out of the narrative. This is in part due to the kind of slippages around authorship and categorization that I will analyze in this chapter, but also in part due to the ways in which cinema has become a screen upon which anxieties over Palestinian identity and nationalism are projected. When I refer to Palestinian cinema, I am therefore referring to films made by filmmakers of Palestinian ethnic heritage, regardless of their citizenship, nationality, or administrative status in any given territory or nation-state, and regardless of the film's il/legibility as Palestinian "national cinema."

## *Occupied Palestine* as Remake

While the previous chapter addressed the grassroots circulation of *Occupied Palestine* as part of the AAUG's mail-order multimedia rental program, this chapter examines the work performed by Koff's film within the discourse on Palestine in the United States through an analysis of the controversies that surrounded the film's theatrical exhibition and later broadcast on public television stations nationwide in the 1980s. After nearly thirty years of being lost and forgotten, *Occupied Palestine* has been resurrected to critical acclaim in the last decade, largely due to the film's reexhibition within the global Palestine-themed film festival circuit. For example, the London Palestine Film Festival featured the newly digitized film for its 2013 festival season, followed by the Boston Palestine Film Festival in 2014, each complete with a postscreening question-and-answer session with Koff. Since this resurrection, the film has been celebrated by film critics, academics, and activists alike as an exceptional example of Palestine solidarity cinematic activism in practice—in terms of both the challenges the film faced and its triumphs.[21]

*Occupied Palestine* is by no means the earliest example of a Palestine film, and several scholars have written about the longer history of Palestinian cinema and solidarity cinema. For example, Nadia Yaqub's *Palestinian Cinema in the Days of Revolution* (2018) privileges Palestinian authorship and historicizes the work of the Palestine Film Unit, Third World Newsreel, the United Nations, and various Third Cinema movements that had been making and circulating revolutionary films about the Palestinian crisis (and specifically from the Palestinian perspective) since the Nakba. Alternately, Terri Ginsberg's *Visualizing the Palestinian Struggle: Towards a Critical Analytic of Palestine Solidarity Film* meditates on a body of films made to promote solidarity with the Palestinian liberation struggle, essentially identifying Palestine solidarity films less as a distinct entity and more as a filmmaking mode recognized though "critical analysis of that cinema's ideological orientation and structural praxis with respect to its political aesthetics and discursive scope."[22]

I am not interested in exceptionalizing *Occupied Palestine* as standing apart from the greater body of Palestine solidarity cinema. However, its inception and production, its attempted exhibition, and its contested broadcast on PBS afford a rich example of both Arab American cinematic activism in action *and* the subjugation of Arab American intellectual and organizational labor within Palestine solidarity cinema more generally. By privileging and focusing on the Arab American actors involved with *Occupied Palestine*'s exhibition and broadcast, we can see that the controversies surrounding this film were used as an opportunity to implement some of the AAUG's cinematic activism strategies outlined in the previous chapter, including the promotion of Palestinian and Arab American scholars and activists within certain forms of US mass media—namely, mainstream print news and public television. This chapter is therefore primarily concerned with Koff's film as a strategic text within a larger movement of Arab American cinematic activism for Palestine, and how the controversy surrounding its exhibition and broadcast, as well as its reception and representation amid overlapping media publics, created an opportunity to exercise some of the AAUG's grassroots cinematic activism strategies, but on a much larger scale. At the same time, analysis of the production and reception of *Occupied Palestine* also offers a case study for understanding the erasure of Arab American activist and academic labor, thereby also providing an example of how compulsory Zionism informs the reception of Palestine films.

As my previous analysis of its circulation through the AAUG demonstrates, in the face of widespread attempted censorship, blacklisting, and threats of violence against the film's audience, the grassroots distribution of *Occupied Palestine* in the United States was the result of Arab American scholars and activists leveraging the power of the AAUG's organizational structure, intellectual commitments, and activist praxis. One of the AAUG's Public Affairs Committee's main directives was to encourage members to actively engage with US mass media, whether through writing letters to the editors of major newspapers or serving as representatives for local print, radio, and television news outlets seeking comment on current affairs pertinent to the organization's mission. As discussed in the previous chapter, the AAUG also strategically produced and distributed media as a vehicle for the organization's scholarly discourse on Palestine and Zionism. Through these combined efforts, engagements with film and media—whether through multimedia production or in response to it—were central to the AAUG's strategies and methods for promoting public intellectualism, and *Occupied Palestine*'s production, distribution, and broadcast in the United States offers a rich example of these methods and strategies in action.

Although *Occupied Palestine* is not, on the surface, an Arab- or Arab-American-made film, this particular film's form and content, its initial theatrical exhibition, and its later repackaging for broadcast on PBS stations in the mid-1980s offer an example of how Arab American institutions and cinematic activism practices have been simultaneously integral to and subjugated within Palestine solidarity cinema history. Through a close analysis of the film's reception, primarily through the print news discourse surrounding the controversy over its broadcast on PBS, I argue that the film's contested exhibition in the United States both facilitated an opportunity for the wider dissemination of Arab American academic critique through mass media and simultaneously perpetuated a liberal form of compulsory Zionism that obscured the work of Arab and Arab American scholars and activists whose intellectual labor helped shape the film and whose organizational labor helped make the film available to various media publics in the United States.

This chapter therefore serves to recuperate the Palestinian and Arab American intellectual content and labor that made a film like *Occupied Palestine* possible. I argue that *Occupied Palestine* was shaped by the AAUG's multimedia texts and scholarship: the filmstrips *Palestine Is the Issue* (1974) and *Palestinians: Holding On* (1976), as well as scholarship such as Edward Said's *The Question of Palestine* (1979), Abdeen Jabara's *Zionism and Racism* (1976), and Ibrahim Abu-Lughod's edited volume *The Transformation of Palestine* (1971). Put another way, I argue that *Occupied Palestine* is a loose remake of the AAUG filmstrips. Although the blacklisting of the film prevented it from a wider theatrical exhibition in the United States after its premiere in 1981, the film's resurfacing on public television in 1986 afforded an opportunity to put the AAUG's grassroots strategies into action through the liberal-oriented mass media platform of PBS.

## *Holding On* to *Occupied Palestine*

*Occupied Palestine* was not conceived in a vacuum. The following section offers some historical context for understanding how a film like *Occupied Palestine* emerged from a longer genealogy of Arab American scholar-activism that has largely gone uncredited in discussions of Palestine films. As previously mentioned, in 2013 *Occupied Palestine* experienced a resurgence of interest among activists and scholars alike. Koff's film has since received an abundance of praise for its sympathetic portrayal of the Palestinian people and their struggle for justice. I seek to contextualize the newfound critical reception of *Occupied Palestine* by situating the film within the genealogy of Arab American cinematic activism as detailed in the previous chapter. In the following section, I examine not only how Koff's film was influenced by the emergent Arab American studies scholarly discourse on Palestine and Zionism but also how *Occupied Palestine* could be considered a remake of the AAUG's educational filmstrips *Palestine Is the Issue* (1974) and *Palestinians: Holding On* (1976), which go uncredited in Koff's film. My evidence for this is rooted in a triangulated textual and visual analysis of these three media texts in comparison to key scholarly texts produced by AAUG scholars prior to and contemporaneously with those media texts.

How did Koff come to make this film? When considering how and why people not of Arab descent in the United States came to consciousness and educated themselves on the issue of Palestine during the 1970s and 1980s, it is difficult *not* to point to some form of Arab American scholarship, activism, or media methods—namely, the resources, both human and textual, made available through the AAUG. Although Koff was already ensconced in social and political justice discourses on colonialism and racism, the production of a film like *Occupied Palestine* would have required substantial research, not to mention networking with Palestinians in the occupied territories and Israelis working against the occupation. And in order to make a film intended to fill a representational void, Koff would have needed to understand what kinds of film and media from the Palestinian perspective already existed and circulated in the United States.

In *Visualizing the Palestinian Struggle: Towards a Critical Analytic of Palestine Solidarity Film,* Terri Ginsberg notes that Koff had been in communication with AAUG members, most notably civil rights attorney Abdeen Jabara.[23] Given that it was the AAUG Public Affairs Committee's official policy and practice to utilize the filmstrips whenever possible for the express purpose of educating sympathetic "fellow Americans," if Koff had been in contact with Jabara and others from the AAUG, then he likely would have, at the very least, been made aware of, if not outright screened, the AAUG filmstrips. Given these connections, and the narrative, formal, and rhetorical similarities between Koff's film and the AAUG filmstrips, it is plausible that Koff scripted and produced *Occupied Palestine* based on engagement with AAUG academic literature and multimedia texts on Palestine and Zionism. A comparative analysis of the argument, narrative, and visual methods of *Occupied Palestine* in relation to *Palestine Is the Issue* and *Palestinians: Holding On,* in relation to academic arguments produced by AAUG members during this same period, as well as Koff's own contributions to Arab studies, supports this claim.[24]

There are three major overlapping narratives, arguments, and methods across the AAUG filmstrips and Koff's film: Each media text emphasizes the financial relationship between the United States and Israel, draws on Zionist primary source documents to highlight how ethnic cleansing is inherent to Zionist statecraft, and utilizes Palestinian first-person accounts of ethnic cleansing events. These overlaps manifest in nearly identical narrative arcs, the most compelling of which exist within *Holding On* and *Occupied,* in a set of scenes that recount the ethnic cleansing of the Palestinian villages of Yalu, Beit Nuba, and Imwas in 1967, and the Jewish National Fund's subsequent establishment of Canada Park. Both *Holding On* and *Occupied* utilize voiceover narration of firsthand accounts of the Israeli military's violence toward Palestinian villages paired with archival and contemporary imagery of the village landscapes. Although the two texts represent strikingly similar narratives, characters, arguments, and imagery, they each deliver that information in opposite narrative order to one another.

Through split screen text and image slides, *Holding On* walks spectators through the logic of settler colonialism and provides an exegesis of Israel's legislative basis for ethnic cleansing. A series of slides presents the text of various Israeli laws, including the 1948 Emergency Articles for the Exploitation of Uncultivated Lands, the Law on the Acquisition of Absentees' Property of 1950, and the Security Area Emergency Laws of 1949. Referred to collectively from here onward as the Absentee laws, together, when enforced through Zionist paramilitary and Israeli military intimidation and outright violence, these laws functioned to dispossess and seize Palestinian land and property. The first in this series of three textual slides addresses the Emergency Articles for the Exploitation of Uncultivated Lands. The law appears as a heading in bold, followed by a brief explanation: "Hands 'abandoned' property to Jews for cultivation, ultimately reverting to State ownership." A single black-and-white photograph is displayed simultaneously on the right depicting an arid, "empty" field, framed by a small pile of rubble in the foreground and a row of olive trees in the background (Figure 3).

Figure 3. A frame from the filmstrip *Palestinians: Holding On* (1976). Copyright the Association of Arab American University Graduates.

At first glance this slide appears visually unremarkable and wholly utilitarian, designed with the sole purpose of informing the viewer of such a law. To a Eurocentric, colonial viewer of the landscape image in this slide, "cultivated" lands are legible primarily through a symmetrical and orderly agrarian grid of intelligibility. As such, the image of open space is perceived as "uncultivated." However, in viewing the image through the lens of indigenous Palestinian land management, the row of olive trees in the background and open space in the foreground are indeed indicative of a cultivated landscape suitable for olive harvesting. This slide depicts not only Israel's founding mythology of "a land without people for a people without land" and "making the desert bloom," but also reveals that such mythology was manifested by a set of laws specifically designed to realize it. The law's phrasing is laden with signification: "Uncultivated Lands" conjures a mental image of a wild, untamed landscape, abandoned by civilization, uncultured, a desert deserted, indeed, without people there to care for and cultivate it. Likewise, "Emergency Articles" signifies an emergent state of exception, both in terms of human condition and the body politic of a would-be nation-state, harkening to the crisis of European Jewish refugees in the wake of the Holocaust, the proverbial people without land. The aesthetic of the bisected screen therefore functions to remind the viewer of how this mythology is manufactured through a discriminatory legal system designed to invisibilize indigenous land practices, vacate the Palestinian landscape, and repopulate it as Israel.

From this sequence of slides representing Israel's Absentee laws, the filmstrip moves on to provide an estimated value of US$113 billion (as of 1976) of Palestinian property seized by Israel (Figure 4).[25] The filmstrip then moves into a sequence of still images illustrating the ethnic cleansing of three villages on the outskirts of Jerusalem in 1967. The split screen sequence depicts photographs of village ruins alongside close-up photographic portraits of elderly Palestinian men and women, symbolic of the people who had once inhabited the landscape on screen. This image sequence is paired with a narration of first-person oral history accounts by Palestinian victims of ethnic cleansing of the villages of Yalu, Beit Nuba, and Imwas in 1967, along with narrator Allen Carr's explanation of Israeli soldiers' rape and murder of Palestinian villagers. A particularly unsettling sequence

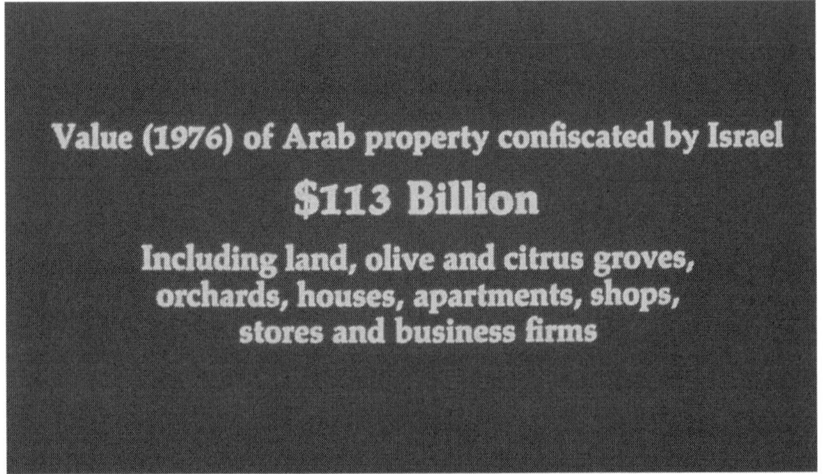


Figure 4. A frame from the filmstrip *Palestinians: Holding On* (1976). Copyright the Association of Arab American University Graduates.

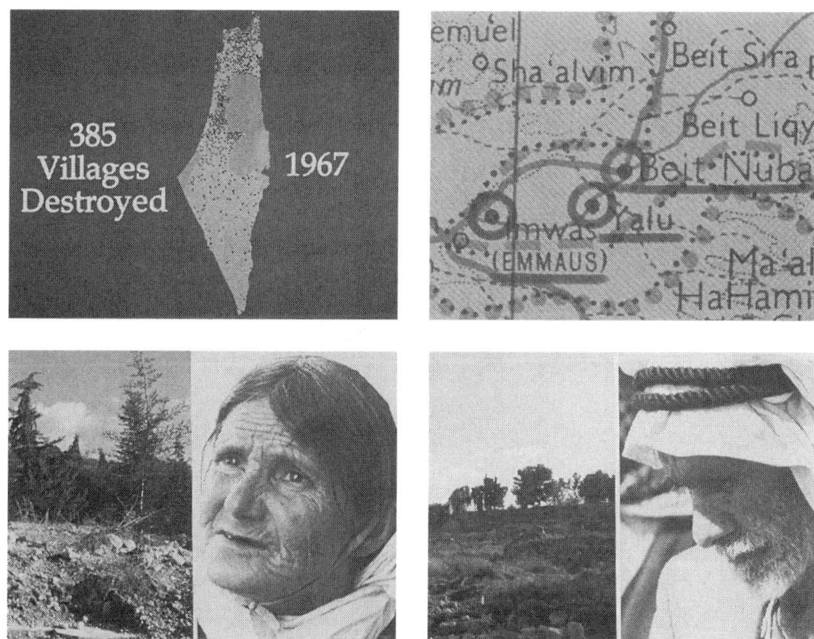


Figure 5. Frames from the filmstrip *Palestinians: Holding On* (1976). Copyright the Association of Arab American University Graduates.

ensues, beginning with mundane photographs of stone rubble amid a young pine forest as Carr narrates the historical account of how the Israeli military bulldozed the homes of elderly and disabled villagers, the inhabitants still inside and left to perish under the stone (Figure 5). The land is thus made uncultivated through the dispersed rubble. It has been violently evacuated of life, forcefully depopulated. It has, in essence, been primed for the Absentee laws.

The sequence closes with a photograph of the contemporary Canada Park sign in Hebrew and English in the foreground, stone rubble and young pine trees in the background (Figure 6). Through this sequence, *Holding On* guides the spectator through a critically distant and intellectualized discussion of Zionist ideological investment in ethnic cleansing and the Israeli state's legal apparatus to achieve those ideological aims, before plunging the viewer into a graphic narrative of the human toll of the Zionist project.

Figure 6. A frame from the filmstrip *Palestinians: Holding On* (1976). Copyright the Association of Arab American University Graduates.

The narrative described above offers an example of how to identify a film as within the genre of Palestine film. In large part it comes down to the concept of form, which Kenneth Burke argues is about the creation and satisfaction of desire.[26] In viewing any media sympathetic to the Palestinian liberation struggle, a certain desire exists to *see* the material results and human cost of Zionist political ideology in action. Palestine films as a genre, then, appeal to spectators for their promise to furnish representations, whether visually, rhetorically, or subtextually, of Palestinian suffering in relation to Zionism. Indeed, this is where the rhetorical structure of compulsory Zionism enters the fray of genre categorization. Compulsory Zionism as a rhetorical structure can indeed exist within the categories of Palestine film, by continually foregrounding a narrative about Zionism and requiring the objectification of Palestinian suffering as evidence of Zionism's inherent violence.

*Occupied Palestine* renders this same narrative sequence, but in reverse order, beginning with the contemporary conditions of the land and working backward through the violent events that transpired there, before closing with a discussion of the state's Absentee laws and legal framework for ethnic cleansing. *Occupied Palestine*'s scene begins with a sequence of observational shots of a dedication ceremony for a new settlement sponsored by Canadian funders on the outskirts of Jerusalem. The dedication ceremony speaker tells a story of triumphant pioneers settling land and beginning anew, a familiar colonial narrative for North American spectators. The scene transitions to still shots of Canada Park, a woodland park in Jerusalem established by the Jewish National Fund in honor of Canadian funders. The camera depicts the park as a serene, even peaceful place with soft golden light filtering through pine trees to illuminate empty and inviting picnic tables. The sound of birds softly chirping amid the branches is interrupted by a single gunshot. A caption then graces the bottom of the screen: "Amos Kenan, 'Report on the Razing of Villages . . .' 1967," as a dramatic voiceover—read by British actor Ian Holm—details the Israeli army's demolition and expulsion of a Palestinian village in 1967. As the camera tracks through the park, showing picnic tables, campsites, and a children's swing set, Holm narrates Kenan's testimony:

> At noon the first bulldozer arrived and pulled down the first house. Within ten minutes, it was turned into rubble, including its entire contents. The olive trees, cypress trees, all were uprooted. We were ordered to block the entrances to the village and prevent the inhabitants from returning. The order was to shoot over their heads. We asked the officers why the refugees were sent from one place to another. They told us this was good for them—they should go—moreover, why should we care about the Arabs, anyway? The platoon commander said simply that they were to be driven out. We drove them out.

This narration prompts the viewer to imagine the atrocities described and envision what is absent from the landscape as depicted on screen. Through a distinct absence of empathetic imagery, the work of visualizing the atrocity is performed through the viewer's imaginative interpretation of the voiceover narration, producing what Ginsberg refers to as a "contemporaneity effect."[27] This technique is continued throughout the scene, as the camera cuts to a medium shot of a young Palestinian woman who narrates her experience of witnessing her own village being demolished over the course of several days, including the horror in hearing of a disabled elderly man who could not flee his home and was thus buried alive as the Israeli army razed his home (Figure 5). The camera cuts back to the bucolic images of Canada Park, and as we see this landscape for the second time, what had first appeared warm and appealing suddenly takes on a sinister sense of haunting as we come to understand that the same emptiness that had made this scenery so inviting was in fact necessitated through ethnic cleansing.

The Palestinian woman interviewee goes on to describe all the amenities that once existed in her village—a textile shop, a grocery, a pharmacy, two schools—as the camera meditates on a series of archival black-and-white photographs of the village's white stone houses cascading down a hillside, a family portrait showing three generations, and finally two women in traditional village dresses standing amid olive trees. She laments: "It was just like any other Arab village; it had all the requirements of life." The camera cuts again to Canada Park with captions explaining the Jewish National Fund's establishment of the park in 1976 on the lands of Yalu, Beit Nuba, and Imwas, three villages razed in 1967 that had a total of 10,000 residents. The interspersing of contemporary scenes of Canada Park with archival images and voiceovers of firsthand accounts and Palestinian experiences of expulsion serves an important pedagogical purpose. This segment of the film trains the audience to see that which is visual, but not visible, throughout the film: the absence of the indigenous Palestinian population and the violence of ethnic cleansing that necessitated such an absence. To reinforce this visual argument, *Occupied Palestine* moves into a narrative explanation of the Israeli Absentee laws before providing a series of captions with estimates of the value of Palestinian property seized by Israel since 1967.

Aside from mirroring the narrative, argument, visual methods, and form of *Holding On, Occupied* aestheticizes the AAUG's discourse on Zionist ethnic cleansing by utilizing the same scholarly methods and content of Edward Said's scholarship. As a literary scholar, Said famously utilized close textual analysis of primary sources to make his arguments in *Orientalism* (1978) and *The Question of Palestine* (1979). In *The Question of Palestine,* Said draws on the diaries and published writings of prominent Zionist intellectuals and politicians, namely, Theodor Herzl, Joseph Weitz, and Chaim Weizmann, to demonstrate how ethnic cleansing was always considered an essential means to the Zionist statecraft end.

One scene in *Occupied* is particularly telling of Said's methodology. The camera pans slowly through an abandoned village, partially demolished and desolate, as narrator Holm provides a dramatized voiceover of Joseph Weitz's personal diary entry from December 19, 1940. Weitz, then director of the Jewish National Fund, wrote:

> It must be clear that there is no place for both peoples in this country. If the Arabs leave the country, it will be broad and will be wide open for us. . . . The only solution is Eretz Israel, or at least the Western part of Eretz Israel, without Arabs. There is no room for compromise on this point, and there is no other way than to transfer Arabs from here to the neighboring countries, to transfer them all.

This scene functions as a cinematic rendering of Edward Said's essay "Zionism from the Standpoint of Its Victims," which was published in 1979, the year prior to Koff's filming of *Occupied Palestine,* and which contains this same excerpt from Weitz's published diary. The film works to make Said's argument *visual* by showing the expressly settler-colonial aims of Zionist political ideology and making visible the material effects of colonial power relations between occupier (Israel) and occupied (Palestine).[28] In this way, *Occupied Palestine* aestheticizes the Palestinian condition of absent-presence.[29] This assemblage of scenes and narration performs the pedagogical work of teaching the viewer to *see* Palestine beneath the screen of contemporary Israel. By drawing upon the mythology of "a people without land for a land without people" in conjunction with visual evidence of Palestinian historical existence in the landscape through the depiction of the village architecture and archival photographs, *Occupied Palestine* is illustrating—and making visible—the Palestinian legal status of present-absentee and in doing so aestheticizes Palestine as occupied by Zionism.

Returning to the question of the AAUG's influence on *Occupied* and its distribution throughout the United States, the following section addresses how these media texts' emphasis on the Palestinian condition of absent-presence becomes increasingly important when we consider the *reception* of *Occupied* in particular, and Palestine films in general, as documented within the mainstream press in the United States.

## Arab American Cinematic Activism in Mass Media

Although attempts in the 1980s and 1990s to screen independent films and reportage that challenged the compulsory Zionism of mainstream media were met with strong resistance from spectators, Zionist activists and organizations, and media producers alike, such controversies also pointed to the possibility for new forms of activism based on film, media, and visual culture. *Occupied Palestine* would be cast into the national spotlight once more when in 1986 San Francisco's PBS station, KQED, included the film in a new program designed for national broadcast: *Flashpoint.* It is likely that the AAUG facilitated the inclusion of *Occupied Palestine* in the *Flashpoint* episode. A letter from Khalil E. Jahshan to Nabila Shehadeh (both on the AAUG board of directors at the time) confirms that the film's producer, Vanessa Redgrave, had authorized the AAUG's use of the film "to produce a special television program to be aired in California."[30] Given the date of the letter (1983) and an estimated production timeline for the *Flashpoint* broadcast, along with the fact that KQED is based in San Francisco and Shehadeh's mailing address was in the Bay Area, it is plausible that the AAUG was the source for *Flashpoint*'s use of the film.

As an institution, public television is a dynamic and fraught site for considering the ways in which mass media itself constitutes a public sphere.[31] Historically envisioned as the antidote to the homogenous cultural wasteland of network broadcasting and all its commercial interests, public television was meant to serve "the public good," by providing content in the service of democratic ideals.[32] However, "public" is in some ways a misnomer, since contemporary public television is predominantly funded through private foundations and neither the institution nor its content are produced or run democratically. As Laurie Ouellette makes clear, public television was historically not produced "by" the people, it was produced "for" the people, with the paternalistic intention of constructing "good citizenship" through spectatorship.[33] Ouellette argues that public television, perhaps more so than any other mass medium, was designed as an instrument of Foucauldian governmentality, replete with the intention to discipline through a discourse on democracy and citizenship.[34] This governmentality manifested through public television programming's "two-step flow" model of content delivery: Educated "opinion leaders" (typically white men) curate information and communicate it to the masses to convey tastes, opinions, and ways of thinking about the world commensurate with legitimate civic engagement and in the service of the public (democratic) good.[35]

The format of the *Flashpoint* broadcast adhered to this two-step flow model. Hosted by KQED reporter Stephen Talbot, *Flashpoint* was designed as a nationally broadcast opinion-editorial style show intended "to create a kind of 'free speech television'" to stir debate around controversial contemporary issues by presenting partisan perspectives accompanied by commentary.[36] The topic of the first installment of the show was on the issue of abortion: *Flashpoint: The Abortion Battle.*[37] For the second installment, *Flashpoint: Israel and the Palestinians,* KQED paired two thirty-minute Israeli-made documentaries, *Two Settlements* and *Peace Conflict,* with an hour-long, edited-for-television version of *Occupied Palestine. Flashpoint* was scheduled to air on the historically significant date of April 9, 1986, which coincided with the thirty-eighth anniversary of the massacre at the Palestinian village of Deir Yassin, where in 1948 Zionist paramilitary gangs, led by future Israeli prime minister Menachem Begin, massacred between 93 and 170 villagers.[38] The Deir Yassin Massacre is one of the most well-known atrocities of the Nakba, and its representation within the discourse on Palestine has become symbolic of the ways in which the establishment of the Israeli state is rooted in the violence of ethnic cleansing.

The *Flashpoint* program was essentially structured in three acts, with one film per act, complete with epilogue, three interludes, and prologue. The epilogue consists of Talbot introducing the topic for the evening's program, including a spartan declaration of nonpartisan "facts" about the circumstances in Palestine and Israel and the content of the films contained within the program. After each film, the viewer is subjected to a rhetorical interlude: A question is posed to the audience by way of a caption, followed by sound bites from the partisan experts, Rashid Khalidi and Ehud Olmert, who then provide commentary and (presumably) answers to said question. Khalidi's and Olmert's comments are edited together in such a way as to suggest that they are in conversation with one another, yet the content of their speech suggests they never even spoke to one another during the filming of these segments. The prologue consists of a pastiche "debate" between Khalidi and Olmert, followed by closing remarks from Talbot.

This neatly packaged program was sent to all PBS stations in the United States with the intention to air as a stand-alone show. However, as television reviewers began to prescreen the program and learned of several local PBS stations rejecting the programming on the basis that it purveyed a pro-Palestinian point of view, an ensuing debate unfolded in the national and local press in the weeks leading up to the scheduled airdate. Perhaps as a rejection of the two-step flow model *within* the PBS institution itself, many local PBS stations opted to air an addendum to *Flashpoint* in the shape of their own, locally produced partisan debate in reaction to the KQED program.[39]

The Khalidi-Olmert debate and the locally produced postbroadcast debates offer telling examples of how compulsory Zionism forces Arab American and Palestine solidarity activists into a stifling dialectic with Zionists. However, when we view *Flashpoint*'s Khalidi-Olmert debate and the locally produced debates through the framework of cinematic activism, different outcomes and effects are made apparent. The PBS broadcast of *Occupied Palestine* within the *Flashpoint* program afforded a critical opportunity to rally the AAUG's media strategies, namely, the Public Affairs Committee's speakers bureau, in the service of conveying the AAUG discourse on Palestine and Israel. As discussed in the previous chapter, intimate, living-room-based media exhibition was one of the cinematic activism strategies that the AAUG's Public Affairs Committee advocated for with the organization's filmstrips in the 1970s. Unlike the filmstrips, the audiences for which were likely quite small, the broadcast of *Occupied Palestine,* along with the accompanying Khalidi-Olmert debate and the locally produced debates, brought the faces and voices of Palestinians and Arab American activists (in the shape of "opinion leaders" no less) directly into liberal American living rooms.[40] The PBS broadcast therefore afforded an unprecedented opportunity to implement the AAUG's grassroots cinematic activism strategy through the mass medium of public television. The context of PBS in turn imbued not only the issue of Palestine but also the Palestinian perspective with a kind of legitimacy as something of "public interest" and ostensibly therefore also of "the public good."

The downside, however, of the locally produced debate segments, is that while the media texts of the AAUG filmstrips and the circulation of Koff's *Occupied Palestine* functioned to alleviate the burden of representation from individual shoulders, the representation of local Palestinians and Arab Americans on PBS as activists or opinion leaders rendered them in the untenable position of native informant, not to mention a highly visible target for harassment within their local communities.[41] Unlike the AAUG filmstrip screenings, the PBS broadcast meant less control over spectators' reception of the material, and also left the program and its content subject to print news media's reportage and mediation of it all.

## Discursive Colonization: Palestine Film in the News

The film's premiere at the 1981 SFIFF was just the start of the controversy that would surround this film for the better part of a decade. Although the screening eventually continued on the evening of its premiere, the specter of violence marked the film as not just controversial but also dangerous. This sentiment was reproduced discursively through film reviews, opinion editorials, and press coverage surrounding the film, which had lasting effects on its availability in the United States. As the controversies surrounding *Occupied Palestine*'s broadcast on PBS unfolded in the local and national press, such as *The Boston Globe, The New York Times,* the *San Francisco Chronicle,* and the *Los Angeles Times* in the weeks before and after the broadcast, it became clear that the majority of the criticism levied at *Flashpoint* was aimed at *Occupied Palestine.* The content of that criticism, however, offers unique insight as to how, in terms of reception, the cultural politics of Palestinian liberation and solidarity and the genre of Palestine films can be unwittingly appropriated into the service of compulsory Zionism.

Cited as "lacking sufficient context," producers at 34 of 308 PBS stations, including those serving some of PBS's largest audiences like New York City's WNET and Washington, D.C.'s WETA, refused to air the *Flashpoint* program.[42] In an opinion editorial in *The New York Times,* journalist John Corry weighed in on the *Flashpoint* debate, calling *Occupied Palestine* "anti-Israeli" and going so far as to accuse the film of being antisemitic propaganda "not far removed here from the films produced under the Third Reich."[43] Corry asserted that images of razed Palestinian villages accompanied by a voiceover of Israeli soldier Amos Kenan's diary entry describing the ethnic cleansing and massacre of Deir Yassin in 1948, and footage of a US Zionist fundraising dinner interspersed with images of right-wing religious settlers handling some of the $600 million worth of machine guns privately financed by American Jewish donors, "looked like old-fashioned anti-Semitism dressed up in a new political nomenclature."[44] Corry's criticism of the film equated critiques of Zionist political ideology and statecraft with the most extreme form of European antisemitism.

What is perhaps most interesting about *Occupied Palestine*'s reception and treatment in the press both at its premiere in 1981 and during the PBS controversy of 1986 is how it was referred to by many journalists as simultaneously an antisemitic film, a Nazi propaganda film, and a Palestinian film. For example, despite filmmaker Koff's self-proclaimed identity as Jewish American, the film was decried ahead of its initial premiere in San Francisco as antisemitic, with a "filmic air of Nazism" and "representing propaganda more than objective documentation."[45] Nearly a month before the intended PBS broadcast in 1986, the *San Francisco Chronicle* and *The Washington Post* both published articles that described the program as consisting of two Israeli films and one Palestinian film.[46] The day after the broadcast, Steve Daley of the *Chicago Tribune* characterized *Flashpoint* as a view of "the Middle East through the eyes of Israeli and Palestinian filmmakers" as represented through "three 'partisan' films—two Israeli and one Palestinian."[47] Although still referring to *Occupied Palestine* as "the Palestinian portion" of the broadcast, John Stanley of the *San Francisco Chronicle* pointed out that although the film is sympathetic to the Palestinian cause, it is not in fact a Palestinian cultural production or self-representation, stating without irony that "one of the more startling things about the Palestinian portion of the presentation is that it was produced by a Jewish American, David Koff, who grew up in a middle class Los Angeles family."[48] This kind of characterization of *Occupied Palestine* as a *Palestinian* film, ergo Koff as a Palestinian filmmaker, is significant because it serves as a form of discursive colonization by displacing Palestinian cultural producers from the field of Palestinian cultural production.

This repeated categorization of *Occupied Palestine* as Palestinian either in terms of authorship or content raises an important question regarding genre: Is *Occupied Palestine* a Palestinian film or a Palestine solidarity film? To call *Occupied* a Palestinian film and Koff a Palestinian filmmaker based on the content of his film calls to mind Edward Said's rhetorical request for "permission to narrate."[49] The discursive colonization taking place through the misrepresentation of Koff and his film as Palestinian functions to supplant Palestinian subjectivity with Jewish American subjectivity, constituting a further occupation of Palestine. Such displacement reinforces and normalizes the colonial paternalism so often used to justify the censorship of Palestinian self-representation and the Orientalist production of knowledge of Palestine and Palestinians as unworthy and indeed incapable of self-representation and self-determination. This discursive displacement is reflected in the visuality of *Occupied Palestine* itself, as representations of Palestinian voices and experiences are often framed, sometimes quite literally/visually, through or positioned in relation to Zionism and occupation. This is exemplified through the film's primary focus on Zionist ideology, settlements, and occupation, relegating Palestine and Palestinians to a secondary focus.

After establishing ethnic cleansing and settler colonization as frames through which to view the film, midway through the film the narrative focuses more acutely on the Palestinian experience of occupation. The film shifts toward showing the material realities of life under occupation for Palestinians who survived the expulsion and ethnic cleansing of 1948 and 1967, illustrating the contemporary material realities that are the direct result of the historical atrocities described earlier in the film. After remaining visually absent from the landscape represented in the first half of the film, Palestinian subjects are visibly placed back into the landscape of historic Palestine by way of the film's visual composition and mise-en-scène. The pastoral beauty of earlier shots is replaced by scenes of rubble from demolished homes, fields of untilled farmland gone to seed, keffiyeh-clad old men smoking in front of storefronts, and stone-throwing Palestinian youth being chased by Israeli soldiers armed with semiautomatic rifles.

Throughout *Occupied Palestine,* images of Palestine are visually framed through the infrastructure of occupation. In one example, in a single take, the camera is fixed on a tight shot of Palestinian homes amid lush trees. As the camera slowly zooms out, we see the structures grow smaller and smaller. Slowly, the shot's frame is overtaken by a settlement façade under construction. The distant homes that the spectator had once been so close to become mere specks in a landscape, now framed through a hulking settlement archway. Through these visual techniques, *Occupied Palestine* establishes an occupied aesthetic—and the ethnic cleansing and settler colonization that it comprises—as a framework through which to understand the land, people, and stories depicted in the film. The visual representation of

Palestine, then, is aestheticized as occupation, meaning that Palestine films become primarily recognizable as such through reference to the political circumstances of Israeli occupation. The misrepresentation of categorizing Palestine films as nationally or ethnically *Palestinian*, therefore, has much larger implications in terms of a filmmaker or film's legibility as nationally or ethnically Palestinian. For this reason, I propose reframing the discussion of cinematic activism for Palestine in terms of Palestinian cinema as a body of films made by Palestinian filmmakers and in terms of the genre of Palestine films as films that focus on Palestine.

*Occupied Palestine* is a pathbreaking film, and it is important to interrogate its role in both challenging and reproducing ideas about Palestine and Palestinians as victims whose existence as "a people" formed in reaction to the Israeli state.[50] Films such as *Occupied Palestine* have performed the work of making visible the subjugated experiences of Palestinians, and in doing so have produced an aesthetic of occupation that has made the topic of Palestine more recognizable and indeed more palatable to a US audience. Furthermore, its resurrection within the Palestine-themed film festival circuit thirty years after its initial ill-fated release offers a clear example of the mainstreaming of Palestine at work: A solidarity film that was once subjugated and censored has, over time, become unfettered and celebrated.

The aestheticization of Palestine as occupation has, at times, worked to marginalize Palestinian self-representation. Palestinian filmmakers whose work offers more heterogeneous and polyvalent stories of Palestine and Palestinianness that do not necessarily take the occupation as their central focus are at times marginalized within the category of Palestinian cinema.[51] For films that focus on Palestine and that are sympathetic to the Palestinian perspective—whether or not the filmmaker identifies as Palestinian—to be labeled and perceived as Palestinian films is to further dispossess Palestinians from the right to tell and represent their own stories. The representation of *Occupied Palestine* in the mainstream US press as a Palestinian film indicates the extent to which Zionism occupies the discourse on Palestine, so much so that Palestinians are displaced from the field of their own cultural productions.

To clarify: I do not wish to demonize Koff. He was a radical documentarian opposed to colonization and exploitation, and it is critical to recognize his contributions to the genre of Palestine films. Koff could not have anticipated the reception of *Occupied Palestine* as a Palestinian film, nor do I believe his intention was to displace Palestinian cultural producers from the field of Palestinian representation. Indeed, he was passionate about racial and political justice and devoted his career to producing anticolonial and antiracist documentary films for the edification of US society. Furthermore, the remake of the AAUG filmstrips into a professional documentary feature film served a strategic purpose in terms of form: The recognizable convention of documentary film simultaneously produces and fulfills a desire to understand the conditions of occupied Palestine in a manner far more engaging and intelligible than the AAUG filmstrips. The film's reception in the mainstream press has very little to do with Koff's intentions and political stakes as a filmmaker and everything to do with how compulsory Zionism structures US culture and the narratives circulated therein.

# 3 An *Uprising* at *The Perfect Moment*

## *Exhibiting Palestinian Cinema in the 1990s Culture Wars*

In 1991 the curators of *Uprising: Film and Video on the Palestinian Resistance* withdrew their film series from its planned exhibition at the Institute of Contemporary Art (ICA) in Boston. Elia Suleiman, a Palestinian filmmaker and cocurator of *Uprising,* cited censorship as the reason for the withdrawal. *Uprising* consisted of eight film and video art pieces, ranging from feature-length films such as Mai Masri's documentary *Children of Fire* and Michel Khleifi's autobiographical narrative, *Canticle of the Stones,* to Suleiman and Jayce Salloum's collaborative video art montage *Intifada: Introduction to the End of an Argument.* Just a year before the *Uprising* controversy, the ICA had garnered a reputation as a champion of free speech for its steadfast support of *The Perfect Moment,* a postmortem retrospective of Robert Mapplethorpe's photography. Despite immense pressure from conservative groups and politicians who demanded the removal of the Mapplethorpe show's sexually explicit content, the ICA insisted on art's capability of speaking for itself and that any argument otherwise was an espousal of censorship.[1]

Yet barely a year later, the ICA exceptionalized Palestinian cinema when the institution attempted to impose a panel discussion on the programming of *Uprising.* Citing a lack of "balance" and a need to "contextualize" the films, the ICA ventured to place Suleiman in political debate over Palestine and Israel with Harvard Law School professor and staunch Zionist Alan Dershowitz.[2] Such a move suggested that when it came to the question of Palestine, art could *not* in fact speak for itself. The ICA's treatment of *Uprising* exemplifies how compulsory Zionism is enforced through cultural institutions by way of mediating or proscribing the discourse on Palestine. Suleiman's withdrawal of the series reflects how Palestinian artists and activists have leveraged cinema and media as a tool by which to challenge that institutional mediation, assert Palestinian self-determination, and cultivate a sense of political solidarity with other marginalized groups.

Where chapters 1 and 2 trace the process of mainstreaming Palestinian liberation and solidarity politics from a point of taboo and grassroots exhibition and distribution to the very beginnings of inclusion within liberal multicultural mass media, this chapter focuses on how that "inclusion" within liberal multicultural institutions in the United States remained contentious in the 1990s. The controversy stoked over the planned exhibition of Palestinian cinema at the ICA afforded an opportunity to harness controversy for the sake of publicity, and in doing so revealed the machinations of compulsory Zionism to wider audiences and would-be allies. The *Uprising* controversy marks a moment of simultaneous convergence and divergence, wherein Palestinian liberation and solidarity politics and gay and lesbian cultural politics met within the realm of the US culture wars of the 1990s.[3] This incident and the resultant juxtaposition of these sets of politics exemplifies how compulsory Zionism has been enforced in the US context through multicultural discourses predicated on celebrating difference as a machination of empire[4] and neoliberal multicultural discourses working to "designate some forms of humanity as less worthy than others."[5] Contestations on multiculturalism in US entertainment media and cultural institutions, especially during the culture wars of the 1990s, stemmed from two oppositional forces. On one side were liberals seeking to increase representational parity in terms of race, ethnicity, gender, and sexuality, and on the other side were conservatives seeking to maintain the status quo by obstructing and objecting to liberal attempts to diversify media and cultural representations. Put another way, the struggle over the place of multiculturalism within the mainstream was a struggle over cultural hegemony. As such, this chapter tells of more than just a moment of confluence and relationality between gay and lesbian cultural politics and Palestinian liberation and solidarity politics; it shows how Palestinian subjectivity, cultural politics, and cultural productions have been positioned as that which subverts the norm, the abject "other," and have been constructed as "politically queer."

The controversy over *Uprising* not only demonstrates how compulsory Zionism underpinned the 1990s US culture wars over race, sex, and representation by attempting to force Palestinian cinema to be in conversation with Dershowitz's Zionist views, but also reveals how compulsory Zionism has been central to the production of homonormativity that operates in the service of neoliberal multiculturalism. Jodi Melamed defines neoliberal multiculturalism as "a central ideology and mode of social organization that seeks to manage racial contradictions on a national and international scale for US-led neoliberalism" and that "consistently portrays acts of force required for neoliberal restructuring to be humanitarian."[6] The Mapplethorpe controversy exemplifies how the multicultural movement of the 1990s seemingly worked to challenge representations and institutions that, in the words of Evelyn Alsultany, "appeared to be neutral while in fact powerfully naturalizing inequalities."[7] From this context, the enforcement of compulsory Zionism through calls for "balance" appeared as liberal multicultural common sense. What good liberal of the 1990s would oppose balance? As a rhetorical strategy, the call for balance was akin to the conservative strategy to muzzle and defame multiculturalism through accusations of "political correctness." The phrase "politically correct" is to the 1990s what the word "woke" is in the 2020s. Ella Shohat and Robert Stam understand the discourse on political correctness in the 1990s as "a displaced attempt to control a leftist project" and "regulate relations between communities."[8] In the case of *Uprising* and the ICA's attempt to enforce compulsory Zionism, the call for "balance" revealed how the contradictions inherent to neoliberal multiculturalism have privileged some while denigrating others.

At the peak of the *Uprising* controversy in May 1991, *The Boston Globe* ran a political cartoon depicting how the homonormativity central to both compulsory Zionism and neoliberal multiculturalism had informed the ICA's treatment of Palestinian cinema in the wake of the Mapplethorpe controversy. Drawn by Paul Szep and titled "Another great show at the ICA," the cartoon features two Semitically stylized men in business suits in the middle of a physical fight (Figure 7). The men are positioned in the middle of a large, framed painting that lies face down, the canvas torn around them, indicating that the work of art has fallen from the exhibition wall and onto the brawling men. The caption on the wall where the painting had presumably once been displayed reads "Palestinian Film Series." The cartoon men are so engrossed in their struggle that they neither notice nor care that the art

*Another great show at the ICA*

Figure 7. An editorial cartoon by Paul Szep published in *The Boston Globe,* May 3, 1991. Courtesy of Paul Szep and Copyright Creators Syndicate, Inc.

over which they fight has been destroyed in the process. Another, intact artwork hangs in the background, adjacent to the fallen Palestinian art and brawling men, with the caption "Mapplethorpe."

Szep's political cartoon indicates how controversies over Palestinian liberation and solidarity politics and gay and lesbian cultural politics were positioned in relation to one another in the culture war arena. Through this relationality, Palestinian artists, activists, and allies in the United States have used art, film, and media to identify the contradictions inherent in multicultural discourse, cultivate coalitional social justice politics, and resist the subjugation of Palestinian cultural politics in the US context. Furthermore, the Szep cartoon visualizes neoliberal multiculturalism at work. Through struggles over representation, compulsory Zionism has aided in the ascension of homonormativity, or a kind of LGBTQ+ subjectivity that does "not contest dominant heteronormative assumptions and institutions, but upholds and sustains them, while promising the possibility of a demobilized gay constituency."[9] As a certain kind of gay cultural politics ascended into mainstream acceptability through the Mapplethorpe controversy, Palestinian cultural politics were sacrificed on the altar of political correctness. In this moment, as the ICA's backing of *The Perfect Moment* was taken as a win in the culture war between conservatives, on the one hand, and liberal multiculturalists, on the other, Palestinian liberation and solidarity politics were rendered, in a sense, queerer than queer.

This chapter intervenes in much of the scholarship on LGBTQ+-Palestinian solidarity politics and antipinkwashing that has focused predominantly on the post-9/11 period.[10] While contemporary leftist queer solidarity activism around Palestine certainly picked up momentum and gained visibility in the post-9/11 era, the overwhelming focus on this period dehistoricizes the development of gay and lesbian and Palestinian relational politics that *pre-date* the rise of Israeli pinkwashing.[11] Such dehistoricization makes it seem as though Israel's decision to focus its propaganda on LGBTQ+ film culture in the 2000s emerged simply from the creative minds of Israel's public relations managers. This, I believe, gives Israel too much credit. This chapter demonstrates that Israel's pinkwashing strategy was born of the state's very real fear of a growing and powerful force: burgeoning gay and lesbian consciousness about Palestinian liberation and solidarity politics and its representation in the mainstream US public sphere. Examining the ICA incidents therefore reframes our understanding of the rise of Israeli pinkwashing in the United States as *itself* a reaction to the growth of relational politics (and the potential foundations for solidarity) between gay and lesbian and Palestinian artists and activists in the 1990s, and the threat such politics posed to the neoliberal multicultural status quo. One method for maintaining that status quo has been the enforcement of compulsory Zionism.

The media discourses and cultural productions that constituted these overlapping controversies at the ICA illustrate three interrelated arguments about the relationships between today's LGBTQ+ cultural politics and Palestinian cultural politics in the US context. First, this chapter historicizes a highly visible moment when cinema emerged as a critical site for the production and management of gay and lesbian and Palestinian relational politics. Second, the post-9/11 proliferation of leftist LGBTQ+-Palestinian solidarity politics in the US context is deeply rooted in the culture wars of the 1990s, and the emergence of Israeli pinkwashing as an official state public relations strategy should be understood as a reaction to this increasingly visible relationality and solidarity. Through this latter point, this chapter provides a greater historical context for understanding *why* the state of Israel focused its pinkwashing campaigns in the early 2000s so heavily on LGBTQ+ film culture and, in turn, why Palestine solidarity politics emerged as a central issue to leftist queer activism in the twenty-first century.

## Representational *Uprising:* The Occupation from the Perspective of the Palestinian Child

The struggle over Mapplethorpe's show was in essence a proxy war over social welfare, as *artistic* value became a metric for *human* value. Arguments to protect or neglect the rights of gender, racial, and sexual minority groups to freedom of expression and to social welfare rested on those groups' abilities to demonstrate their cultural contributions. The production of culture, then, not only became about minority freedom of expression but also became a key to entering the safe house of humanity and the rights afforded therein. Suleiman would go on to explicitly make this same argument during the *Uprising* controversy. Just as Mapplethorpe used the tools and aesthetic tastes of elite, dominant culture to recuperate gay humanity during the AIDS crisis in a way that was heralded by elite art institutions, likewise, in a context wherein compulsory Zionism legitimized the death and oppression of Palestinian civilians, Suleiman and his *Uprising* compatriots used film and media production to gain some control over the representation of Palestine in the United States while representing the issue of Palestine as worthy of US attention *because* of Palestinian artistic merit. The following section explores how this is so by focusing on two films from the *Uprising* series: *Children of Fire* and *Intifada: Introduction to the End of an Argument.* But to understand the significance of these films, it is necessary to first situate them in two specific contexts: US film and media representations of Palestine, and Palestinian governance and struggles for self-determination in the 1990s.

The urgency over representation that the *Uprising* debate signified can be linked to previous failures of political negotiation and simultaneously foreshadowed the anxiety and disappointments that would occur during political negotiations later in the 1990s. Palestinian narrative and art cinema emerged to international critical acclaim during the early 1980s, a decade bookended by the 1978 Camp David Peace Accords and the 1993 Oslo Peace Accords. Camp David and Oslo, referred to collectively from here onward as the "peace process," were foremost concerned with political representation. During Camp David, Israel refused to recognize or negotiate with the Palestine Liberation Organization (PLO) as a representative of the Palestinian people and instead attempted to broker peace deals with the governments of Jordan and Egypt, which had held administrative control over the West Bank and Gaza Strip, respectively, prior to the start of the Israeli occupation in 1967. Palestinian political self-representation was therefore absent from the Camp David Accords while the question of Palestinian self-determination was left in the hands of everyone but the Palestinians themselves.

Since the peace process of the 1970s was largely concerned with the question of political representation (or lack thereof), it is fitting that Palestinian artists in the 1980s and 1990s would take up concerns over representation of a different kind, namely, the aesthetic and the cultural. Aesthetic and cultural representation became a means for disenfranchised Palestinians to assert power and demand self-determination in ways that the US and Israeli governments and societies could recognize as nonviolent. The films in the *Uprising* series therefore clarify how and why the question of aesthetic self-representation has been so central to the expression of self-determination, particularly in the context of the United States, a country whose government has wielded inordinate control over the so-called peace process.

Given these contexts, Masri's *Children of Fire* was unique both within the *Uprising* series and amid the broader representational landscape. Furthermore, the film's inclusion in the *Uprising* series afforded an opportunity to screen the film in one of Boston's premier cultural institutions, thereby elevating the import of the film's message. Filmed in the cinema verité style, Masri took a participatory approach to the film's subject and its methodology, which afforded a radically different representation of Palestine, the likes of which US audiences would not likely have been exposed to previously. Filmed in 1989 in the West Bank city of Nablus, *Children of Fire* offers a uniquely Palestinian viewpoint of the occupation, both in form and in content.

*Children of Fire* opens with Masri attempting for the fifth unsuccessful time to enter Nablus, her father's hometown. We first encounter Masri as she argues with an Israeli soldier after she has been denied entry at the city's main entrance, a checkpoint controlled by the Israeli military. As Masri argues with the soldiers, it becomes apparent that the soldiers perceive the film's very production as a threat to the Israeli military's control of the occupation. Frustrated by the repeated denial of entry, Masri and her crew hire a taxi to take them into the city through the winding mountain back roads instead. Nestled in the northern region of the occupied West Bank, Nablus garnered the nickname *jabal al-nar,* "mountain of fire," for its long history of resistance under Ottoman, British, and Israeli rule.[12] From this opening scene Masri establishes herself as the exilic narrator barred from her familial homeland and, as an act of resistance, on a journey of return through the mountain of fire. It is through Masri's dual subjectivity as filmmaker and Palestinian in exile that we see the occupation in far more intimate terms than anything broadcast on US televisual news at the time.

Although Masri is a native speaker of Arabic, she narrates the film in English, indicating its intention for an Anglophone audience. In the first minutes, Masri explains her motivations for returning to her familial home in the role of filmmaker: "Nablus has been on the news a lot. For most people, it's more trouble in a faraway place. But to me, this is happening to the people I know." Masri's narration over stock news footage of the intifada—children throwing stones and waving the Palestinian flag, youth clashing with the Israeli military, all seen through the thick black smoke of burning rubber tires—functions to personalize the Palestinian experience for US viewers. Given the film's placement within the *Uprising* series and in the context of a prestigious cultural institution such as the ICA, Masri's personalization grounds the viewer in the realm of subjectivity in order to preemptively defuse accusations of bias that may be levied by US viewers who have been trained to expect journalistic objectivity with regard to the documentary form itself. This personalization, which emphasizes the use of "the camera less as revolutionary weapon than as monitor of the gendered and sexualized realms" of anticolonial struggle, marks

*Children of Fire,* both in content and in style, as what Shohat refers to as a "post–third worldist feminist text."[13] Furthermore, through its making, its content, and later its attempted exhibition, *Children of Fire* exemplifies Palestinian attempts to subvert compulsory Zionism through an appeal to culture war discourses over freedom of expression and, as demonstrated below, the sanctity of the child.

Masri and her crew base themselves at her uncle's apartment in Nablus, and the film's narrative unfolds from this domestic space. The camera is trained on Masri and executive producer Jean Khalil Chamoun as they anxiously look out a window, a large boom microphone expectantly extended to record the sound of conflict from the street below. The camera cuts to a long shot from the perspective of the apartment window to show a group of Israeli soldiers aggressively breaking through doors and entering homes with semiautomatic rifles drawn, hunting for someone. It is from this perspective of the Palestinian home under siege that *Children of Fire* shatters the dominant perception of Palestine. We see this quite literally in visual terms as the camera cuts to a bullet hole in one of the apartment's windows. This is not the vision of Palestine that US spectators would have been familiar with: There are no burning tires, no stone-throwing youth in black-and-white keffiyeh scarves, and no tanks or army jeeps in this frame. Instead, we see an unremarkable view of a quiet side street, a relatively mundane scene rendered spectacular and foreboding through the shards of glass. Here the visuality of *Children of Fire* is representative of what Hamid Dabashi refers to as the Palestinian aesthetic of "traumatic realism," and it is through this "aesthetic under duress" that *Children of Fire* poses an intervention to the existing regime of representation.[14]

From this space of the Palestinian home under siege, we see women's and children's experiences of the occupation and its social and emotional effects. Masri explains that her uncle's teenage neighbor, Ayman, had just been shot and killed by the Israeli military. A handheld camera follows Masri into the neighbor's apartment as she makes her way through the crowd of mourners to give her condolences to Ayman's mother. Masri narrates through voice-over: "I come to mourn as a neighbor, and yet I brought a camera with me. I feel that the camera is violating their grief, but I know they'd all want Ayman's story to be told." Conscious of her outsider gaze as filmmaker and wary of objectifying Palestinian grief, Masri subsequently shifts the film's focus away from her own subjectivity and toward the experiences of Palestinian women and children *as told by* women and children themselves.

The film is largely framed through an extended interview with Ayman's ten-year-old neighbor, Hanna, who provides a firsthand account of a childhood under occupation. Scenes of the army's brutality against children—beatings, arrests, the deployment of rubber bullets and live ammunition against unarmed civilians, tear gas assaults—are interspersed with Hanna's drawings depicting these same images in her own hand. The interview with Hanna and her self-representations of an occupied childhood are further illustrated through footage of young boys engaged in an imaginative play game of "soldiers and fighters," complete with the reenactment of dragging a wounded friend through the street. Stills of Hanna's drawings of children throwing stones are juxtaposed with footage of a teenage girl as she is handcuffed and dragged—screaming in terror—into a military jeep. The jeep speeds away as the girl's mother chases after it with arms wide open, wailing in vain, her daughter's fate unknown. The camera returns to Hanna's illustrations of dead bodies being carried through the street before cutting again to a live shot of children marching at the head of a funeral procession.

Hanna's drawings serve as an aesthetic framing device to illustrate how crucial Palestinian self-representation is to understanding the power dynamics of the Israeli occupation and the material realities of occupied Palestinian life. One particularly telling sequence of shots alternating between Hanna's drawings and live-action scenes makes this argument in visual terms. The scene begins with a close-up of Hanna. The camera is positioned at the level of her face before cutting to an over-the-shoulder shot, indicating that the viewer is not only positioned as Hanna's peer but is literally watching from her perspective (Figure 8). What we see from Hanna's perspective is her own visual representation of the intifada interspersed with live-action shots mirroring her illustrations. While a US audience may have seen similar scenes as part of editorial news coverage of the intifada, what is unique about this sequence is that it reframes the occupation from the perspective of a Palestinian child, privileging Palestinian self-representation over Western editorial representation.

Figure 8. Stills from Mai Masri's documentary film *Children of Fire* (1990) depicting protagonist Hanna drawing the first intifada. Copyright Nour Productions.

Hanna's drawings represent the brutality of the occupation and demonstrate how Palestinian resistance to the occupation operates on a visual level. Burning tires are a recurring motif in both Hanna's drawings and US media coverage of the intifada. By the early 1990s, imagery of keffiyeh-clad Palestinian youth waving the Palestinian flag and slinging rocks at Israeli soldiers through a screen of red flames and thick black smoke had become ubiquitous in US news reportage on Palestine. Yet this motif of flames and smoke is afforded new meaning through Hanna's perspective; we learn that the intifada is a visually oriented form of resistance. Her drawings illustrate how Palestinian youth resist the occupation through a technique of "concealment," which Gil Hochberg identifies as one of the key visual organizing principles necessary for political control, empowerment, and transformation within the context of Israeli occupation.[15] With the field of vision obstructed by the smoke of burning tires, Palestinian youth are concealed and protected from the lethal sight lines of Israeli military rifles while the bright red and green of the Palestinian national colors remain defiantly visible as the Palestinian flag waves through the smoke, fanning the flames further (Figure 9).

I view this personalized, self-representative aesthetic not merely as a stylistic choice but as an appeal to US viewers deeply preoccupied with concerns over the relationship between children and freedom of expression. By framing the occupation through the lens of childhood and amplifying the subjective perspective of the content, Masri's film played to two particular, although adversarial, US audiences: the conservative right and the liberal multicultural left, two groups

Figure 9. Stills from Mai Masri's documentary film *Children of Fire* (1990) depicting protagonist Hanna's drawings of the first intifada. Copyright Nour Productions.

entrenched in an ongoing culture war wherein, as I demonstrate through analysis of the Mapplethorpe controversy, concerns over a balance between freedom of expression, minority representation, and children's emotional, intellectual, and physical safety had been a major point of contention.

## A *Moment* of Crisis: Domestic Culture Wars and US Imperialism

The embroiled concerns over children and minority representation that would arise surrounding *Uprising,* and Masri's film in particular, revealed to observers how compulsory Zionism masquerades as inclusionary multiculturalism while upholding the neoliberal status quo and all its accompanying exclusions. The Mapplethorpe show generated so much ire, both in defamation and defense of the work, partly because it touched some of the most sensitive nerves in the US culture wars: sexuality, race, and children. Although Mapplethorpe's photography and mixed-media work ranged in content, conservatives criticized him for a relatively small subset of his portraiture work, which included seminude portraits of young children, classical nudes of athletes and bodybuilders, and explicit images of genitalia, sexual acts, and BDSM practices. It was the images of children, and concerns over children's exposure to the adjacent sexual imagery, that garnered some of the most outrage from conservatives. The First Amendment Common Sense Alliance—a coalition of conservative groups including Citizens for the Family First, Morality in the Media, and the Catholic League for Religious and Civil Rights—opposed *The Perfect Moment* show on the grounds that it juxtaposed "five graphic homoerotic images and two photographs of nude or partially nude children."[16] Championing the crusade in Congress was Republican senator Jesse Helms of North Carolina, who proposed legislation stipulating that federal funds could not be used to support "obscene or indecent materials, including . . . depictions of sadomasochism, homoeroticism, the exploitation of children, or individuals engaged in sex acts." As the Mapplethorpe controversy escalated, some institutions canceled the exhibition for fear it would affect their financial stability, especially given the US government's trend toward the neoliberal economic policies of fiscal austerity and privatization, which already threatened the security of public arts funding.[17]

In a move that implied an attempt to "balance" conservative pressures with the struggle in Congress over federal funding, the ICA imposed a one-time age-restrictive admission policy for the show, which limited admission to no one under the age of eighteen without the accompaniment of an adult.[18] The restrictive admission policy did not sit well with free speech activists, such as George Pappas, a local city councillor and artist, who was quoted in *The Boston Globe*: "By putting a restriction on it, you're implying that there is something offensive about it."[19] Indeed, the imposition of an age requirement smacked of political correctness and neoliberal multiculturalist compromise: The policy simultaneously upheld dominant (white, heteronormative, conservative, Christian) assumptions about the sanctity of the child while ushering (white, masculinist) gay cultural production into the galleries of homonormativity.

The controversy over *The Perfect Moment* must also be understood within the larger domestic and international contexts. Mapplethorpe's death from AIDS-related illness in 1989 imbued his work with a greater sense of representational purpose as activists came to view the US government's treatment of the communities most affected by HIV and AIDS as negligent at best and genocidal at worst.[20] During this time, video—the medium of choice for *Uprising*—emerged as increasingly important within US-based AIDS art activism and anticolonial, third world liberation documentary movements alike, largely because of its affordability and ease of transportability.[21] As Jih-Fei Cheng argues, the video afterlives of women and queers of color who worked to relate the AIDS activism movement to larger political issues, such as war and imperialism, remain today in their archived form as a "living testament to collective will against the perpetuation of state oppression and colonial terror."[22] The medium of video, therefore, came to symbolize the power of art and media to make underrepresented causes, such as AIDS and Palestine, visible within a regime of representation designed to exclude them.

Working within the more traditional medium of gelatin silver photography, Mapplethorpe became an easy subject to uphold as a multicultural poster child, and white curators praised his representations of Black men as dignified and powerful.[23] In contrast to the handheld aesthetics of contemporaneous AIDS videos produced by and for women and people of color, as chronicled by Alexandra Juhasz in *AIDS TV*, Mapplethorpe's formally masterful photographic technique legitimized the expression of homonormativity by emulating the art world's conservative aesthetic standards and reproducing what Kobena Mercer and Isaac Julien have critiqued as the anthropological and pornographic objectification of the Black male body.[24] The defense of Mapplethorpe as multicultural icon, then, exemplifies how, in Melamed's words, the word *multicultural* itself "signifies as antiracist even as it becomes a way of ascribing racialized privilege to some forms of humanity . . . [and] the category of whiteness and its privileges are displaced into the category of multiculturalism."[25] The ICA's defense of Mapplethorpe and subsequent denigration of Suleiman and his fellow Palestinian video artists and filmmakers exemplifies this displacement of white privilege *as* multiculturalism.

The ICA's defense of Mapplethorpe buoyed the rise of homonormativity, and with that defense came the need for a new target to denigrate in the culture war arena. The controversies surrounding the figure of the child in *The Perfect Moment* coincided with a larger international context of US imperial expansion and military intervention in the Southwest Asia and North Africa (SWANA) region, as marked by the start of the First Gulf War in 1990 and subsequent US invasion of Iraq in 1991. Just as the figure of the child was to be protected from the sexual degeneracy of gay subjectivity, so did the US public need protection from the racial degeneracy of the oriental other: the Arab. Within such overlapping contexts, the ascension of homonormativity coincides with the normalization of US empire, laying the groundwork for "the strange coupling of civil rights and national security," or what Chandan Reddy identifies later during the Obama presidency as "freedom with violence."[26] The domestic culture war over freedom of expression and civil rights solidified homonormative subjectivity as a privileged status as the struggle over Palestinian self-representation during the *Uprising* controversy became a foil for the US empire's struggle to dominate the SWANA region.

This dual movement of the rise of homonormativity, on the one hand, and the rendering of Palestinian liberation and solidarity politics as politically queer, on the other, hinged on the figure of the child. Just as in the Mapplethorpe controversy, *Children of Fire*'s representations of children drew the greatest criticism. A closer analysis of this shared criticism helps clarify how compulsory Zionism positions Palestinian subjectivity as politically queer. In both cases, the representations of children were decried as harmful, yet the key difference lay in who the object of that harm was. In the case of *The Perfect Moment,* conservatives criticized Mapplethorpe's representation of children as harmful both to those children represented in the images themselves and to potential child spectators. In the case of *Children of Fire,* however, Masri's representation of Palestinian children was decried, in the words of *Boston Globe* staff writer Matthew Gilbert, as "manipulative and vindictive,"[27] suggesting that, despite the film's depictions of Israeli military violence inflicted on Palestinian children, the true objects of harm were the film's would-be (adult) spectators.

Gilbert went on to suggest that *Children of Fire* suffered from "overkill,"[28] a criticism that could rightly have been aimed at the Israeli military's violence toward Palestinian children but instead was levied at the filmmaker's representation of Palestinian children as subjects worthy of protection. Gilbert's criticism constructed the Palestinian child not as the object of harm but as the perpetrator of harm. His paternalistic review of *Children of Fire* strategically infantilized the film's potential US audience, placing those potential spectators in the position of the child in need of protection from the dangerous, degenerate Arab other. In doing so, *The Boston Globe* lumped Palestinian cultural productions and the politics they represented into the same camp of moral degeneracy that heterosexist conservatives had relegated Mapplethorpe to. Palestine, it would seem, was not merely in league with queerness; in relation to the ICA's staunch defense of gay representations, the museum's enforcement of compulsory Zionism rendered the issue of Palestine beyond the realm of acceptable multiculturalism, or put another way, queerer than queer. This implicit association of Palestine with queerness might also account for why the First Amendment Common Sense Alliance, the very group that demanded the censorship of Mapplethorpe's show in the name of saving children from alleged harm, remained silent when the ICA attempted to censor the images of Palestinian children in need of protection from the harms of military occupation as depicted in *Children of Fire.*

This question of childhood innocence and protection appears elsewhere in the *Uprising* series, most notably in Suleiman and Salloum's experimental video art piece *Intifada: Introduction to the End of an Argument.* I turn now to *Intifada* to further elaborate how the *Uprising* show attempted to challenge the compulsory Zionism of the United States through intertextual representations of issues within the contemporaneous US culture wars. *Children of Fire* and *Intifada* worked synergistically to appeal to the discourse on children within the US culture wars in order to recalibrate the viewer's moral compass on the question of Palestine. If *Children of Fire* furnished a radically different perspective on Palestinian self-representation amid the plethora of documentary and editorial representations that merely treated Palestine as an object of report, *Intifada* turned the aesthetic of Palestinian self-representation on its head. Suleiman and Salloum combined original video footage with edited montages of mainstream news reportage on Palestine, alongside Hollywood and Israeli film, television, and cartoon stereotypes of Arabs and Muslims, to provide a scathing critique of the role of visual culture in supporting US political duplicity in the SWANA region and compulsory Zionism on the domestic front. Wholly unlike a documentary or narrative film, *Intifada* offered an even more radically different aesthetic of Palestinian self-representation than *Children of Fire.*

Although *Intifada* is more akin to experimental video art, such a genre does not preclude the making of an argument, which even Gilbert himself noted in his favorable review of the film: "The movie allows a clear view of Hollywood stereotyping, and hints at the insidious ways the entertainment media filters into news coverage. . . . 'Intifada' also questions the notion of propaganda itself."[29] *Intifada* consists predominantly of material taken from broadcast television news reports, Hollywood and Israeli films, and archival footage, yet large portions of the film consist of the filmmaker's own footage: scenes of driving around Palestine, interviews with family members, and mundane street scenes. It is through these quotidian scenes that *Intifada,* not unlike *Children of Fire,* provides a transformative self-representation in the service of the *Uprising* series' larger argument to humanize the Palestinian people through cultural production.

The film opens with a shot of treetops and the corner of a residential building as seen from a third-story window. A woman's voice softly sings in Arabic as we watch the tree leaves rustling in a slight breeze. We hear the woman stumble over the lyrics before giving a slight grunt of an embarrassed laugh, then states in English, still in a sing-song voice: "I don't know the tune to this." She continues singing awkwardly in Arabic, then switches again to English, continuing to flub the lyrics before breaking out into a cheerful laugh. The woman's voice-over fades out as a muffled recording of the song she had been singing fades in, along with the sound of crickets, before the woman's voice returns to sing along. This opening introduces US viewers to an unfamiliar and almost silly version of Palestine, a version that is socially awkward, genuine, lighthearted, and even romantic. *Intifada* disarms potential critics by asserting itself as Art with a capital A. The quotidian nature of this opening stands in sharp contrast to the view of Palestine depicted in the montage of mainstream media footage that follows.

As if in anticipation of Gilbert's criticism of *Children of Fire, Intifada*'s juxtaposition of original footage and mainstream media conveys a rebuttal to Gilbert's critique of Masri's film by providing an argument for the protection of Palestinian children from none other than children's television icon Fred Rogers, of the Emmy Award–winning public television show *Mister Rogers' Neighborhood.* Midway through *Intifada,* amid a montage of US television news clips on the occupation, including images of Palestinian children running away from an Israeli tank while news anchors pontificate about "terrorism" via voice-over, the screen cuts to black for a moment of silence before showing a clip from *Mister Rogers' Neighborhood,* wherein Rogers states in his gentle and measured way: "I've been terribly concerned about the graphic display of violence which the mass media has been showing recently, and I plead for your protection and support of your young children."[30]

Taken in the context of *Intifada,* Rogers's plea strategically contextualized the Palestinian issue in a way that could speak to two distinct US audiences at once: the public-television-watching, liberal multiculturalist crowd on the one hand, and the conservative, save-the-children crowd on the other. Coming on the heels of the Mapplethorpe debate, the films in the *Uprising* series made the issue of Palestine relevant to a US audience by making the struggle over Palestinian self-determination relatable to an audience steeped in a culture war over children's safety. It must be understood, then, that the curatorial decision-making behind *Uprising* is what made the show so provocative, in that it played to liberal multiculturalist argumentation in defense of freedom of expression while challenging conservatives to follow through in their crusade to defend children from harm. Together, *Intifada* and *Children of Fire* attempted to cast the culture war discourses back onto a US audience in order to render the Palestinian issue legible to and worthy of a bipartisan US audience's attention.

## The Controversy: Relating the Palestinian and the Queer

*Uprising* was originally scheduled for 1990, but as the United States engaged in the First Gulf War during the latter half of 1990 and prepared to invade Iraq in January 1991, the ICA delayed the series due to what museum administrators characterized to Suleiman as the "general mood of the country."[31] Even if by spring of 1991 the Gulf War ground invasion had officially ended, that "mood" apparently lingered. *Uprising* was thrust into the media spotlight in April when Steve Grossman, vice chairman of the ICA board of directors, resigned from his role in protest of *Uprising*'s alleged lack of "educational context."[32] Grossman was not just a major figure on the ICA board; he also held powerful positions elsewhere within Boston's political culture. At the time of his resignation, Grossman served as vice president of the American Israel Public Affairs Committee (AIPAC) and chairman of the Massachusetts Democratic Party.[33] These roles positioned him as a well-connected fundraiser and political advocate for the ICA, and his resignation had the potential to leave the museum financially and politically vulnerable at a time of increased attacks against and attempts to defund art institutions over the nature and meaning of freedom of expression.

Grossman was not the sole actor pressuring the ICA. Leonard Zakim, then director of the New England branch of the Anti-Defamation League (ADL), was also a key figure in this controversy. Quoted in *The Boston Globe,* Zakim was "concerned about the seemingly one-sided nature of it. . . . It makes sense to have a responsible educational context."[34] Zakim further demanded that Suleiman engage in a political debate with Dershowitz, to "balance" the opinions and representations presented in the series with a Zionist perspective. Grossman's and Zakim's roles within organizations such as AIPAC and the ADL, respectively, are key to understanding the significance of their pressure on the ICA. The ADL and AIPAC exemplify the institutional aspect of compulsory Zionism, or what Nadine Naber, Eman Desouky, and Lina Baroudi refer to as a coordinated network of special interest groups operating under the pretense of civil rights, faith-based, and multicultural advocacy, and working to "maintain a unified pro-Israel position, silencing criticism of Israeli policy and demonizing its critics."[35]

Zakim's suggestion that it would be irresponsible to expose the Boston public to the Palestinian films, combined with Grossman's insistence on the museum's educational mission, melded into a rhetoric about "complexity" and created a sense of moral imperative: "The mission of the ICA is heavily educational in nature, and these films require an educational context. With something as complex as the Palestinian question, understanding only comes from discussion and debate."[36] Charges of "complexity" have often been used as a rhetorical strategy to stymie substantive discourse on Palestine. Such "complexity" is in fact manufactured by creating confusion and obscurity around the topic through accusations that the issue of Palestine is too political, sensitive, or otherwise untouchable.[37] The complexity rhetoric is therefore exemplary of how politically correct calls for balance are indeed thinly veiled attempts to censor and derail leftist causes. "Complexity," in other words, is the liberal multicultural rhetoric of compulsory Zionism.

The rhetoric of "balance," and its accomplice "complexity," placed the ICA in a difficult position. Elizabeth Sussman, the museum's acting director at the time, cosigned this notion of complexity in her statements to *The Boston Globe*: "Since the issue is more complex than we had planned, we want to honor the complexity by having a discussion."[38] The ICA's readiness to "honor the complexity" exemplifies how compulsory Zionism permeates US cultural institutions in ways that force Palestinian voices into an inequitable dyad, as the occupied (Palestine) must yield its representational sovereignty to its occupier (Israel).

But why, after having successfully fended off the compulsory heterosexists during the Mapplethorpe controversy a year previously, did the ICA succumb to compulsory Zionism? Although the ICA had weathered the Mapplethorpe storm relatively unscathed, Grossman's departure left the institution vulnerable to the legion of conservative critics who loitered around arts institutions in the 1990s. For Grossman to accuse the *Uprising* series of "political propaganda"[39] was to, by extension, cast doubt on the integrity and value of the museum's entire curatorial decision-making process, thereby opening up previous and future exhibits to similar accusations. With Grossman's departure, the ICA needed to enforce compulsory Zionism as a way not only to withstand the pressures of AIPAC and the ADL but also to defend and *maintain* its previous victory in the struggle over freedom of expression. This is indeed how compulsory Zionism operates as neoliberal multiculturalism: To maintain the value of gay art and protect a newly acceptable homonormativity, Palestinian artists had to be devalued and, indeed, disciplined. For this reason, even after Grossman's resignation, the ICA attempted to forestall any aftershocks over the Mapplethorpe controversy by continuing with the plan—unbeknownst to the curators—to impose the Dershowitz-helmed panel espousing a Zionist viewpoint on the *Uprising* series.[40]

In this moment, free speech advocates who had come to Mapplethorpe's defense came to the defense of Suleiman and the *Uprising* show. James D'Entremont of the Boston Coalition for Freedom of Expression, a group that had defended Mapplethorpe, characterized the ICA as "inconsistent and disturbing" in its treatment of *Uprising* in the wake of *The Perfect Moment.*[41] John Reinstein of the American Civil Liberties Union also validated Suleiman's accusation of censorship, stating that "if the panel was standing by itself, that would be different. But the problem is the cause and effect. The artist has a legitimate claim because of the linkage of the panel to the film series."[42]

Some free speech advocates drew even more direct parallels between the ICA's uneven treatment of gay and Palestinian artists' struggles. In a letter to the editor in *The Boston Globe* titled "Off Balance at the ICA," a Suffolk University communications professor, Gerald Peary, criticized the ICA for capitulating to Zionist demands. In what he characterized as a double standard endemic to the demand for "a balancing panel—including, presumably, someone espousing an anti-Palestinian point of view," Peary pointed to how the request for balance reveals the ICA's contradictions in its aims to protect some by denigrating others.[43] In closing his letter, Peary noted the ICA's plans for a gay and lesbian film festival later that year and, to emphasize his point, asked, "Will there be those who demand a balancing panel of respected heterosexuals?" In placing the issues of gay and lesbian and Palestinian self-representation in allied relation to each other, Zionism and heterosexism became legible as related ideological mechanisms with shared investments in domination, power, and control over underrepresented subjects. An unexpected consequence of this controversy, then, was to make clear to the US public how compulsory Zionism functions to discipline both Palestinians and LGBTQ+ people by identifying the overlaps and relationalities between LGBTQ+ and Palestinian struggles for freedom of expression and self-determination. The ICA's treatment of the *Uprising* show, however, further solidified Palestinian subjectivity as politically queer in relation to the norms of compulsory Zionism.

In this pivotal moment, Palestinian artists gained critical support from other art institutions embroiled in the culture war over gay-, lesbian-, and AIDS-related art. Artists Space, the renowned New York gallery, which in 1989 had its $10,000 National Endowment for the Arts grant temporarily revoked for its exhibition of the AIDS-themed show *Witnesses: Against Our Vanishing*[44] and where *Uprising* had originally been exhibited in 1990, stood by the film series and publicly condemned the ICA, stating, "We deplore the use of the Palestinian or any other culture to create a false controversy for opportunistic ends."[45] Susan Wyatt, executive director of Artists Space, defended the exhibition of Palestinian cinema: "It is important for art to speak for itself. [Suleiman's] culture should be seen as a culture with its own identity. It doesn't need to be apologized for or linked to another program."[46]

Suleiman made the connection to the Mapplethorpe controversy explicit in a set of *Boston Globe* interviews: "One tactic of oppression is to deny a voice, to wipe out a culture. If you're beautiful, if you have paintings and films and art, it is hard to legitimize your murder,"[47] and "a place that protected against censorship when it came to Robert Mapplethorpe is practicing censorship on us."[48] Suleiman's reference to "murder" followed by the direct invocation of Mapplethorpe further highlighted the need for a relational analysis between gay and lesbian people and people with HIV/AIDS in the United States and the Palestinians under Israeli occupation by speaking to the necropolitical conditions that these groups struggle to survive under.[49] Indeed, the right-wing attempts to censor AIDS-related arts activism came at a time when the AIDS movement had taken up the word *genocide* to describe the US government's necropolitical negligence toward the epidemic and the marginalized communities it predominantly affected,[50] while Palestinian activists, scholars, and international human rights organizations had started using the word to describe the magnitude of violence the Israeli military perpetrated against Palestinian and Lebanese civilians during the 1980s.[51] Suleiman's implied framework of genocide served as a critical point of resistance to calls for "balance," thereby reframing the debate into a question not just of self-representation but of self-determination and cultural survival in the face of necropolitical state violence.

## Neoliberal Multiculturalism: Replacing One Queer with Another

Since the curators were also the distributors of most of the *Uprising* films, they subsequently pulled their films from the ICA in protest of the Dershowitz panel.[52] *Canticle of the Stones,* however, had been distributed by the Seattle-based Arab Film Distribution, and its screening was slated to continue along with the panel, which was intended to, in the words of Sussman, "focus on the question of how artistic programs should or should not be contextualized in a public setting."[53] In speaking to the press, Sussman suggested that such panels were a common component of the museum's programming, although other, unnamed ICA board and staff members refuted that claim.[54] Once Arab Film Distribution was informed of the exceptional circumstances under which *Canticle of the Stones* was to be screened, it pulled the last remaining film from the scheduled screening.[55]

With the withdrawal of the *Uprising* films also came the cancellation of the panel discussion with Dershowitz. However, the ICA continued with its plan for another film series, *Images of Palestinians in Israeli Cinema and Video.* The print news representation of the ICA's treatment of *Uprising* and *Images* tells an incomplete story that obscures the institution's pervasive attempts to control Palestinian self-representation and suppress critiques of Zionism. Before critics such as Grossman and Zakim had even insisted that the ICA balance Palestinian self-representations with Israeli perspectives, Suleiman had been working with Ella Shohat, a Jewish-Iraqi/Mizrahi cinema scholar, to curate a companion exhibition on critical representations of the Zionist imaging of Palestine, highlighting new engagements with Palestinians within emerging alternative Israeli cinema.[56]

The *Images* series was based on Shohat's academic book *Israeli Cinema: East/West and the Politics of Representation* (1989), which had also been the subject of intense controversy in the late 1980s and 1990s, both in Israel and within mainstream Jewish spaces.[57] Shohat's personal subjectivity and identity as an Arab Jew is significant here, and her position in this controversy illuminates the neoliberal multicultural machinations of compulsory Zionism. *Images* originated as a collaborative project between Suleiman and Shohat, as a companion to the *Uprising* show, not the balancing counterweight that it was represented as in *The Boston Globe.*[58] Given the misrepresentation of *Images* in the press as a response to Zionist critiques of and in turn a replacement for *Uprising,* one can argue that the identities of the curators reified a rhetoric of "population exchange." Since 1948, Zionist population exchange rhetoric was intended to derail concerns about and absolve Israeli responsibility for indigenous Palestinian displacement by replacing the narrative of Palestinian displacement with a narrative about Jewish exodus from Arab lands and salvation through resettlement in Israel.[59] However, the issue of Arab-Jewish/Mizrahi subjectivity remained marginal within nearly all academic and popular discourses of the 1980s and 1990s.[60] And although Shohat's identity as an Arab Jew was not at all discussed in the press, we might consider its treatment of the ICA controversy as unintentionally echoing a kind of population exchange rhetoric manifesting in US news media through calls for "balance." If, as Shadmi argues, compulsory Zionism constructs Mizrahi subjectivity in the context of Israel as the queer other in need of discipline, then we must understand the denigration of *Uprising* and subsequent celebration of *Images* as an example of how neoliberal multiculturalism seeks to alienate Palestinian subjectivity by rendering it queerer than queer.

Compulsory Zionism in this moment performs the work of neoliberal multiculturalism by upholding *some* abject subjects in order to justify the denigration, expulsion, and erasure of the other, undisciplinable queer. Both before and after the ICA controversy, scholars wrote extensively on how the state of Israel has abused its Mizrahi citizens,[61] and Shohat herself has discussed how Israel's Mizrahim have experienced a kind of cognitive dissonance with regard to their experiences of otherness within Israeli society: "Although such experiences are in some ways typical of refugee and even immigrant communities, what was rather anomalous about this situation, I think, was that we Arab Jews were expected to define this exilic condition as 'coming home.'"[62] Just as the ICA's Mapplethorpe victory represented a homonormative homecoming for gay and lesbian subjectivity, the representation of *Images* as a replacement for *Uprising* makes clear how compulsory Zionism upholds Arab-Jewish subjectivity as a multicultural "decoy" in the denigration, displacement, and erasure of Palestinian self-representation.[63] Indeed, the inordinately positive reception of *Images* in *The Boston Globe* exemplifies this last point. Gilbert, who had previously lambasted the Palestinian filmmakers of the *Uprising* series, lavishly praised *Images,* calling the films "subtle and rational," "effective," "clever," "morally intricate," and overall absent of what he characterized as "the flagrant heartstring manipulations that marred *Uprising*."[64] Although Shohat's scholarship has come under attack both in Israel and in mainstream Jewish American circles, the *Images* series about the representation of Palestinians in Israeli cinema was for the most part celebrated as an American showcase of Israeli openness, indicating how compulsory Zionism operates in the service of neoliberal multiculturalism in order to replace Palestinian subjectivity, as well as Arab-Jewish identity, with an image of an all-inclusive, American-style Israeli democracy.

Aside from selecting the films, Shohat had little control over the *Images* exhibition, and as the controversy over *Uprising* intensified, she publicly withdrew her association with the *Images* show, stating in a press release to *The Boston Globe*: "I want the public to know where I stand in relation to this controversy. . . . I unequivocally support the curators of *Uprising*."[65] In a letter to the ICA, Shohat further challenged the institution to uphold its proclaimed commitment to so-called balanced discourse. She called on the ICA to organize a "courageous public discussion on the myriad forms of subtle and not so subtle modes of censorship operating whenever critical Israeli or Palestinian cultural events are proposed or presented."[66] The ICA continued with its exhibition of *Images* despite Shohat's withdrawal, which included attendance by three of the featured Israeli filmmakers.[67] Ultimately, *Uprising* did screen that same weekend at The Space, an independent gallery in downtown Boston, as well as in October 1991 at Harvard University's Carpenter Center for the Visual Arts.[68]

Much of the post-9/11 discourse on pinkwashing has presumed that the advent of Israel's pinkwashing campaigns prompted an upsurge of LGBTQ+ activism in rejection of it. Such a premise does not account for *why* Israel chose, seemingly from a vacuum, the LGBTQ+ community, and film culture in particular, as primary targets for its public relations campaign in the first place. The *Uprising* controversy offers much-needed historical context in this regard. In her treatise on homonationalism, Jasbir Puar asserts that "queer times require even queerer modalities of thought, analysis, creativity, and expression in order to elaborate upon nationalist, patriotic, and terrorist formations and their imbricated forms of racialized perverse sexualities."[69] If we view the 1990s as the historical context whence the post-9/11 "queer times" arrive, and if "*queerer* modalities" are indeed necessary to challenge homonormativity, then the issue of Palestine fits the bill. The enforcement of compulsory Zionism during the *Uprising* controversy protected the ascension of homonormativity while constructing Palestinian subjectivity as queerer than queer. However, one unintended result of this controversy was the revelation of Palestine solidarity politics as the queerer modality by which to resist homonationalism and the freedom with violence it perpetuates.

The ICA's treatment of the *Uprising* series, in contrast to its defense of *The Perfect Moment* exhibit, exemplifies how compulsory Zionism operates in the United States under the auspices of political correctness and in the service of neoliberal multiculturalism. Although compulsory Zionism's goal during the ICA controversy was to censor and alienate Palestinian self-representation and the cultural politics therein, the relationships between Zionism and heterosexism became readily apparent to a broader US public through the press coverage of these two overlapping controversies. Although radical leftist gay and lesbian activist organizations such as Lesbians and Gays Against Intervention had been working in support of the Palestinian cause for several years before the *Uprising* controversy even made news in 1991, such relational politics existed in the farthest left realms of gay and lesbian activist culture. Indeed, in *Lavender and Red: Liberation and Solidarity in the Gay and Lesbian Left,* Emily Hobson recognizes the emergence of antipinkwashing activism from anti-imperialism activist groups such as Lesbians and Gays Against Intervention;[70] however, a detailed account of Palestine solidarity politics is absent from Hobson's otherwise thorough and transformative historical narrative. The present chapter picks up Hobson's threads to weave the question of Palestine back into the historical tapestry of gay and lesbian cultural politics of the 1990s.

The *Uprising* incident further helps historicize why the Israeli state focused its "Brand Israel" public relations campaigns so heavily on LGBTQ+ film culture in the new millennium. For example, when protests erupted in San Francisco in 2010 and 2011 around the Israeli consulate–sponsored pinkwashing film festival Out in Israel and Frameline: International Lesbian and Gay Film Festival's acceptance of Israeli consulate funding, Israel's consular general to the Pacific Northwest, Akiva Tor, was not entirely wrong when, in a series of interviews with local news, he stated that "a lot of anti-Israel feeling is centered in LGBT communities" and "our LGBT citizens are among our most creative, so it's logical they'd be represented in a film festival."[71] Though his stereotypical generalization of LGBTQ+ people as "most creative" is problematic, his statement indicates that Israel's public relations managers had done their research. What Tor is in fact referencing here is a much longer relationship between gay and lesbian and Palestinian artists and activists that cohered in highly visible and publicized ways specifically around arts and cinema. The present chapter locates one of the origin points for such visibility in cinematic activism for Palestine.

# 4 It's an Honor Just to Be Nominated

## *Palestinian Liberation and Solidarity Politics in Hollywood Award Shows, 1978–2024*

> "Suicide bombers, Mossad agents, gay cowboys, country singers, literary lions, a bullheaded CIA agent, and a transsexual on a road trip were among the cast of characters in films nominated Tuesday for Academy Awards."
>
> —David Germain, "Oscar Says Yes to 'Paradise Now': 'Munich' Nominated in Five Categories," *The Jerusalem Post,* February 1, 2006

On April 4, 1978, Yasser Arafat, then leader of the Palestine Liberation Organization (PLO), sent Oscar-winning film director Fred Zinnemann a telegram thanking the renowned filmmaker for helping to represent the Palestinian liberation cause to a live television audience of thirty million viewers. Arafat was referring to Vanessa Redgrave's Oscar acceptance speech at the Academy Awards ceremony the previous evening for her performance in the titular role of Zinnemann's Holocaust drama, *Julia* (1977). During her speech, Redgrave infamously lambasted members of the Jewish Defense League (JDL), whom she referred to as "Zionist hoodlums," for their months-long campaign of harassment and intimidation in opposition to her cinematic activism in solidarity with the Palestinian liberation struggle.[1] Arafat's telegram is, to use our contemporary parlance, an epic example of trolling. The tone is celebratory and cordial: Arafat wished Zinnemann the best of luck in his next production, while also urging Zinnemann to, in the interest of representational equity, take up the Black liberation cause in his future film projects. Arafat ended the missive by informing Zinnemann, likely to

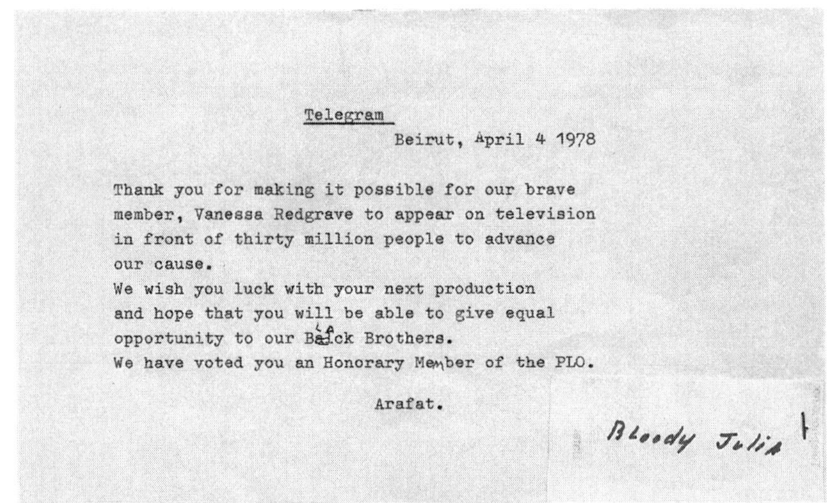

Telegram

Beirut, April 4 1978

Thank you for making it possible for our brave
member, Vanessa Redgrave to appear on television
in front of thirty million people to advance
our cause.
We wish you luck with your next production
and hope that you will be able to give equal
opportunity to our Black Brothers.
We have voted you an Honorary Member of the PLO.

Arafat.

Bloody Julia

Figure 10. A telegram sent to Hollywood film director Fred Zinnemann from PLO chairman Yasser Arafat the day after Vanessa Redgrave won an Oscar for her role in Zinnemann's Holocaust drama, *Julia.* Copyright the Fred Zinnemann estate.

the filmmaker's chagrin, that he had been voted an honorary member of the PLO. In the telegram's margin, Zinnemann offered a succinct comment, writing in red felt-tipped pen on a scrap of paper stapled to the corner: "Bloody Julia" (Figure 10).[2]

Where the previous chapters traced the process of mainstreaming from taboo to inclusion through the wider dissemination of Palestinian cinema and Palestine films in US mass media and elite institutions, this chapter examines what is perhaps the most massive of the various mass media platforms examined in this book: Hollywood award ceremonies and their multimillion-viewer live television broadcasts. Doing so helps to track how, within the process of mainstreaming, inclusion transitions into normalization.

The materials analyzed in this chapter consist of the archived papers of director Fred Zinnemann, print news articles, and the video recordings of award ceremonies themselves. The scholarship of Evelyn Alsultany, Melani McAlister, and Jack Shaheen has demonstrated just how thoroughly Hollywood cinema has dehumanized Palestinians and as such Hollywood has long since offered a prime site for the study of institutionalized compulsory Zionism. However, as highly publicized and annual moments of spectacle, Hollywood award ceremonies and the treatment of the topic of Palestine and Palestinian cinema within these ceremonies across a span of over forty years provide key insight into how the discourse on Palestine has changed over time within the context of mainstream US media institutions and the Hollywood film industry. Indeed, Tony Shaw and Giora Goodman's recent publication *Hollywood and Israel: A History* reveals an anxiety over these changes:

> Hollywood has been one of the great cultural gluing agents in the [US-Israel] alliance, forging and magnifying pro-Israel sentiments in American society on screen and lobbying for the Jewish state. . . . In the twenty-first century, new voices in and around the celebrity capital have treated Israel in ways that could not have been imagined decades earlier. These voices reflect a growing division over Israel among Americans, including Jews, and have had serious implications for the special relationship between the United States and Israel.[3]

The close reading of archival materials and award ceremony footage and speeches examined in this chapter unsettles the idea of Hollywood's monolithic compulsory Zionism. I argue that award ceremonies have been strategically leveraged to reveal fissures in that monolithic façade, sometimes to stoke spectacle in the interest of capital, and sometimes to assert contradiction in the interest of humanity. In turn, this chapter demonstrates how the seeds of the "growing division," of which Shaw and Goodman speak, in US society more broadly but specifically within Hollywood, were planted and in fact germinated decades prior to the turn of the twenty-first century.

Arafat's telegram also unsettles the previously held academic arguments about how the Palestinian liberation movement and its accompanying film units conceived of Palestinian cinema primarily in the tradition of Third Cinema.[4] Likewise, although much scholarly attention has been paid to the Redgrave spectacle at the Academy Awards in 1978, key aspects of the Redgrave controversy have been overlooked. This chapter historicizes how Hollywood's treatment of the topic of Palestine and its treatment of Palestinian cinema within Hollywood's machinations—both as institution and as industry—have changed between 1978 and 2024. I focus on six significant moments in Hollywood award ceremony history wherein the topic of Palestine and Palestinian cinema is explicitly addressed within those award ceremonies, in particular the Academy Awards (Oscars) and the Golden Globe Awards, in order to highlight how the institution and industry of Hollywood have slowly been leveraged in the service of cinematic activism for Palestine, for better or worse. In doing so, this chapter also poses an intervention to the prevalent academic understandings of Hollywood's relationship to Israel, Zionism, and the Palestinian struggle for liberation.

The history of how and when the topic of Palestine has entered, as well as Palestinian cinema's inclusion within, these Hollywood awards shows offers insight into how the representation of Palestinian cinema, in coordination with the content of Palestinian cinema itself, constitutes a discourse for the production of knowledge about Palestine for spectators historically considered at best unsympathetic and at worst hostile to the Palestinian cause. The distribution of that discourse through Hollywood award shows has proved critical in moving the topic of Palestinian liberation from the wings of the US public sphere to the main stage. Whereas public expressions of sympathy toward Palestinians and a willingness to even acknowledge Palestinian cinema were once considered taboo and unspeakable within Hollywood, Palestine solidarity and engagement with the Palestinian cinematic movement have now been adopted as part of Hollywood's risk management calculations in the interest of protecting profit maximization. Put another way, Hollywood's treatment of Palestinian cinema in the twenty-first century reflects the industry's cynical use of Palestinian cinema as a symbol of DEI and a way to navigate what Alsultany refers to as the cycle of "crisis diversity."[5]

With broadcast audiences ranging from roughly twenty million to forty million viewers in the United States alone, Hollywood awards shows offer interesting sites for analysis of how Hollywood addresses—literally and figuratively—contentious social and political issues.[6] These awards shows are sites wherein the industry ritualistically manufactures competition, produces spectacle, and bestows much coveted validation. The conferring of these awards endows their recipients with a form of legitimacy, bestowed by some of the most elite and powerful players in the global film industry. That legitimacy in turn has potential to translate into greater cultural and monetary value and, ultimately, capital. A core stake in this nexus of competition, spectacle, and validation is that of bankability. Award nomination and winning not only confer a sense of legitimacy and status for the recipient but also forecast a winner's future bankability within an industry that seeks to recapitalize that status. In these ways, Hollywood awards ceremonies are reflective of a political economy of prestige in that the process of endowing legitimacy and validation through award nomination and granting intrinsically relates to the industry's business interests of risk reduction and profit maximization.[7] As a result, one consequence of this shift is that the kinds of Palestinian films that have gained traction, legitimacy, and cultural capital through Hollywood institutions (and by extension the US mainstream) are more homogenous, didactic, and sometimes more sensationalistic, and do not necessarily reflect the increasing diversity of the Palestinian cinematic movement. Although much of Palestinian cinema has historically been produced outside of the reach of Hollywood, the Palestinian cinematic movement has experienced a distribution boom throughout the United States since 2006, in part due to the success of Hany Abu-Assad's *Paradise Now* in acquiring an Oscar nomination and winning a Golden Globe Award, and in part to changes in distribution and viewing technology, such as the advent of streaming. As a result of that success and subsequent development of the Palestinian cinematic movement, Palestinian films have enjoyed greater visibility and circulation within more mainstream film markets within the United States. As such, a homogenized version of Palestinian cinema as it is promoted through Hollywood awards shows therefore has much greater implications for what kind of content and narratives get the green light for production (especially within Hollywood), the reach of Palestinian cinema within US markets and audiences, and who is and who is not considered a Palestinian filmmaker.

The perception of the legitimacy of these award-granting institutions themselves, particularly with regard to the Academy Awards, has been intensely scrutinized in the twenty-first century in relation to shifting discourses on racial and gender equity within Hollywood and US society. It is therefore important to also consider how the presence or absence of Palestinian cinema within these awards ceremonies is embroiled within larger conversations about institutionalized racism, sexism, homophobia, and transphobia in the United States.[8] A subargument of this chapter, therefore, is that Hollywood's increased inclusion of Palestinian cinema within its award-granting apparatuses is less indicative of a dramatic shift in cultural or political attitudes toward Palestine and Palestinian liberation among Hollywood elites, and more indicative of Hollywood's cynical use of Palestinian cinema as a form of DEI insurance to counteract its racist, sexist, homophobic, and transphobic liabilities.

Examining how Palestinian cinema is excluded from or included in, as well as how Palestine overall is referred to and represented within, these Hollywood awards ceremonies, the broadcast of those ceremonies on television, and their accompanying news coverage illuminates how cinematic activism has changed the discourse on Palestine in the United States over the past fifty years. More specifically, I argue that within Hollywood's political economy, the representation of Palestine and Palestinian cinema has moved from a position of risk and liability to one in the service of risk management. Within these awards shows, the topic of Palestine has seen it all, going from taboo and unspeakable to begrudgingly included within a liberal multicultural frame, to center stage as a choregraphed confrontation, to a victorious spectacle, and eventually to a diffuse utterance of normalization, and, most recently, ultimately back to contentious spectacle. The progression of Palestinian cinema's representation within these awards shows tracks how cinematic activism has at once functioned to legitimize the topic of Palestinian liberation and solidarity for mainstream US audiences, but has also expedited a commodification of Palestinian representation within Hollywood. This process of commodification threatens to reduce Palestinian representation to a type of cultural capital and an object in the service of "virtue signaling" within Hollywood and social media.[9] In sum, the topic of Palestine in Hollywood and its attendant publics is not only represented but is now (strangely) valued as an emerging market, while also leveraged cynically as a counterweight within the political economy and culture wars in the United States over race, gender, and sexuality. Still, important albeit downplayed changes have occurred in terms of Hollywood's treatment of the topic of Palestinian liberation, Israel, and Zionism, and those changes signal potential for major changes in the cultural and financial sustainability of Israel's apartheid regime.

This chapter examines a series of flashpoints when the topic of Palestine or Palestinian cinema has been represented and contested within and surrounding Hollywood award ceremonies. Those examples span over forty years and include, in chronological order, Redgrave's Oscar acceptance speech in 1978, Elia Suleiman's challenge to the Academy's rules excluding Palestinian cinema from submission eligibility in 2002, the Oscar nomination and Golden Globe win of Abu-Assad's film *Paradise Now* in 2006, the relative normalization of Palestinian films as Oscar nominees between 2014 and 2021, the specter of Palestine in the Academy's lawsuit over the Israeli government's subversive attempt to use the Oscars for a propaganda stunt in 2016, and lastly, Jonathan Glazer's 2024 Oscar acceptance speech for his Holocaust film *The Zone of Interest,* in which he condemned the cynical use of the Holocaust as justification for genocide.

This chapter interrogates the effectiveness of this progression, particularly in terms of whether these shifts in the treatment of Palestine solidarity speech and Palestinian cinema within some of Hollywood's most powerful institutions are indicative of any cultural, institutional, or material changes with regard to Palestinian liberation and solidarity politics within the Hollywood industry. On the one hand, the increasing regularity of Palestinian cinema's nominations within these elite award competitions does a certain kind of work to normalize the speakability of Palestine to a broadcast audience of tens of millions of viewers in ways that were previously impossible. While this normalization may be useful in reducing the taboo around the mere mention of Palestine, it does little else in the way of cinematic activism in that it does not function to convey substantive information about the Palestinian condition or provide directives for further engagement, knowledge acquisition, or action. On the other hand, there is evidence that this shift toward normalization within these awards shows is less indicative of a cultural shift in support of Palestine and more suggests that hardline support for the state of Israel is increasingly being viewed as a liability in the context of high-risk capitalist enterprises such as film production. The Academy's attempt to distance itself from the Israeli propaganda stunt executed through the Distinctive Assets swag bags in 2016 suggests a skittishness around situations that have potential to lead to economic damages, such as a consumer boycott.

It is important to consider the context of neoliberal capitalism when questioning how and why sympathetic representations of Palestine have succeeded in circulating within mainstream media in the United States. Fifty years ago it was nearly impossible to even speak the word *Palestine* in the United States—in regular social interaction, let alone within the context of the Academy Awards—without inviting severe censure, ostracism, and sometimes even violence.[10] To be clear, merely speaking the word *Palestine* on the Oscar stage by no means constitutes a form of activism, nor does it change the material reality of Palestinian life under Israeli apartheid. This case study shows that the normalization of the word *Palestine* in the context of Hollywood awards ceremonies, and by extension US mainstream culture, has very little to do with a recognition of Palestinian cinema's artistic value, and even less to do with recognition of Palestinian human value or rights to self-determination. The Academy's changing treatment of Palestinian cinema has not hinged on questions of equitable representation or humanitarianism. Instead, this change shows how the inclusion and normalization of Palestinian cinema within Hollywood awards ceremonies was enabled through a recognition of a Palestinian film *industry* willing and able to engage within a global capitalist marketplace of cinema. This chapter therefore examines how and why the mere speakability of the word *Palestine* was normalized within Hollywood's ritualistic ceremonies of recognition and legitimization.

Arab American studies has long treated Hollywood with criticism and skepticism due to what in many ways has been discussed as Hollywood's monolithic Zionism. The following section offers a starting point from which to complicate that narrative.

## The Redgrave Incident

While scholars have focused intensely on Redgrave's Oscar speech of 1978, less attention has been paid to the discourse surrounding the speech.[11] *Julia* was based on a chapter of Lillian Hellman's memoir *Pentimento,* which recounts the story of a wealthy American woman known as "Julia" who was studying medicine in Vienna in the 1930s and subsequently became an antifascist activist and money smuggler for the anti-Nazi resistance movement in Germany.[12] Helmed by the highly renowned Zinnemann and cast with high-profile Hollywood and European stars such as the then-staunchly Zionist Jane Fonda,[13] Jason Robards, Maximillian Schell, and Meryl Streep in her film debut,

*Julia* was a favorite for Oscar success. Despite the Oscar fanfare, *Julia,* or rather, Redgrave, was proving to be a thorn in Zinnemann's side. The same year *Julia* was produced, Redgrave produced and narrated *The Palestinian* (1977), a documentary film promoting the Palestinian liberation struggle that featured an interview with PLO leader Yasser Arafat. Members of the JDL, a right-wing extremist group that the FBI classifies as a terrorist organization, picketed outside of the Oscars ceremony in protest of Redgrave's Oscar nomination, complete with burning Redgrave and Arafat in effigy (Figure 11).[14] JDL members had spent the better part of the 1970s terrorizing the Arab community of Los Angeles with physical assaults and bombings.[15] Although not as violent as their targeting of the Arab American community, the JDL treated *Julia* as guilty by association and terrorized film screenings in protest of Redgrave's politics.

*Julia* and *The Palestinian* were produced during the same time period, and both were released in 1977, but tensions over Redgrave's radical leftist politics existed between Zinnemann and Redgrave well before *Julia* even went into production. In a meeting between the actress, director Zinnemann, and screenwriter Alvin Sargent, Redgrave

Figure 11. The Jewish Defense League burns an effigy of Vanessa Redgrave. AP Photo/Doug Pizac.

objected to script rewrites that she perceived as depoliticizing Julia's radical leftist ethos and actions. Redgrave felt that Julia's character was reduced to that of a "nice girl, a humanitarian, but not a passionate fighter against social injustice."[16] Thanks to screenwriter Sargent's mediation between the actress and director, Zinnemann ultimately agreed to "sharpen" the representation of Julia's passion for social justice, but he also made it a point to remind Redgrave of the terms upon which he assumed they had agreed when she signed on to the film:

> I reminded her of our first discussion in New York when I said that I did *not* want *Julia* to be a political film, to which, I thought, she agreed. Further, I said that I wanted Julia to be an active anti-fascist, but *not* an active anti-capitalist. I said that Vanessa would have to accept this and agree to it without reservation, otherwise I didn't see how she could be in the film. To this she said that she would "give it a think."[17]

Indeed, Zinnemann was hyperaware of how Redgrave's politics might cast a shadow of political controversy over *Julia*'s reception and its Oscar prospects. From the beginning of its release in the United States, *Julia* and its production studio, Twentieth Century Fox (Fox), were the target of the JDL's ire. In a more sophomoric example of JDL terrorism, the group released a dozen mice into a crowded theater during a screening of *Julia* in New York City, greatly distressing spectators and disrupting the screening.[18]

The JDL attempted to pressure Fox to make a public statement vowing never to hire Redgrave again and threatened to picket theaters exhibiting *Julia* if the studio did not comply. The JDL's blacklist demand of Fox hit a tender nerve in Hollywood, one that sparked an animated debate in the industry's trade journals *Variety* and *The Hollywood Reporter*, as well as in the *Los Angeles Times*. Fox executives staunchly refused that request, stating that

> not many years ago, this country, this state, and this industry in particular experienced a tragic period when people were refused employment because of their political beliefs. While Fox as a company, and the individuals that work here, do not agree with Redgrave's political philosophy, we totally reject, and will not be

> blackmailed into supporting, any policy of refusing to employ any person because of their political beliefs. We have therefore refused to issue the statement demanded.[19]

Various figures from the film and media industry weighed in through letters to the editor sections to defend Redgrave's right to free speech and reject censorship, including filmmaker John Landis, journalist Les Rodney, and voice actor Larry Robinson.[20] Additionally, Chester L. Migden, the national executive secretary of the Screen Actors Guild (SAG), one of Hollywood's largest and most powerful labor unions, penned a public letter to Fox president Dennis Stanfill throwing SAG's support behind the studio's position. In the letter, Migden asserted: "We are not making any judgement of Miss Redgrave's position. We all reserve the right to quarrel with her views, but to start the old game of blacklisting must be immediately, totally and firmly rejected at the outset. Our board here expressed its views supporting your position and concurred by rejecting as intolerable blacklisting for political or any other reason."[21] Fox had to balance the highly sensitive and Hollywood-specific subject of censorship and blacklisting while attempting to distance itself from Redgrave's politics and therefore avoid the JDL's harassment. Ahead of the Oscar broadcast the studio prepared a press statement to be released the day after the Oscars "in the event Vanessa issues a statement that we don't want her to," disavowing Redgrave's speech, yet "accepting" her right as a private citizen to freedom of expression.[22]

Indeed, when Redgrave won the Oscar for Best Supporting Actress, she seized the opportunity to deliver the following speech on live television:

> My dear colleagues, I thank you very, very much for this tribute to my work. I think that Jane Fonda and I have done the best work of our lives and I think this was in part due to our director, Fred Zinnemann. And I also think it's in part because we believed and we believe in what we were expressing. Two, out of millions, who gave their lives and were prepared to sacrifice everything in the fight against fascist and racist Nazi Germany. And I salute you and I pay tribute to you and I think you should be very proud that in the last few weeks you've stood firm and you have refused to

> be intimidated by the threats of a small bunch of Zionist hoodlums whose behavior is an insult to the stature of Jews all over the world and to their great and heroic record of struggle against fascism and oppression. And I salute that record, and I salute all of you for having stood firm and dealt a final blow against that period when Nixon and McCarthy launched a worldwide witch hunt against those who tried to express in their lives and their work the truth that they believed in. I salute you, and I thank you, and I pledge to you that I will continue to fight against anti-Semitism and fascism.[23]

To this day, Redgrave's speech is remembered as causing "the most political ceremony in Academy history."[24] Though her speech is most often recalled in popular memory with regard to her support of the Palestinian people, she does not mention the words *Palestine* or *Palestinians* at all during her speech. Rather, she weaves a rhetorical web of connections between racism, fascism, McCarthyism, and Zionism, drawing audible gasps, hisses, and boos from the Academy audience. At Redgrave's simultaneous condemnation of Nazi Germany, Nixon's McCarthyism, and "Zionist hoodlums," the Academy collectively clutched its pearls in disbelief over such an association. Many perceived the phrase "Zionist hoodlums" not as a reference to the JDL extremists protesting outside of the pavilion, but as, at best, a rebuke of Israel, and at worst, as antisemitism.

What is less commonly remembered about the Redgrave incident is how it also revealed an ambivalence among Academy members over the interplay between three sensitive topics within Hollywood: free speech, the insistence on a binary between art and politics, and support for Israel. This ambivalence became evidenced during the ceremony itself, when presenting the award for Best Adapted Screenplay, screenwriter Paddy Chayefsky rebuked Redgrave by condemning the use of the Academy Awards as a platform for "political propaganda," to which he received robust applause. However, what happened next is largely absent from public memory and academic analysis of this moment. In receiving the Best Adapted Screenplay award for *Julia,* Alvin Sargent offered a counterpoint to Chayefsky's angry pontification. After thanking mentors, colleagues, and the film's cast and crew (including Redgrave), Sargent took a moment to remind the audience of the moral imperative behind the film. He offered thanks to one final person who, in his words,

> is more responsible for this than anyone else, and that is a lady whose name, or was called, Julia. And for all the things that she stands for, I like to think that this Oscar represents those things and the *free expression* of all our good thoughts and feelings and loves *no matter who we are or what we have to say.*[25]

I interpret the latter part of this statement as Sargent giving a word of caution to his peers in relation to their reaction to Redgrave, and it is reasonable to believe that Sargent perhaps held a more open mind regarding Redgrave's politics. After all, Sargent worked closely with Redgrave and Zinnemann in finding a balance between Zinnemann's desire for an apolitical Holocaust film and Redgrave's insistence on honoring her character's political values. In the aforementioned meeting between Zinnemann, Redgrave, and Sargent, Zinnemann noted: "It is the lot of the writer always to be in the middle, and Alvin was no exception. He was impressed by some of Vanessa's arguments and he will try to sharpen the specific points on which we agreed."[26]

In his acceptance speech, Sargent also subtly reminded the audience, and perhaps specifically Chayefsky, of Hollywood's righteous fight against McCarthyist censorship and the industry's long history of rejecting the selective application of the right to freedom of expression "no matter who we are or what we have to say." A similar sentiment was echoed by journalist Denis Hamill in *Los Angeles Herald Examiner* coverage of the ceremony the following day:

> Paddy Chayefsky is a hypocrite when he stood up to criticize Vanessa Redgrave for using her speaking time . . . to make a political statement. Anyone who castigates another person for exercising her right to free speech is making a political statement. . . . He was pontificating.

It would have been very easy for the Academy, out of spite or in punishment of her views on Palestine, to not grant Redgrave the Oscar. In her speech, Redgrave essentially thanked the Academy for not yielding to the outside pressure of an extremist group, for standing by its commitments to freedom of expression, and for prioritizing artistic merit over political difference. Surely if Redgrave had *not* won the Oscar there would have been speculation that such a snub was politically motivated. What likely upset Academy audience members so greatly that evening was not the fact that Redgrave won, or that she held political beliefs that many deeply opposed, but that she publicly acknowledged—to an audience of millions—the possibility of dissent within Hollywood's seemingly unequivocal Zionist façade. What was perhaps even more upsetting to Hollywood's Zionists, to the point that it has been ignored in nearly all academic and news media accounts of the incident, though, was that renowned screenwriter Sargent took a moment out of his own ninety seconds of fame to essentially back Redgrave up.

Returning to Arafat's telegram to Fred Zinnemann, the spectacle over Zionism and Palestine during and around the 1978 Oscars ceremony is significant for pinpointing the advent of two radical changes that would not fully come to fruition until decades later. The first change being that Redgrave, with the support of screenwriter Sargent and journalist Hamill, exposed ambivalence within Hollywood over what had previously been represented to the US and international publics as monolithic Zionism. This small fissure of ambivalence in the façade of monolithic Zionism would grow over the years and ultimately manifest as outright dissent by the second decade of the twenty-first century.

Arafat's telegram also indicates a pivot within the Palestinian liberation movement's understanding of and vision for cinema's role in advancing the cause. In the telegram, Arafat thanks Zinnemann for "making it possible for our brave member, Vanessa Redgrave to appear on television in front of thirty million people to advance our cause." The word *Palestine* or *Palestinian* was never uttered once during the Oscars ceremony, and yet the PLO perceived this moment as a victory for the cause. This moment does indeed mark a pivotal moment in the representation of Palestine solidarity within mainstream media, in part due to the massive scale of the broadcast. That particular Oscars ceremony received 39.73 million US viewers, a number that excludes any international viewership.

Oscars aside, the 1970s were an especially productive time for cinematic activism for Palestine. Palestinian cinema of the third period (1968–1982) did not fully circulate to US audiences, let alone make it to US television broadcast. With the establishment of the Palestine Film Unit (PFU) in 1968, cinematic activism (although not necessarily named as such) had been made an official strategy of the Palestinian liberation movement.[27] In terms of Gertz and Khleifi's periodization of Palestinian cinema, the end of the 1970s coincides with the winding down of the third period of the Palestinian cinematic movement. The third period was devoted almost entirely to producing and circulating the cinema of revolution. The PFU was one of the PLO's cinematic propaganda units charged with narrativizing the Palestinian revolutionary struggle, particularly designed for audiences consisting of other Third World liberation factions and Marxist-Leninist resistance movements. The content of the third period mirrors the intended audience of third world liberation movements, therefore placing third period Palestinian cinema solidly within the category of Third Cinema, which can loosely be understood as cinema of resistance by the Third World for the Third World.

However, the 1970s is also when the Palestinian liberation movement, broadly speaking, began attempting to harness the power of mass media. The Palestine Film Unit was established by 1968, and by 1972 the PLO had established the Department of Culture and Media, and both the Democratic Front for the Liberation of Palestine and the Popular Front for the Liberation of Palestine had established film units.[28] The result was a period of prolific Palestinian cinema and Palestine film production and its dissemination to Third Cinema–oriented film festivals worldwide.[29] But it was not enough to disseminate cinema of revolution to already radicalized audiences, and the Palestinian liberation movement understood more radical acts of resistance, such as airplane hijackings, as media spectacles designed to draw in a much wider spectatorship, especially among Western audiences. While filmmakers of the third period were largely committed to the project of Third Cinema, the Arafat telegram suggests that those in positions of power within the liberation movement saw the potential afforded through strategic engagement with Western mass media, including those associated with Hollywood, such as Redgrave. Arafat celebrating the dissemination of the discourse on Palestinian liberation through the highly visible and commercial platform of the Academy Awards exemplifies a pivot away from the Third Cinema politics of the third period and, at the very least, a kind of righteous excitement at the prospect of

Palestinian liberation being represented to a mainstream US television audience. While the PFU certainly sought to speak to and in conversation with other Third World liberation struggles, the PLO's partnership with Redgrave indicates an interest in leveraging the spectacle of Hollywood celebrity to distribute Palestinian liberation and solidarity politics to a wider, more mainstream US audience.

The 1970s and early 1980s were also a period of extreme violence against Palestinian artists and cultural producers, Palestinian activists, and solidarity activists in the US context. Cinematic activism for Palestine or anyone or anything *perceived* as associated with that cinematic activism (including Zinnemann's film *Julia*) were specifically targeted by bomb threats, bombings, and other forms of harassment and disruption. Some examples include the bombing of a Los Angeles theater in the early dawn hours of June 15, 1978, ahead of a scheduled screening of Redgrave's *The Palestinian,* the mice at the *Julia* screening in New York City, and the 1981 bomb threat against David Koff's *Occupied Palestine* at the Castro Theatre as discussed in chapter 2. The Palestinian cinematic movement experienced significant tragedies in the 1970s and 1980s, including the accidental deaths of Lebanese filmmaker Gary Garabedian in 1968 and Palestinian filmmaker Hany Jawhariyyah in 1976, and the partial paralysis of Palestinian filmmaker Sulafa Jadallah in 1970 when someone on set accidentally shot her.[30] The 1970s and 1980s were also a period wherein violent efforts were made to silence Palestinian artists and cultural producers. For example, Palestinian writer and Popular Front for the Liberation of Palestine (PFLP) spokesman Ghassan Kanafani was assassinated in 1972, and Palestinian cartoonist Naji al-Ali was assassinated in 1987.[31] In sum, the 1960s through the 1980s was a period wherein the prolific cultural production and cinematic activism within the broader Palestinian liberation movement was met with both outright violence and suppression, but also plagued by tragic accidents under the conditions of colonialism and exile. The nail in the coffin of the third period of Palestinian cinema came during the 1982 Israeli invasion of Lebanon, during which the massive archive of Palestinian cinema housed in Beirut disappeared.[32]

Yet as the era of revolutionary Palestinian cinema of the third period came to a close, the era of Palestinian art-house cinema of the fourth period blossomed, beginning in 1980 with Michel Khleifi's experimental hybrid documentary–narrative film *Fertile Memory,* followed by *Wedding in Galilee* in 1987, and the beginnings of several now-prominent Palestinian filmmaker and actor careers in the 1990s, such as filmmakers Rashid Masharawi, Mai Masri, Hany Abu-Assad, and Elia Suleiman, and actors Mohammad Bakri and Hiam Abbas. With the advent of the fourth period also came the advent of the Palestinian art-house film and the circulation and recognition of Palestinian cinema within the larger political and cultural economy of international cinema through elite venues such as the Cannes Film Festival and its litany of prestigious awards.

The Redgrave incident is just one in a series of examples of how the debate over Palestine and Zionism has played out on a mainstream, mass media platform, in this case through a live international television broadcast of the Academy Awards ceremony. The following section examines how Palestinian filmmakers of the fourth period, in a departure from the Palestinian cinematic movement's third period ethos, literally and figuratively capitalize on the fissure revealed through the Redgrave incident by lobbying the Academy for the inclusion of Palestinian cinema in the Oscar nomination process.

## Suleiman and Goliath

In 1978 the Redgrave Oscar controversy pivoted on a word entirely left unspoken. Twenty-two years later, Palestinian filmmaker Elia Suleiman essentially asked the Academy for, in the words of Edward Said, "permission to narrate."[33] In 2002 Suleiman attempted to submit his narrative film *Divine Intervention* (2002) for consideration in the category of Best Foreign Language Film. *Divine Intervention* is the second of a trilogy of films by Suleiman that—informed by his family history and personal experiences of apartheid, exile, and return—represent an absurdist and darkly comical take on Palestinian life under Israeli rule. The film focuses on the mundane daily life of the silent protagonist—E. S., played by Suleiman himself—in the Palestinian town of Nazareth (in the northern region of what is now the state of Israel). Through static shots of carefully stylized mise-en-scène, we follow E. S. through the boring, rote, and at times ridiculous happenings of daily life, including regular parked car rendezvous at an Israeli army checkpoint with his lover, a West Bank resident unable to enter Israel, for five precious minutes of intimate hand fondling.

Many of Suleiman's films employ magical realism as a means by which the film's characters circumnavigate, thwart, and mock the quotidian humiliation, inconvenience, and degradation under Israeli apartheid. In one of *Divine Intervention*'s most famous scenes, while parked with his lover at the checkpoint, E. S. inflates a red balloon adorned with the face of Arafat. E. S. releases the balloon to be carried by the wind over the checkpoint, over the incensed yet dumbfounded Israeli soldiers, until it reaches the Al-Aqsa Mosque (the Dome of the Rock) in Jerusalem, pausing at the pinnacle as this warped facsimile of Arafat's charismatic smile circles one of Palestine's most potent national symbols. In the wake of the Oslo Accords' catastrophic failure and the Palestinian Authority's inability (indeed, some would even say unwillingness) to adequately represent the Palestinian people, the balloon scene is itself a comment on the possibilities, limits, and im/probabilities of Palestinian representation (political, cinematic, or otherwise). This scene is also a clear example of how Suleiman's films are saturated with postmodern themes, such as Baudrillardian hyperreality, image distortion, preoccupation with ideology, and mistrust and even mockery of grand narratives.

Despite *Divine Intervention*'s international critical acclaim, the Academy determined that Suleiman's film was ineligible for submission. The point of contention between Suleiman and the Academy did not revolve around questions of artistic merit or talent; rather, the issue hinged on semantics and—in a fantastically ironic way—one of the hallmarks of modernity that Suleiman's film itself critiques: bureaucracy.[34] According to the 2002 Academy rulebook, in order to be eligible for submission to this category,

> The film must be first released in the country of origin . . . and first publicly exhibited by means of 35mm or 70mm for at least seven consecutive days in a commercial motion picture theater for the profit of the producer and exhibitor, advertised and exploited during its eligibility run in a manner considered normal and customary to the industry.[35]

In the eyes of the Academy, taking its cue from the United Nations, Palestine was not a UN member-state, therefore it was not a "country," and therefore *Divine Intervention* did not meet the basic eligibility requirements to be considered for nomination in the category of Best Foreign Language Film.[36] Despite the fact that Palestine has held UN observer status since 1974 and that the Academy had previously bent its own rules to include submissions from other contested territories (such as Hong Kong, Puerto Rico, and Taiwan), the Academy stood by the rules to exclude *Divine Intervention* from consideration in the nomination process.[37] Given how eligibility for submission was contingent upon UN member-nation status, the controversy called attention to how the category name itself was a misnomer. With the enforcement of this rule, and the Academy's willingness to occasionally bend it, the Best Foreign Language Film category became not only an arbiter of international taste but also an adjudicator of national legitimacy.

While much of the controversy surrounding Suleiman's bid for eligibility hinged on the Academy's refusal to recognize Palestine as a country, the film faced specifically nation-state-based institutional and infrastructural barriers to achieving Oscar eligibility. The Academy's rulebook stipulated that a film must have been put forward by said country's national film selection committee, of which Palestine had none at the time. The film must have also screened "in a commercial motion picture theater for the profit of the producer and exhibitor, advertised and exploited during its eligibility run in a manner considered normal and customary to the industry."[38] This latter rule set an impossibly high bar for Palestinian cinema to meet. At the time of Suleiman's bid, the Second Intifada (and the Israeli army's violent suppression of it) was raging in the occupied Palestinian territories; the only operating theaters had been closed due to the Second Intifada, or, as was the case in Gaza, set ablaze by religious fundamentalists.[39] If by some miracle Suleiman had been able to exhibit his film for one whole week in the middle of a veritable war zone, the probability of advertising the film within the Palestinian territories in a manner that could have met Hollywood norms was, to put it in accordance with Suleiman's cinematic aesthetic, absurd.

It is important to clarify here that Suleiman did not actually officially submit his film in 2002, but rather was dissuaded from submitting it, as it would have faced certain rejection. This certain rejection was, according to Academy communications director John Pavlik, due in part to the "undefined nature of 'Palestine'" and given the lack of a national selection committee submitting the film on Palestine's behalf.[40] For this reason, Suleiman withheld his submission in order to lobby the Academy to once again make an exception for a film made under ongoing conditions of colonialism. And there was indeed reason to believe that Suleiman could successfully argue his case, as Pavlik admitted to the press that for the purposes of submission eligibility, "the question of whether Palestine is a country is open."[41]

Although the first rule for eligibility within the category traffics in the abstract language of "country," the remaining criteria for eligibility revolve entirely around the construct of a national cinema sutured to a nation-state. Pavlik's admission to the Academy's openness around the question of Palestine's status was deeply troubling to Morton Klein, then president of the Zionist Organization of America. Klein staunchly opposed the Academy's openness to consider Suleiman's request, stating in *The Jewish Exponent*: "I think it would be deeply disappointing if [the Academy] would recognize a film from an area that is not a UN sanctioned country." In Klein's view, the Academy's willingness to even consider *Divine Intervention* for submission would "give legitimacy, or at least the perception of legitimacy, to this terrorist regime" and would be tantamount to giving "a stamp of approval, or any kind of credibility, to this vicious regime."[42] For Klein, the ultimate concern here was that the Academy of Motion Picture Arts and Sciences (AMPAS) held the power to anoint Palestinian cinema as a *national* cinema, even in the absence of a sovereign nation-state.

Arab American civil rights organizers, the Arab American press, and Palestinian political actors condemned the Academy's colonialist rules for film submission. Feda Abdellhady Nasser, a counselor for the Permanent Observer Mission of Palestine to the United Nations, criticized the Academy's dismissal of *Divine Intervention,* stating in a *Los Angeles Times* article, "What it comes down to is that the Palestinian people, in addition to the denial of their rights . . . are now being denied the ability to compete in a competition that judges artistic and cultural expression." In an op-ed in *USA Today,* Palestinian American lawyer, media analyst, and activist Sherri Muzher was more pointed in her assessment of the academy's handling of the film: "The academy's refusal to consider *Divine Intervention* shows that it is far from being an impartial, apolitical body. Although Hollywood is no stranger to world events and free speech, controversy at the Oscars should never include such censorship." Filmmaker Suleiman also critiqued the Academy's simultaneous compartmentalization and collapsing of the categories of "national cinema" and "foreign language cinema," when in *The New York Times* and *USA Today*, he stated: "Cinema is the negation of the notion of nationalism. . . . Of course, if there's a denial of Palestinianism as a cultural or national entity, then you fight for it. But, in fact, cinema is yearning to cross those boundaries all the time." Suleiman defended the value of his film not merely as evidence of Palestine's existence but, perhaps more importantly, as an art form through which to transcend geopolitical and material reality and indulge in the universal pleasure of cinema.

Under pressure from Suleiman and Arab American civil rights groups, the Academy reconsidered its exclusion of Palestinian cinema during the following submission year. And although the Academy ultimately did allow *Divine Intervention* to be submitted for consideration, Pavlik publicly made perfectly clear that the Academy was not attempting to make a political statement: "We're not trying to be the UN and say that Palestine is a country. We're saying that there's a film *industry* that considers itself Palestinian, and it has come up with a film worthy of submission. . . . This year the committee decided to treat Palestine as an exception in the same way we treat Hong Kong as an exception."[43] The Academy's recognition of Suleiman's film as the product of an industry anointed Palestinian cinema with a kind of power considered far more legitimate than a nation-state. The legitimacy of Palestinian cinema in this moment originated not in terms of nationalism but in that it acknowledged the existence of a Palestinian film *industry*.

Why should it have mattered whether the Academy deemed Palestinian cinema eligible for Oscar nomination? As an institution, the Oscars have long since proven to be the cultural arm of white supremacy, as evidenced by the Academy's longstanding reluctance to nominate and award filmmakers and actors of color.[44] Palestinian cinema, and by extension Palestinian nationalism, does not need the recognition of a Eurocentric institution such as the Academy in order to be deemed valid or valuable. And, in the words of Sherri Muzher, who wrote on this particular controversy, "the brutality of Israel's occupation wouldn't dissipate if the academy recognized a Palestinian film."[45] Amid the violence of military occupation, including home demolitions, child imprisonment, and unprecedented land grabs, a squabble over bureaucratic gatekeeping in Hollywood indeed seems out of sync with the priorities of the Palestinian liberation struggle.

Yet the controversy over *Divine Intervention*'s submission eligibility mattered, and indeed still matters, because it posed a series of important questions to a mass audience in a novel way: If Palestinian films are allowed to be submitted to a category devoted to inter*national* cinema, is Palestine a nation? After all, representation, wrote Said, is the "issue always lurking near the question of Palestine."[46] Suleiman's quarrel with the Academy was more than just a struggle over Palestinian cinema's eligibility for institutional recognition. It was a struggle over Palestinian cinema's legibility as a national cinematic movement, the legitimization of Palestine as a nation, and the representation of that nationalism to a mainstream American public through the Academy Awards ceremony broadcast. Palestinian cinema's inclusion at the Academy Awards afforded a soapbox from which to project the legitimacy of Palestinian nationalism to one of the largest broadcast audiences in the United States. However, the Academy's acceptance of Palestinian cinema did not rest on Palestinian cinema's status as a national cinema; it rested on questions of political economy.

## Palestine in Hollywood's Political Economy

If Morton Klein's greatest concern over the Academy's consideration of Palestinian cinema rested on a question of national legitimacy, then Pavlik's justification for accepting the submission on the grounds of "industry" probably did not assuage Klein's concerns. Suleiman and champions of Palestinian cinema emphasized the rights to freedom of expression alongside universalist notions of art's role in the production of a common humanity. Yet Pavlik, and by extension the Academy at large, took a far less impassioned approach to the submission decision. The Academy's willingness to reconsider *Divine Intervention*'s eligibility, was, according to Pavlik, not about nationalism, legitimacy, or sovereignty. Nor was it about recognizing cinema as a producer and product of common humanity. The Academy's decision was far more vulgar, at least in the Marxist sense. This was about "industry," and therefore capital.

The controversy around Suleiman's attempted Oscar nomination bid offers a starting point from which to understand how and why

Palestinian cinema has, at different times, been rejected or accepted within Hollywood's political economy depending on how that cinema affects the industry's bottom line. If we examine Hollywood award shows as the institutional face of the industry's power, we can therefore understand award shows as the pageantry of risk management. Risk assessment, argues James McMahon, intrinsically demands that "assessments of a film's social significance be translated, with a degree of confidence, into quantitative expectations about the film's future income."[47] To borrow McMahon's language, Hollywood award shows' representation of the topic of Palestine and Palestinian cinema has always been accompanied by attempts to assess Palestine's social significance, and in turn calculate that significance into a quantitative expectation around the cost or benefit of that representation. The Academy's willingness in 2003 to recognize Palestinian cinema in terms of a Palestinian film *industry* suggests that some of the most powerful figures in Hollywood took a very close look at the Palestinian geopolitical situation in the first decade of the twenty-first century in relation to the burgeoning body of Palestinian filmmaking, weighed the probability of Palestinian cinema as an emergent industry and market, and ultimately decided that the long-term benefit of accepting Palestinian cinema outweighed the short-term cost. The Academy quietly banked its tacit inclusion of Palestinian cinema in a slow-growing cultural investment account, the dividends of which, I wager, have not yet paid off. In the meantime, Suleiman's victory in 2003 set the stage for Palestinian cinema's triumphant return to the Oscar discourse with Abu-Assad's Oscar nomination and Golden Globe win in 2006.

## Palestinian Cinema in *Paradise*

*Paradise Now* is lauded as the first Palestinian film to be nominated for an Academy Award.[48] Each year, the Academy accepts film submissions from around the world to be considered for nomination in the category of Best International Feature Film (which until 2020 had been named Best Foreign Language Film).[49] An Oscar nomination is itself considered a huge feat, and as the saying goes, it's an honor just to be nominated. The stakes for nonanglophone international films are especially high in terms of distribution to new markets and exposure to new audiences. For international filmmakers, Oscar nomination signifies the final round in a vetting process on behalf of predominantly anglophone US audiences that are not typically eager to consume films with subtitles and that may be considered narratively or aesthetically "foreign," and entices those potential audiences to the box office through an appeal to cosmopolitanism. An Oscar nod, therefore, is critical to getting international, nonanglophone films circulating within the US market. In 2006 Abu-Assad's narrative film *Paradise Now* (2005) received just such a nod and reaped the circulation and exposure benefits that it afforded. *Paradise Now* was nominated for both an Academy Award and a Golden Globe Award (which it won) in the category of Best Foreign Language Film, and as a result, *Paradise Now* became the highest grossing Palestine film by a Palestinian director at the US box office to date.[50]

As celebratory as this sounds, the reception and treatment of *Paradise Now* in Hollywood was uneven and contentious. The film's nomination for both a Golden Globe and an Oscar not only resurrected Zionist ire and controversy from years prior over Suleiman's Oscar bid, but that ire and controversy were now amplified as Klein's concerns over Palestinian national legitimacy played out through a heated debate over how to classify *Paradise Now* in terms of "country of origin." While the Golden Globes chose to represent the film as from "Palestine," the Academy classified *Paradise Now* on the Oscar stage as hailing from "The Palestinian Territories," a decision that seemed to please very few of the stakeholders in this particular argument—Palestinian and Zionist alike.

The debate over semantics was just the beginning of this spectacle. When *Paradise Now* won the Golden Globe Award for Best Foreign Language Film in January 2006, the film's brief moment of live television broadcast fame was besmirched by an affective display of compulsory Zionism. The presenters for the category that evening were Sarah Jessica Parker, herself nominated that evening in the category of Best Actress in a Musical or Comedy for her role in *The Family Stone,* and Matthew McConaughey, her costar in the romantic comedy scheduled for release later that spring, *Failure to Launch* (2006). As the duo crossed the stage, McConaughey in a standard black tuxedo, Parker in a floor-length black gown, the camera cut to a shot of Parker's husband, actor and vocal Zionist Matthew Broderick, who gave his wife an encouraging wink, as if to assuage whatever anxiety she felt. Parker began the presentation by stating "On a show with such a worldwide audience, this is a most important category," laying bare the stakes of the moment before McConaughey announced the category title.

Before continuing with a close reading of this television broadcast moment, it is important to more fully contextualize the significance of Sarah Jessica Parker serving as announcer for this particular category during this particular year. According to the Hollywood Foreign Press Association (HFPA), the Golden Globe Award–granting organization, "presenters are selected and assigned by the show's producers and our production partner [Dick Clark Productions] in conjunction with our broadcast partner," and assignments are usually given to presenters a few weeks prior to the show.[51] Parker was known to be a staunch supporter of Israel and outspoken against suicide bombings. Less than a year before this broadcast, journalist and former *60 Minutes* producer Abigail Pogrebin published the book *Stars of David: Prominent Jews Talk About Being Jewish,* which featured an interview with Parker. In the interview, Parker speaks openly about many things, including her nonreligious upbringing, curiosity about the Jewish faith, ambivalence toward organized religion, and her sense of Jewish cultural identity before delving into her thoughts and feelings about Israel and suicide bombings. Responding to what Pogrebin frames as "the crisis in Israel," Parker states:

> It makes you identify. I feel much more strongly about the situation there and I feel foolish about it too because I don't know the history. But I do know that I feel defensive when people say "How can Israel go in with tanks?" What are they supposed to do? Children are being killed by people willing to strap bombs to their bodies and walk into the public market. So Israel's response to this is to protect its people. I am not an Ariel Sharon fan, but what are the Israelis supposed to do? Just be decent? . . . It makes you really much more of a Jew.[52]

Here Parker relates how her sense of Jewish identity is amplified by her sense of outrage over suicide bombings in Israel and that her defensiveness in reaction to criticism of Israel's military violence is justified based on the "indecency" of suicide bombing. Regardless of her distaste for certain Israeli politicians, specifically Ariel Sharon, for Parker there is no justification for violent resistance. Parker's personal and political opinions about Palestinian suicide bombings made her a polemical candidate for presenter of this particular award category. Assigning her to the role of presenter suggests an attempt by the show's producers to stage a dialectic, whether in the interest of preserving the "balance" of compulsory Zionism or in the hope of producing a spectacle to generate interest and potentially boost ratings for the ailing award show format.

As a nominee that year, it would not have been unusual for Parker to also serve as a presenter. What was unusual, however, was the show's break from its established editing conventions for the show's live broadcast. Award show broadcasts follow certain conventions when it comes to live editing for a television audience, regardless of category. Cutaways during acceptance speeches are ubiquitous, providing reaction shots of people either mentioned by the speaker or people significant to the speaker, such as their partner or children. These reaction shots function not only to break up the monotony of the acceptance speech but also to stoke emotional investment and sentimentality for the winner by showing the affective responses of the winner's colleagues and family members. Knowing Parker's personal and political opinions and the conventions of award show editing is key to understanding how Abu-Assad's acceptance speech that evening became a spectacle of compulsory Zionism.

Parker began listing the nominees by announcing the first two. She then turned to McConaughey, and mouthed something inaudible as McConaughey nodded his head and in his quintessential McConaughey way drawled out a slow "yeah." McConaughey then proceeded to announce "*Paradise Now,* Palestine," as Parker stood by adorned with her impeccable smile. Not wanting to seem imbalanced or unorderly in their announcement labor, Parker then subtly prompted McConaughey to announce the next nominee as well, to which he obliged before passing the last nominee on to her. McConaughey then opened the envelope and the two announced the winner in unison, repeating the previous phrase: "*Paradise Now,* Palestine." The camera cut to Abu-Assad and the film's producer Bero Beyer as they made their way to the stage, weaving through the cloistered tables full of nominees and guests, many of whom seemed to clap tepidly, some of whom chose not to clap at all. Upon arrival on stage, Abu-Assad shook Parker's hand upon accepting the award and a handshake from McConaughey, then proceeded to the microphone. For those watching the broadcast on television, Abu-Assad began his acceptance speech framed by Golden Globe graphics and a caption reading: "*Paradise Now,* Palestine, Foreign Language Film." A mere seven seconds into his acceptance speech, the camera cut away not to Abu-Assad's colleagues or family, but to Parker and McConaughey, as if searching for some kind of reaction. Indeed, the camera cut to the presenters just in time to capture McConaughey stroking Parker's upper back, as if comforting her in a moment of distress, before cutting back to Abu-Assad.

Cutaways serve particular affective purposes in the production of live media events. For example, a cutaway to the winner's colleagues, friends, or family functions to promote sentimentality, while cutaways to co-nominees seek to construct the winner and losers either as esteemed colleagues or as hostile rivals. I contend that in this instance, the cut to Parker functions in this latter vein, but less in the service of stoking hostility and more in the service of generating sympathy not for Parker, but—within the context of Parker's previously stated opinions—sympathy for the victims of suicide bombings, Israelis more broadly, and by extension all Jewish people. The cut from Abu-Assad to Parker exemplifies what Daniel Dayan and Elihu Katz refer to as "the conquest script" in the production of live media events such as award ceremony broadcasts. The conquest script is a style of live media production that emphasizes, sometimes metaphorically, the breaking or redefining of tradition.[53] Although only lasting two seconds, the cut to a reaction from Parker reveals how in an unprecedented moment marked by the inclusion and legitimization of Palestinian cinema within the context of an industry known for its hegemonic Zionism, Zionist feelings must be represented in the interest of amplifying a sense of defeat for the old ways and a sense of victory for that which is construed as the conqueror. If the purpose of the reaction shot in award show acceptance speeches is to generate a particular affective response, and the conquest script is leveraged to signal a radical change in the order of things, then this moment in Golden Globe history functioned to signal Palestinian metaphorical uprising within the context of Hollywood on the one hand and stoke Zionist fears of Palestinian uprising in Israel on the other hand.

Cutting to Parker during Abu-Assad's speech also suggests a somewhat desperate attempt by Golden Globe producers to generate spectacle. And frankly, the show was in need of something spectacular. Award show viewership had been steadily decreasing in the twenty-first century.[54] Lengthy award ceremonies spanning three to four hours (not including the red carpet preshow broadcast) have increasingly been in stiff competition with more enticing network and cable programming. Indeed, the 2005 Golden Globe Award Show broadcast during its annual Sunday night time slot lost an estimated 10 million viewers—one-third of its audience from the previous year—to the television show *Desperate Housewives.* This ratings blow prompted the producers to move the 2006 award show to Monday evening to avoid a repeat of that loss. Still, the 2006 show was only able to recuperate 2 million of the lost viewers, as well as an additional 2 million in 2007, before dropping off a ratings cliff in 2008 with a loss of 14 million viewers—two-thirds of the previous year's viewers. I draw attention to these viewership ratings discrepancies to highlight one of the ways in which compulsory Zionism is leveraged in Hollywood in the interest of producing a spectacle. That spectacle, in turn, is leveraged for two purposes: in service of profit maximization by attempting to lure viewers with the promise of political drama on live television, and in service of shoring up a Zionist narrative. Attempts such as that within the Golden Globes to establish a polemic and dialectic also function to, in a roundabout way, bolster the idea that Israel is a liberal democracy, the rationale being that Israel is indeed democratic because Palestinian representation is not only tolerated, it is celebrated within even some of the most Zionist institutions. Compulsory Zionism therefore manifests in Hollywood award ceremonies through an illusion of inclusion, the enforcement and manufacturing of a contentious dialectic between Palestine and Zionism, and exploiting that dialectic for profit.

The spectacle of Zionist fragility at the Golden Globe Awards in January 2006 is just one example of how this dialectic and spectacle are produced within Hollywood awards shows. Three months after the Golden Globes ceremony, Academy Award producers made a move directly out of the Golden Globes' compulsory Zionism playbook in straying from its conventions in the visual staging and presentation of the nominations in the Best Foreign Language Film category at the Oscar ceremony. Generally, the norm for presenting nominations in each category—whether for a film, actor, or otherwise—is standardized across award shows. During the presentation of any given award, each nominee is announced individually by the presenter, and that announcement is accompanied by a graphic depicting a textual description of the category title and nominee (actor name, film title, etc.) and, as is the case with films, either a still from the movie, a short clip, or the film's publicity poster. This graphic is displayed on television screens as the presenter reads the list of nominees, typically with the same graphic displayed on a large screen behind the presenter for the benefit of the live audience. During the 2006 show, Oscars producers broke from this format for the Best Foreign Language Film category and instead presented two film posters on screen at once. The result: The poster for *Paradise Now* appeared on screen to an international audience of tens of millions of viewers alongside the poster for *Sophie Scholl: The Final Days,* a German historical drama based on the story of German anti-Nazi activist Sophie Scholl, her capture by the Gestapo, conviction for treason, and execution by guillotine in 1943 (Figure 12).

Figure 12. Posters for the Oscar-nominated films *Sophie Scholl: The Final Days* (2005) and *Paradise Now* (2005).

There are several ways the Oscars producers' staged dialectic of *Paradise Now* and *Sophie Scholl* can be interpreted. On the surface, it is legitimate to be outraged that the first official Oscar nomination for Palestinian cinema (specifically as a representative of *national* cinema), was forced to share its moment with another film. Likewise, the forcing of a Palestinian film into competitive relation to a Holocaust film functions to shore up what Michael Rothberg refers to as "competitive memory," wherein the memory of the Holocaust is used to overshadow the discourse on Palestinian liberation. This competitive memory framework functions to pacify the otherwise racist logic that the creation of an ethnoreligious supremacist state is necessary to atone for the crimes of another ethnoreligious supremacist state.

However, in keeping with the work of Rothberg on collective memory, another, more generous interpretation of this dialectical dyad is possible. Tony Shaw and Giora Goodman have historicized the industry's financial and ideological support for Israel. However, as demonstrated through my previous close reading of the Redgrave affair, disagreement and dissent over Hollywood's position in relation to Israel and Palestine have indeed been percolating for decades. If the Redgrave affair represents the first hairline fracture in the supposed monolithic façade of compulsory Zionism within Hollywood, then the Oscars' treatment of *Paradise Now* can be viewed as further compromise of that structural integrity. And the wearing down of that structural integrity indeed stems from the inside of the façade.

A side-by-side consideration of the two films reveals a subversive message in their simultaneous presentation on the Oscar stage, one that is more akin to Alvin Sargent's cautioning of the Oscar audience some twenty-eight years prior. Both films tell stories of resistance to state violence, and the protagonists of both films are framed as making the ultimate, altruistic sacrifice for the greater good of resistance and justice. Pairing the two together represents, in visual terms, Rothberg's concept of "multidirectional memory," bringing to the surface myriad questions about the relational histories of genocide and state violence while simultaneously representing two radically different modes of resistance: nonviolent (*Sophie Scholl*) and violent (*Paradise Now*). Given that the Holocaust ultimately ended with the creation of the state of Israel as restitution while the Israeli occupation and apartheid oppression of Palestinians continues, it is tempting to infer that the films' co-presentation was intended to compare (and cast judgement) on the circumstances represented in each film. After all, Scholl was framed, in history and in the film, as a nonviolent resistance activist unjustly murdered by a fascist state. In contrast, the character of Said in *Paradise Now,* who chooses violent resistance in the film, was always already a stand-in for the generic caricature of "the terrorist" that US audiences would have been familiar with. And while both Said and Sophie's actions lead to their deaths, Said's death is considered one of self-destruction, an indirect yet *avoidable* consequence of state violence. In contrast, Sophie's death by guillotine is perceived as a direct and almost unavoidable *result* of state violence.

Until the creation of the state of Israel in 1948, the word *terrorism* in mainstream US and European print news was not solely synonymous with Arab or Islamic fundamentalism as it became so in the late twentieth and early twenty-first centuries. Prior to 1948, in US and European news the word was primarily used in reference to Zionist paramilitary activity (such as bombings) during the British Mandate period in Palestine.[55] While members of those same Zionist paramilitary groups such as Haganah, Lehi, and Irgun (responsible for the infamous massacre of Palestinian civilians at Deir Yassin), would go on to become celebrated Israeli war heroes and politicians, the martyrs whom Said is meant to represent in *Paradise Now* are defamed as terrorists, expelled from the realm of humanity, and condemned to the realm of the monstrous. To that end, I interpret the pairing of *Paradise Now* and *Sophie Scholl* as a prompt for the Oscar audience, and the Academy more specifically, to consider these films and their characters not as antagonists of one another but as complements to one another in historical and ongoing struggles against state violence. To put it more simply, while the Oscars' representational dyad of *Sophie Scholl* and *Paradise Now* robs Palestinians of autonomous self-representation, such a dyad can also be interpreted as a kind of visual solidarity between two films, both of which represent resistance struggles against genocide.

Still, the awkward dialectical staging of these two films—each in their own right deserving of their own moments in the spotlight—functions to deny Palestine of representational autonomy and self-determination. The vast majority of television viewers likely did not undertake such a close reading as I have outlined above. While the inclusion of Palestinian cinema within Hollywood award shows indeed helped to expose wider and more mainstream US moviegoing audiences to the very concept of Palestine as a nation complete with a national cinema, the manufactured dyad presented that evening at the Oscars, like the Golden Globes three months before it, reinforced compulsory Zionism by denying the possibility of Palestinian self-representation without the requisite Zionist authorization of that representation.

Since 2006, two other Palestinian films have been nominated for Oscars: Abu-Assad's *Omar* (2013) in the category of International Film and Farah Nabulsi's *The Present* (2020) in the category of Live Action Short. Neither won the award.

## Snubbing Zionist Swag

Hollywood awarding institutions' treatment of Palestinian cinema and the topic of Palestine has changed significantly over the past forty years. Since 2015 the Academy Awards in particular has been more intensely criticized for its role in perpetuating institutionalized racism and sexism. Celebrities and activists began publicly scrutinizing the Academy under the racial and gender justice spotlights between 2015 and 2018 with the advent of the social media hashtag activism campaigns #OscarsSoWhite (2015), #MeToo (2017), and #TimesUp (2018).[56] These hashtag activism campaigns reflected larger intersectional and transnational social movements gaining momentum in the United States at the time, particularly the Black Lives Matter movement. Leftist Black Americans and Palestinians have a long history of solidarity and social movement mobilization, most notably exemplified through the Black radical tradition, the black internationalism movement, and the Black Panther Party.[57] But in 2014 Black-Palestinian solidarity politics became part of a more mainstream conversation in the United States as the uprising in Ferguson, Missouri, in protest of Michael Brown's murder by the Ferguson Police Department coincided with one of Israel's deadliest military assaults on the Palestinian civilian population in the Gaza Strip. Although not a new solidarity, Black activists in the United States and Palestinians in Gaza exchanged messages of solidarity through the highly visible and widely circulatable social media platforms of Twitter and Instagram, placing

Black-Palestine solidarity at the forefront of the mainstream racial justice discourse in the United States for the first time.

In March 2014 Hany Abu-Assad's film *Omar* (2013) became the second Palestinian film to compete in the category of Best International Feature (formerly known as Best Foreign Language Film). Later that same summer, Israel's assault on Gaza and the Ferguson uprising consumed the US news media cycle, and transnational racial justice politics were at the forefront of the US culture war discourse. In December 2014 the Oscars announced the all-white acting nominations for the 2015 Academy Awards ceremony, prompting media strategist April Reign to launch the #OscarsSoWhite hashtag activism campaign and prominent Black filmmakers such as Spike Lee and Ava DuVernay to boycott the 2015 Oscars ceremony.

The all-white nomination docket would be repeated in the 2016 Oscars ceremony, and that same year AMPAS made a public attempt to distance the Oscars from Israeli state violence. Every year, awards show attendees (nominees and presenters alike) are offered luxury "swag bags" chock-full of extravagant goods and services.[58] In 2016 one of those bags was from Distinctive Assets, a company distributing the "Everybody Wins" gift bags to Oscar nominees that included a gift certificate for plastic surgery, a sex toy, a marijuana vaporizer, and an all-expenses-paid trip to Israel funded by the Israeli Ministry of Tourism.[59] The Academy filed a lawsuit against Distinctive Assets, with the primary complaint being that Distinctive Assets had been "falsely representing that its extravagant 'gift bags' [are] redistributed by the Academy, at its direction, or with its endorsement or approval."[60] Objecting to the "less than wholesome nature of some of the products contained in the bags," the lawsuit cites a Distinctive Assets post on Twitter (now X) from February 5, 2016 (which has since been deleted) which featured an article with the headline "Inside the Absurd $200k Oscar Gift Bag: Vapes, Trip to Israel, and a Vampire Breast Lift." The Academy made its claims on moral grounds and the misuse of the Oscar trademark. However, over the years these gift bags have regularly included items which could be perceived as "less than wholesome" or otherwise problematic, depending on one's moral values, such as discounts for plastic surgery, condoms, weight loss supplements, cannabidiol (also called CBD) products, and the title of Lord or Lady of Glencoe and a small plot of land in Scotland (which deeply angered many Scottish people). Of the twenty-five Oscar nominees to receive the gift bag trip offer, all but one turned down the offer.[61]

## Gaza as *Zone of Interest*

The final flashpoint of this chapter occurs in 2024 in the post–October 7 context. Since October 7, 2023, mass public protests in solidarity with the Palestinian people and in condemnation of Israel and the US government have become commonplace in the United States, with activists particularly focused on disrupting business as usual. Ahead of the 2024 Oscar ceremony, the *Los Angeles Times* reported that the Academy Awards producers had taken extra precautions to prevent disruption, with the presence of two thousand private security officers patrolling in and around the ceremony. The Los Angeles Police Department cordoned off the streets surrounding the Dolby Theatre with chain-link fencing while a legion of cops donning riot helmets and batons stood at the ready to confront protesters.

Palestinian liberation and solidarity activists indeed succeeded in disrupting the Oscars' business as usual in 2024. A protest organized by Film Workers for Palestine and Screen Actors Guild—American Federation of Television and Radio Artists (SAG-AFTRA) for Ceasefire that originated at the Cinerama Dome on Sunset Boulevard marched nearly one mile to the Dolby Theatre, the site of the awards ceremony (Figure 13). Despite the Academy's and LAPD's efforts, this anti-spectatorial traffic-blocking protest caused a thirty-minute delay to the start of the 2024 Academy Award ceremony. The protesters succeeded in bringing business as usual to a literal standstill as celebrities stuck in the protest traffic abandoned their limousines and resorted to walking several blocks to the Dolby Theatre, and video footage of Oscar attendees hurrying awkwardly through the protest crowd circulated throughout social media.

Palestine solidarity was also represented inside the 2024 ceremony itself through a variety of visual and vocal means. Celebrities such as Mahershala Ali, Ava DuVernay, Billie Eilish, Mark Ruffalo, Riz Ahmed, and Ramy Youssef donned red buttons symbolizing their support for a ceasefire as signatories of a collective letter signed by the group Artists4Ceasefire. When interviewed on the red-carpet entrance to

Figure 13. *Top:* Protesters line up holding letters and symbols reading "Eyes on Rafah." AP Photo/Etienne Laurent. *Bottom:* Demonstrators protest in support of Palestinians near the Dolby Theatre during the 96th Academy Awards in Los Angeles, California, on March 10, 2024. Photo by RINGO CHIU/AFP via Getty Images.

the ceremony, Egyptian American actor and television director Ramy Youssef leveraged his interview spots with the entertainment press to point out the button and explain that it symbolizes the collective call of over four hundred Hollywood signatories for an immediate and permanent ceasefire.[62]

When the ceremony finally kicked off, the usual suspense of wondering who will win was accompanied by another speculative question: Who, if anyone, would pull a Redgrave that evening? Just as in the case of Redgrave, it was the makers of a Holocaust film who would politically confront the audience. Winning the Oscar for Best International Feature for *The Zone of Interest,* director Jonathan Glazer, with the film's producer James Wilson and executive producer Len Blavatnik by his side, graced the Oscar stage and offered the following prewritten remarks:

> All our choices were made to reflect and confront us in the present, not to say look what they did then, rather look what we do now. Our film shows where dehumanization leads at its worst. It's shaped all of our past and present. Right now we stand here as men who refute their Jewishness and the Holocaust being hijacked by an occupation which has led to conflict for so many innocent people. Whether the victims of October the [interrupted by applause] . . . Whether the victims of October the 7th in Israel or the ongoing attack on Gaza, all the victims of this dehumanization, how do we resist? Aleksandra Bystroń-Kołodziejczyk, the girl who glows in the film, as she did in life, chose to. I dedicate this to her memory and her resistance.[63]

Unlike Redgrave in 1978, whose speech elicited boos and hisses from the Academy audience, Glazer's speech was met with encouraging applause and vocalizations of support from the Oscar audience. But outside of the ceremony, on social media and in the press the following day, Glazer was met with harsh criticism, including condemnation from Anti-Defamation League (ADL) CEO Jonathan Greenblatt.[64] It was also revealed after the ceremony that Glazer had not cleared the speech with both of his on-stage colleagues—more specifically, executive producer Len Blavatnik. Blavatnik's presence on stage during Glazer's speech brings the uneasy contradictions of cinematic activism

Figure 14. *From left:* James Wilson, Leonard Blavatnik, and Jonathan Glazer. AP Photo/Chris Pizzello.

for Palestine at the Academy Awards to the fore, wherein human interest is calculated to protect capital interests (Figure 14).

Blavatnik is a billionaire with financial stakes in a number of competing interests and a reputation for throwing his financial power around. Blavatnik's right-wing financial activities include contributing $1 million to Trump's inauguration fund; contributing to political action committees for Republicans Mitch McConnell, Lindsay Graham, and Marco Rubio; and contributing to the defense fund for Democratic New York City mayor and champion of the New York Police Department Eric Adams (who is currently under federal investigation for corruption). While Blavatnik certainly uses his money to support causes and candidates that suit his interests, he also withholds his money for similar aims. For example, in December 2023 Blavatnik was one of several major donors who accused Harvard University's then president Claudine Gay of tolerating antisemitism for failing to crack down on Palestine solidarity activism on campus and announced that he would withhold donations to the university.[65] Though seemingly bipartisan, Blavatnik's donations indicate his political interests and financial investments in maintaining the white supremacist status quo, whether through efforts to erode the US Constitution and protected civil liberties, through support for militarized policing, or through higher education. Meanwhile, Blavatnik's private equity firm, Access Entertainment, is an investor and co-financier of A24 Films. The company has made a name for itself producing left-leaning, award-winning films such as *Moonlight* (2016), *Everything Everywhere All At Once* (2022), and other films and television focused on racial, gender, and sexual minorities and themes of social justice, including the Palestinian American Netflix show *Mo.* In short, Blavatnik is not merely a contentious figure; he is both funding and capitalizing on US culture wars over race, gender, and sexuality, including the culture war over Palestine.

While the flashpoints examined in this chapter are by no means definitive proof of a cultural shift with regard to Hollywood's relationship to Israel, attitudes toward Zionism, or stance on Palestine, they offer critical insights into the shifting parameters of the discourse on Palestine in the United States, as well as insights into both the victories and pitfalls of mainstreaming Palestine through cinematic activism. The Distinctive Assets gift bag controversy and the revelation of the contradictory nature of financiers like Blavatnik suggest that, at the very least, Hollywood institutions and celebrities recognize a shift within the general US public's (and by extension, media consumer's) attitude toward these topics. Undoubtedly the Black Lives Matter, #TimesUp, and #MeToo social movements have made Hollywood aware of how political shifts among moviegoers have potential to interfere with Hollywood's profit margin. The looming threat of a boycott mobilized by the Boycott, Divestment, and Sanctions (BDS) movement has the potential to transform Hollywood's association with the Israeli state into a financial liability. In this sense, whatever ambivalence toward Zionism and the question of Palestine that lurks throughout the Hollywood industry is likely motivated less by concern for human rights, democracy, or any of the other humanistic values the industry claims to advance through the universal power of cinema, and more for protecting the industry's profit maximization potential with respect to the shifting value of Palestinian cinema and the position of Palestine within the US discourse on racial equity within Hollywood's political economy.

# 5 Mainstreaming Palestine

## *Film Festivals and Visibility Politics in the 2010s*

The nervous excitement within me rises with each step I take up the stairs of Boston's Museum of Fine Arts (MFA). Situated on Huntington Avenue across the way from Northeastern University and the Wentworth Institute of Technology, the museum's Greek Revivalism façade is illuminated dramatically, commanding attention in the early darkness of the October evening. Upon entry, I make my way through several galleries, breezing through the Art of Asia, Oceania, and Africa; Works on Paper; and Photography. I make a mental note about the colonial legacy of museum curatorial practices as I pass the folk arts and antiquities encased in glass. I barely glance at the collection of photographic prints from the Pictorialism movement, and in my hurry, I cannot distinguish whether the drawings I pass are by Klimt or Schiele. I rush through the painstakingly controlled exhibitions of fine and folk arts until finally arriving at my destination of choice: a large atrium that houses contemporary art installations, a café and wine bar, the museum's main bookshop, and, most importantly, the Remis Auditorium, a screening room with a seating capacity of almost four hundred. The open space of the atrium is quickly filling with people, many of whom don keffiyeh, the traditional Palestinian scarf. While many of the keffiyeh I see are the traditional black-and-white or red-and-white variety, most people—young and old alike—are rocking the new, hip version of the scarf, made with nontraditional colors: pink, purple, gold, maroon, green, orange, turquoise. The whole rainbow is represented, and no two are alike. Manufactured in the Palestinian-owned and -operated Hirbawi textile factory in the occupied city of Al-Khalil (Hebron) in the West Bank, these scarves are available for purchase at a small table set up in front of the auditorium's entrance. In addition to supporting Palestinian manufacturing, the proceeds from the keffiyeh sales go toward covering basic festival costs. Next to the keffiyeh table, a large vertical banner reads "Boston Palestine Film Festival" (BPFF).

The above scene describes my entrance to the opening night of the ninth annual festival in October 2015. It was the third year in a row in which I attended the festival to screen new films, observe the festival culture, and conduct interviews with organizers and spectators. This space inside the heart of one of the premier US cultural institutions was brimming with excitement, urgency, and Palestinian cultural politics. Notably absent, however, were any outright signs of Zionist protest.[1] No mice of malevolent intentions, as was the case with *Julia* in 1977. No bomb threats befell the MFA, as they did on the Castro Theatre in 1981. No calls for Alan Dershowitz to serve as guest speaker, such as at the Institute of Contemporary Art (ICA) in 1991. And no discourse in the print news about the dangers of the MFA granting Palestine or Palestinians a sense of national "legitimacy," as with Hollywood award shows in 2002 and 2006. It is almost as if it is a perfectly normal thing to exhibit Palestinian cinema and Palestine solidarity cinema.[2]

By this opening night in October 2015, it had been over twenty years since the censorship controversy over Palestinian cinema at Boston's ICA, discussed in chapter 3. As a city with a history of attempts to censor Palestinian cinema and now one of six major cities to host an annual Palestine-themed film festival in North America, Boston offers a case study of how and why cinematic activism has been both mobilized and institutionalized in the service of normalizing a discourse on Palestinian liberation and solidarity politics in the US context. Given that history, the BPFF's exhibition within the MFA is quite a sight to behold; everything about this microjourney into the BPFF tells its spectators, as well as passersby and onlookers, that they are about to experience something of great cultural import. Inside the MFA, Palestinian films and Palestine solidarity films (and the cultural politics therein) comingle with works by renowned contemporary artists, such as Jeppe Hein, Jenny Holzer, Maurizio Nannucci, and Kara Walker, artists who are known for their deployment of cultural commentary through their work. The BPFF's placement at the MFA, in the words of one festival organizer, "mainstreams Palestine and makes this an art festival in a powerful way."[3] After years of controversy over its inclusion within myriad cultural institutions in the United States, Palestinian cinema and Palestine films, it would seem, have arrived. As such, this chapter takes the BPFF as an example of how practices of cinematic activism foment cultural and institutional changes in order to normalize marginalized social movement goals and benefit underrepresented groups. But at the same time, this chapter interrogates and problematizes the use of cinematic activism to mainstream topics and issues such as Palestine that are typically deemed as radical, marginalized, or underrepresented in the United States.

This chapter represents a radical departure from the methods of analysis utilized in the previous four chapters: away from close readings of film and media texts and archival materials and toward ethnographic participant observation and qualitative interviews. This shift in method is necessary to account for how the texts and practices examined in previous chapters have contributed to the transformation of cinematic activism for Palestine and the development of new cinematic activism projects such as Palestine-focused film festivals. The BPFF is in league with a host of other annual Palestine-focused film festivals such as the Chicago Palestine Film Festival, the Houston Palestine Film Festival, and the DC Palestinian Film and Arts Festival, as well as one-off Palestine-focused film festivals such as Outside the Frame: Queers for Palestine Film Festival, and more broadly focused and long-standing Arab-themed film festivals such as the Arab Film Festival in California and Mizna: The Twin Cities Arab Film Festival.

This chapter is based on ethnographic participant observation at the BPFF and Outside the Frame. Over the course of three festival seasons, I attended the BPFF three times between October 2013 and October 2015. During the festival's off months, I conducted interviews with festival participants. This chapter is largely focused on the BPFF's aims, goals, and effects according to twenty-one BPFF participants and is organized around dominant themes that emerged in semistructured interviews. Interviews were analyzed in conjunction with the festival's own publicity materials along with close readings of films and festival-related visual culture. Of the twenty-one participants I interviewed, nine had worked for the festival in the capacity of organizer (five) or volunteer (four) at some point since the festival's founding. Fourteen participants self-identified as Palestinian or Palestinian American, three participants self-identified as Jewish or Jewish American, and the remaining four participants respectively self-identified as Irish American, Indian, Iranian American, and Syrian American.[4] Eight of the people I interviewed were invested in their own arts practice, which included photography, documentary filmmaking, music performance, and creative writing. Three participants were undergraduate or graduate students at the time of our interview, and six were current or former K–12 or postsecondary educators. All interviewee names are pseudonyms. A microprocessual analysis of this diverse set of interviews reveals the ways in which film festivals constitute a major organizing and institutionalizing method of cinematic activism, one that, in the case of Palestinians living in the United States, is used to resist compulsory Zionism and promote the open expression of Palestinian cultural politics from the Palestinian perspective.

According to nineteen of the twenty-one participants, education and cultural connectivity were the two main goals and effects of the festival. At its most basic level, the education imparted through these films, according to my interlocutors, was one of "humanization," that is, making the issue of Palestine more readily understandable, personalized, and relatable for a general US public. Such a process at once works to counteract the dehumanization of Palestinians overwhelmingly represented in US news and entertainment media for decades, while fostering connectivity to other groups, predominantly folks of Southwest Asia and North Africa (SWANA) descent and Jewish people in the United States. The intended educational and cultural connectivity benefits of the festival were not limited to those unfamiliar with the issue of Palestine. Although some expressed hesitancy around the festival "preaching to the choir," in general, people agreed that the pedagogical and social components of the festival were just as important for themselves and the Palestine solidarity activist community as they were for those unfamiliar with Palestine.

Within this discussion on education and connectivity, half of my interlocutors mentioned the role that films and festivals play in terms of a desire to "mainstream" Palestine and how the festival works to "legitimize" support for the Palestinian cause by way of association with elite cultural institutions such as museums and film institutes. Among more than half of my interlocutors there was a particular hope for Palestinian cinema and its distribution through film festivals to perform the work of educating the broader US public by undoing or counteracting mainstream media stereotypes. What is more, most people believed that the BPFF's placement within such a prestigious institution such as the MFA lends legitimacy to the films and Palestinian cultural politics therein. The festival's placement with the MFA also has a kind of element of surprise, in that it is not necessarily the first venue one might anticipate for the exhibition of Palestinian cinema or Palestine films. Ultimately, exhibiting the festival in the MFA is critical to representing Palestine through more mainstream venues.

Regarding cultural connectivity and the Arab American community, the idea of "the festival" invokes the tradition of the Arab American *haflah*. While *haflah* means "party" in Arabic, in the Arab American context the term refers to large community events such as concerts, performances, and other community-oriented celebrations of Arabic arts and culture organized by local Arab American philanthropic organizations, and typically with the intention of fundraising.[5] In the 1980s and 1990s in particular, *haflat* (plural of *haflah*) came to signify prominent cultural events that typically served two purposes: community cultural celebrations of Arab and Arab American music and performing arts, and fundraising events for philanthropic organizations providing humanitarian aid in Arab homelands subjected to colonial and imperial violence, such as Iraq, Lebanon, and Palestine. In this sense, the BPFF operates within a long-standing Arab American tradition of what I refer to as *philanthro-spectatorship,* or the mobilization of spectators toward grassroots philanthropic aims.

## The Boston Context

As made clear through my prior discussion of the academic roots of Arab American activism on Palestine and subsequent grassroots development of cinematic activism in previous chapters, the history of the discourses on Palestine and Zionism in US academe points to the ways in which, in the United States, academic knowledge production colludes with media representations to produce a hegemonic field of meaning about Palestine and Israel.[6] In Metro Boston specifically, the prevalence of Zionism within the liberal political culture that is frequently associated with the region has historically been inscribed through educational institutions—colleges, universities, and K–12 public schools. For example, as a hub for some of the nation's most prestigious postsecondary institutions and boasting one of the highest numbers of colleges per capita, the culture of US academe deeply informs the culture of Metro Boston. When prestigious local universities or their faculty and administrators take political positions, those positions have broad cultural influence. For example, in 1984 Jehuda Reinharz—who was then professor of Jewish history at Brandeis University in Waltham, Massachusetts (and later would become president of Brandeis)—wrote an uncritically positive, widely circulated review of Joan Peters's *New York Times* bestseller *From Time Immemorial,* a profoundly anti-Palestinian book that was critiqued as dangerous and fraudulent by scholars such as Edward Said, Noam Chomsky, and Norman Finkelstein.[7]

Brandeis was established in Waltham in 1948 as a "Jewish-sponsored secular university open to students and faculty of all races and religions."[8] I point to the Brandeis example to explain how influential academe has been in muddying the distinctions between Judaism and Zionism, and in turn conflating criticism of Israel with antisemitism. Conflating Judaism and Zionism is a strategy of compulsory Zionism that equates critiques of the Israeli state with antisemitism, the accusation of which has historically been used to censor Palestine-related scholarship and activism, and that now has become the basis for the criminalization of certain forms of Palestinian liberation activism, such as attempts to outlaw Boycott, Divestment, and Sanctions (BDS). For example, in 2002, nearly two decades after *From Time Immemorial* was published and three years before the official BDS call from Palestinian civil society in 2005, Palestine-focused student activists called for Harvard University's financial divestment from companies that conduct business in illegal Israel settlements in the West Bank. Then president of Harvard Lawrence Summers publicly characterized the student activism as "profoundly anti-Israel" and accused the student movement of antisemitism.[9] Over a decade later in 2014, numerous university presidents throughout the United States, including several in the Boston area such as Harvard University, Boston University, Brandeis University, and the Massachusetts Institute of Technology, publicly denounced the American Studies Association after the organization's membership overwhelmingly passed a resolution to support the Academic and Cultural Boycott of Israel.[10] This lengthy exegesis on the Boston area's academic culture is not as tangential as it may seem. In addition to the main venue of the MFA, the BPFF frequently utilizes various satellite venues for festival screenings, including at Emerson College, Harvard Law School, and Massachusetts College of Art. The academic cultural context is therefore important for understanding how cinematic activism for Palestine at once circumnavigates and is normalized within institutions of compulsory Zionism.

Institutionalized support for Zionism is not limited to higher education; examples can also be found in the area's regional public-school curriculum. For example, the Facing History and Ourselves (FHAO) curriculum has been used system-wide in Boston Public Schools for decades and is part of the curriculum in over 150 public, charter, and private schools across the United States as well as in Canada, Mexico, South Africa, and Great Britain.[11] Founded in the Boston suburb of Brookline, Massachusetts, in 1976, FHAO is a self-described antiracist and conflict resolution–themed youth curriculum that takes the Holocaust as the basis for teaching social justice. The same year as FHAO's founding, Elaine Hagopian served as president of the Association of Arab American University Graduates (AAUG), and she has recalled how FHAO's emphasis on the Holocaust "was too often used to justify Israel" and its violence against Palestinians, and how such curriculum informs the politics of Metro Boston's liberal culture.[12] Holocaust studies scholar Michael Rothberg has critiqued the ways in which the Holocaust has been constructed as a Eurocentric narrative of exceptionalism in the service of defending Zionism. Rothberg notes that in achieving a culturally hegemonic status, such exceptionalist conceptualizations of the Holocaust serve to reinforce a competitive model of collective memory by establishing a hierarchy of oppression and suffering. This hierarchy "obeys a logic of scarcity" to simultaneously create impermeable borders and divisions between struggles that could be allied together while overshadowing and silencing other forms of state violence, trauma, and genocide. The competitive memory model fails to interrogate the intimate relationship between European colonialism, the Holocaust, and present-day political crises in the SWANA region.[13] While the FHAO program attempts to resist this kind of competitive model of racialized oppression by incorporating issues such as Jim Crow, the civil rights movement, the Darfur genocide, and the Armenian genocide, FHAO has produced a series of lesson plans and trainings for educators designed to shape how Palestine and Israel are discussed in school settings. These lesson plans and webinars reinforce problematic understandings of the relationship between Israel and Palestine by referring to it as "the conflict," reducing the political relationship as one of "religious conflict," and reifying the equation of anti-Zionism with antisemitism.[14] In producing K–12 curriculum and teacher trainings that seek to neutralize the colonial relationship between Israel and the Palestinian people, FHAO tacitly promotes compulsory Zionism to K–12 students under the guise of antiracist, social justice–oriented curriculum.

Compulsory Zionism does not just permeate Boston's cultural and educational institutions; it is quite literally manifest in the city's built environment. The Leonard P. Zakim Bunker Hill Memorial Bridge, named in memory of the former director of the New England Anti-Defamation League (ADL) office and Zionist activist discussed in chapter 3, is one of Boston's most visible and prestigious landmarks.[15] This world-famous cable-stayed bridge spans over 1,400 feet to carry ten lanes of the concurrent traffic of Interstate 93 and US Route 1 across the Charles River, making it the world's widest cable-stayed bridge. Referred to in the *Boston Herald* as a "civil rights crusader," Zakim spent decades organizing Boston's Black and Jewish communities around social justice issues, and the bridge's dedication ceremony focused heavily on his role in the cultivation of Metro Boston's liberal political culture.[16] During the ceremony, then mayor of Boston Thomas Menino praised the naming of the bridge for its ability to "showcase the diversity and the unity of race, religion, and personal background that exists in Boston today because of the work of community leaders like Lenny Zakim and because patriots fought long ago in Charlestown to make our country independent."[17] Given Zakim's staunch Zionist stance, the settler-colonial rhetoric that animated the dedication ceremony highlights the irony inherent in the promotion of a colonial and xenophobic ideology such as Zionism as a form of social justice activism. In such a celebration of liberal multiculturalism, the history of indigenous peoples and European conquest—both in the Americas and the Levant—becomes obscured, even erased. I draw out this cultural context of compulsory Zionism in Boston in order to highlight how remarkable it is that the BPFF not only succeeded in its founding, but to this day thrives within an elite cultural institution such as the MFA.

## Founding the Festival

Although it is a relatively small festival when compared to A-list festivals such as Cannes, Sundance, or the Human Rights Watch Film Festival, the BPFF's success comes into sharp relief when viewed within the context of compulsory Zionism and Arab American activism in the Boston area in the decades that preceded its founding. Established in 2006, with the first festival in 2007, the BPFF is an all-volunteer nonprofit organization with three major aims: "to celebrate Palestinian cinema as a cultural and artistic production of a people in exile and under occupation and siege," "to reduce prejudice and discrimination against Middle Eastern people generally and Palestinians in particular" in the post-9/11 United States, and "to instill pride in our Arab-American community" and "provide a link" to Arab heritage, culture, and history for those living in diaspora.[18] As discussed in the previous chapters, controversies surrounding the exhibition of Palestinian cinema from the 1980s and through the first decade of the 2000s served to identify film as a critical terrain of struggle over the question of Palestine, and the Boston area proved to be a locus for such controversies. From those controversies arose an awareness of how festival organizing, curatorial practices, and film exhibition have a unique capacity to subvert compulsory Zionism. It is from that awareness that cinematic activism began to cohere into an organizing strategy.

Despite moments of Palestinian cinema's increased visibility in mainstream US entertainment media between 2002 and 2006, the post-Oslo period was also characterized by a decline in US-based political and social activism around the issue of Palestine.[19] But when Palestinian cinema became more widely visible in the United States through Academy Award and Golden Globe Award nominations in 2006, it proved to be a pivotal moment for the resurrection of Palestine solidarity activism as well. Palestinian American festival cofounder Mary recalls how the festival's organizing was inspired by a sense of cognitive dissonance regarding how Palestine was being represented and discussed in relation to both the realities of Israeli apartheid and regarding the efficacy of Arab American organizing and Palestine solidarity activism. The daughter of Palestinian immigrants, Mary was born and raised in the United States and has been a festival organizer since its inception in 2006. She had been politically active with several Palestine-related grassroots organizations in the 1980s, but described to me how Oslo had revealed deep fissures within the Palestinian liberation and solidarity activism circles she had been a part of. The Palestinian liberation and solidarity activism community she had been involved with predominantly included exilic Palestinian and other Arab professionals—teachers, engineers, doctors, and the like—who were working or studying in the United States, as well as those like herself who had been born and raised in diaspora. She recalled how the Palestine activism she had been working with since the 1980s devolved into factions and essentially "fell apart" with the signing of the Oslo Accords in 1993, and that organizing in the Boston area largely went dormant for the latter half of the decade.[20] During this same period, even the once prominent AAUG began to wither, and the organization ultimately dissolved in 2001.[21]

However, with the turn of the millennium also came the start of the Second Intifada in fall 2000. Palestinians in the occupied West Bank and Gaza Strip once again rose up in protest against the Israeli occupation, and once again, they were met with violent repression by the Israeli military. In addition to the Second Intifada, the September 11, 2001, terror attacks and the subsequent US military invasions of Afghanistan in 2001 and Iraq in 2003 reestablished the SWANA region as the theater within which the US government and various transnational corporations would play out their attempts to assert political hegemony and control over the region's natural resources of oil and gas. In summer 2006, Israel waged a war in Lebanon, which included an aggressive bombing campaign and ground invasion of southern Lebanon—a region heavily populated with Palestinian refugees. As the United States and Israel levied threats and waged wars against countries such as Iraq and Lebanon—both of which play host to large numbers of Palestinian refugees—the desire and need to reconvene Palestine-focused activism in the United States grew urgent: "We felt the blackout on what was happening in Palestine. . . . The media was against us—the control of the Zionist lobby, all of that stuff—just made us invisible. We felt like there were these films coming out [of Palestine] and these are Palestinians telling their own story."[22] However, Mary pointed to a particular frustration she had around what she calls the "react and demonstrate" model of political activism, wherein, in the face of the US and Israel's atrocities against the Arab homelands, the first—and sometimes only—method of activism consisted of protesting, usually in front of the Israeli consulate. She desired a more "proactive" approach and envisioned "a radical departure from 'let's go stand in front of the consulate and have our signs.' I felt like that line of activism was dead. It was going nowhere and we could keep doing it until we're a hundred years old and it's not going to have any impact."[23] This frustration, coupled with excitement around the increased circulation of Palestinian films, is what inspired the festival's organizing.

When *Paradise Now* won the Golden Globe Award for Best Foreign Language Film in 2006, it was lauded as a victory for Palestinian representation in the US mainstream. That victory was short lived as a mere six months later, Israel waged a war against southern Lebanon, an event that stirred public memories among liberals in the United States of Israel's role in the Sabra and Shatila Massacre in the exact same region almost twenty-five years previously.[24] The time was ripe for a cultural intervention, and in 2006 several of my interlocutors formed the organization Tawassul. In Arabic, *tawassul* means closeness, nearness, proximity, and neighborliness. The organization's main goal was to bring Palestinian self-representations—art, cinema, and other cultural productions—to the Boston area with the intention of bringing the issue of Palestine closer to home, so to speak. The hope was that in organizing around the exhibition of Palestinian cultural productions, Tawassul could help to draw a general audience into learning about Palestine and the SWANA region more broadly. Mary recalled, "The guiding principle was: This is not like usiness as usual in terms of political work, this is going to be different, we thought, a better way to reach a mainstream audience to hear what's happening."[25]

The stark contrast that existed between the mainstream US news media's biased coverage of what was happening in the SWANA region[26] combined with the kinds of media attention Palestinian cinema was receiving in the United States in 2006 proved to be a starting point for a new kind of grassroots political activism, that which would be undertaken within the realm of "culture" and focused on issues of cultural representation. The organizers' vision for the festival as a form of political work is in keeping with the literature in cinema and media studies on spectatorship, film festivals, identity, and cultural politics. Cinema has the unique ability, in the words of film scholar Miriam

Hansen, to "function as a matrix for challenging social positions of identity and otherness, as a catalyst for new forms of community and solidarity."[27] Likewise, film festivals, Cindy Hing-Yuk Wong argues, "do not create social issues, but in selection, screening, and reception, they galvanize debates."[28] It was from this context that Tawassul's members undertook the project of organizing a film festival in order to, in the words of Palestinian cofounder Ruba, "do politics through film."[29] I therefore take the BPFF as a case study for understanding the work of cinematic activism within a larger process of mainstreaming representations of Palestinian cultural politics in US media and cultural institutions.

## The Politics of Visibility

As Mary's and Ruba's recollections of the festival's prehistory attest, the pathway to making knowledge about Palestine and empathy with Palestinians accessible to more mainstream US audiences was conceived of in terms of exhibiting Palestinian visual culture. The festival originates, therefore, through an appeal to US visibility politics, meaning that Palestinians must be "'seen' as a potential victim of racism in order to be 'included' in liberal multicultural diversity initiatives."[30] In discussing the racialized hypervisibility of Arab Americans (and those perceived to be) in the immediate aftermath of September 11, scholars have noted that Arab American subjectivity experienced a kind of hypervisibility in the eyes of the state, and that hypervisibility was accompanied by a heightened vulnerability to both vigilantism and state violence. In writing on Arab American subjectivity post-9/11, Nadine Naber writes that "'visibility' is a power-laden project that has the effect of silencing critiques of state violence and the structural inequalities that produce hatred and racism," while objectification is mistaken for inclusion.[31] With regard to the project of cinematic activism for Palestine, the trap of visibility certainly is a bit more complicated, since Palestine and Palestinians continue to actively experience ethnic cleansing and genocide. Visibility is certainly not the be-all and end-all of Palestinian liberation. When it comes to Palestine solidarity activism in the US context, the politics of visibility disproportionately occupy the project of cinematic activism for Palestine.

The early festival organizers posited that run-of-the-mill American cultural complicity with the US government's support for the state of Israel stemmed from a lack of awareness of what was actually taking place in Palestine and Israel. This lack of awareness has been manufactured through the representational regime of compulsory Zionism. When the festival originated in 2006, it was not so much that there was a dearth of visual evidence of Palestinian oppression or that Palestinian visual culture did not exist, but that, as demonstrated in the previous four chapters, the compulsory Zionism of US culture had served to censor such representations through an enforcement of "balance" and "objectivity," wherein Palestine is always co-represented in relation to Israel and a Zionist perspective. The BPFF proved a useful departure from the regime of compulsory Zionism and the enforcement of "balance" by leaning on the liberal multicultural history of ethnic film festivals as constituting a counterpublic sphere.

The BPFF itself, although requiring months of behind-the-scenes labor, is limited to the discrete time-space experience of its exhibition in the fall. Festival advertising, although practical and necessary for any cultural event to attract an audience, has become an important aspect of extending the time-space of the festival experience while also becoming symbolic of how the representational work of the festival reaches beyond the scope of the screening auditorium. Palestinian cofounder Ruba emphasized the intention of making the festival visible through print advertising: "The plan was actually to do politics through film. The plan was: We're going to show Palestinian films, we're going to put ads in the subway, we're going to put ads in *The Boston Globe,* we're going to get reviews in papers so that people would come and watch the films and know that they're there."[32] From the beginning, the festival has run print advertising campaigns on Boston's public transit system, the Massachusetts Bay Transportation Authority, or "the T" for short. Several of my interlocutors recalled vivid memories of their encounters with the festival's advertising campaigns while riding the T, which is how Palestinian American audience member Anton first heard about the festival: "I remember the first time I saw the advertisements on the subway, I was like, *wow*! Boston Palestine Film Festival. What is that? I was really excited that there was something going on about this."[33] While the primary purpose of the festival's advertising may have been merely in the service of publicizing the event, the BPFF print advertisements quickly took on a much greater significance for both the festival itself and the greater Palestine solidarity activism community.

The inaugural festival in 2007 coincided with the fifty-ninth anniversary of the Nakba ("the catastrophe" in Arabic) in 1948 and the fortieth anniversary of the Naksa ("the setback" in Arabic) in 1967. For the BPFF's second year, the organizers took up the Nakba as the festival's main theme, which was reflected in the advertising campaigns. Cofounder Suhail recalled how the advertising campaign in and of itself felt like a victory in the struggle to make Palestine visible in the United States:

> We had the word *Nakba* plastered all over the city [which had] never been done in the mainstream like that. Longtime activists said [they'd] never put the word *Nakba* in any advertising campaign in the city. . . . The city had never seen anything like it. . . . Every major newspaper did an article on us.[34]

This emphasis on visibility and visual culture was intended, in Suhail's words, to represent "social justice [but] from a different way,"[35] and the subway advertisements proved to be a powerful tool for attracting participants and audience members. For example, Mary proudly relayed a story to me from one of the festival's first few years, wherein a couple that had been on their way home from a baseball game at nearby Fenway Park excitedly arrived for a screening at the MFA dressed head to toe in Boston Red Sox apparel after spotting the ads on the T.[36] With a weekly ridership of 1.2 million passengers, advertising on the T is one of the most visible and efficient promotional methods for cultural events in the Metro Boston area.[37] Additionally, all of the BPFF venues are accessible via the T's widespread public transportation system. Notably, the MFA has its own stop along the Green Line light rail route, which provides service to some of Boston's most elite academic institutions, including Northeastern University, the Wentworth Institute of Technology, the Massachusetts College of Art, and the Longwood Medical Center complex, which includes the Harvard University Medical School campus.

The festival's print advertisements have become a regular part of Metro Boston's seasonal advertising campaigns and are a point of pride for both the organizers and festival participants alike. The festival has also worked to maximize the benefits of its advertisements' popularity by taking a participatory approach to its publicity campaigns. In the weeks ahead of opening night, the festival holds a competition through social media, wherein potential festival participants are challenged to post pictures to Twitter and Facebook documenting their encounters with the festival's advertisements for a chance to win a pair of tickets to the screening of their choice. As a form of participatory culture,[38] the BPFF's social media competition helps to further publicize the festival through social media while rewarding participants for their interactive engagement with the festival beyond the time and space of the festival itself.

Audience member Alma commented on how pleased she was to see how the issue of Palestine, as she put it, "infiltrates" Boston's culture through more quotidian forms of visual culture such as the subway advertisements. She explained:

> The T is a working-class public sphere, and that brings a film festival outside of just the league of [the] elite or educated. Is a poster on the T really drawing the attention of everybody? Probably not. . . . But it feels like a presence in a public sphere that's positive. The norm is to see things about Israel everywhere. So I feel the BPFF infiltrates in the sense that it [Palestine] seems everywhere at the time that the festival's happening, when otherwise there's nothing.[39]

Alma's comment about the BPFF's print materials infiltrating the public sphere is evocative of Jurgen Habermas's conception of the public sphere "as a space for the emergence of an inclusive civil society" wherein pressing political, social, and cultural issues are debated.[40] Wong has drawn upon Habermas's conception of the public sphere, as well as on theoretical reinterpretations by Nancy Fraser, Oskar Negt and Alexander Kluge, Miriam Hansen, and Michael Warner, to investigate the wider social and cultural work of film festivals. Wong contends that the sociality and spatiality of festivals (and I would argue festival advertising as well) as sites for open discussion of contested and underrepresented issues "has opened up international organization for the promulgation of liberal human issues like human rights, ecological consciousness, immigration, globalization, and gay identities."[41] With regard to the question of Palestine, substantive discussion of the issue from the Palestinian point of view has historically been restrained in the United States under the very purview of "debate," and the open discussion of Palestine within the greater US public sphere has been tellingly absent. The organization of a Palestine-specific film festival, then, has greater social and political implications that reach far beyond the purview of merely "art" or "culture" and gesture to transformation of the US cultural climate with regard to the issue of Palestine.

## QUIT! the Visibility Politics

Boston is not the only city wherein the project of cinematic activism for Palestinian liberation has played out through public transportation's visual culture. While discussing the significance of the BPFF's advertisements on the T, Alma related what was taking place in Boston to what had also been taking place in San Francisco during the same period. The San Francisco Bay Area has played host to a visual-culture-based tête-à-tête between the Zionist lobby and Palestine solidarity activists, a significant portion of which has revolved around film festivals. For example, in April 2010 a collective of organizations—including Blue Star Public Relations, the Consulate General of Israel to the Pacific Northwest, the Israel Education Initiative, the San Francisco Jewish Film Festival, and the LGBT Alliance of the Jewish Community Federation—cosponsored Out in Israel, a month-long film festival designed to showcase "LGBT culture in Israel and Zionist perspectives."[42] The festival was an example of Israeli pinkwashing, and the Out in Israel advertisements that graced San Francisco's public transit systems quickly became the target of an anonymous culture-jamming collective that goes by the name Street Cred and operates under the banner of a larger arts activism movement called Bay Area Art Queers Unleashing Power (BAAQUP). In an effort to dissuade spectators from attending the Out in Israel film festival, Street Cred employed the technique of culture jamming by appropriating the style and aesthetic of the original Out in Israel advertisements and replacing them with aesthetically similar ads that subvert the original message (Figure 15).

Street Cred's culture jamming in 2010 was the beginning of what would develop into a coordinated cinematic activism campaign over

Figure 15. *Left:* The original Out in Israel Film Festival poster, San Francisco, CA, April 2010. *Right:* The Street Cred/BAAQUP culture-jammed version of the Out in Israel poster, April 2010.

the next several years. Although Out in Israel was a one-off festival, as discussed in chapter 3, Israeli pinkwashing projects such as Brand Israel had homed in on LGBTQ+ visual culture as a site for the dialectic struggle between compulsory Zionism and Palestinian liberation and solidarity politics. The resultant Palestine-focused cinematic activism that emerged in the Bay Area between 2010 and 2014 was markedly different from that undertaken by the BPFF. Though the cinematic activism campaigns in both metro regions were organized around film festivals, the ethos and practices in each city differed considerably. Importantly, the Palestine solidarity cinematic activism in the San Francisco Bay Area differs from that of the Boston area for its emphasis on ideological solidarities, its grounding in a history of leftist queer anti-imperialism, and its deemphasis on visibility politics, identity politics, and cultural authenticity.

In the aftermath of Out in Israel, the Bay Area activist group Queers Undermining Israeli Terrorism! (QUIT!), a mixed group of Arab-, Jewish-, and SWANA-identified leftist queer and transgender activists, focused a BDS campaign on the Frameline Film Festival, the oldest LGBTQ+-focused film festival in the world. QUIT!'s issue with Frameline was not the festival's inclusion of Israeli films, nor was it even necessarily protesting the inclusion of pinkwashing films. Rather, QUIT! objected to the fact that Frameline accepted funding from the state of Israel by way of the Israeli consulate in San Francisco. Doing so, argued QUIT!, made Frameline, and the LGBTQ+ community it purports to represent and support, complicit with colonial violence by normalizing financial relations with a government that numerous international agencies have classified as an apartheid regime.

QUIT! spent numerous years lobbying Frameline, holding anti-spectatorial protests outside of festival screenings, writing press releases, and organizing across other leftist groups in the Bay Area and queer activist groups across the United States and Canada that were similarly organizing to have Israeli funding removed from queer film festivals. Part of that coalition building entailed the organizing of a counter film festival, which was held during the same time as Frameline's opening weekend during the summer of 2015. Outside the Frame: Queers for Palestine Film Festival was a free, three-day Palestine solidarity film festival running concomitantly with Frameline's thirty-ninth annual opening weekend, June 19–21, 2015, at the Brava Theater in San Francisco's Mission District. With eight hundred people in attendance, myself included, Outside the Frame served as a radical alternative to Frameline and showcased not only Palestine solidarity films but a variety of films by filmmakers who refused to submit their films to Frameline in adherence to BDS. Alongside QUIT!'s festival organizing, Street Cred continued its guerilla art campaigns, making Frameline a main target of the collective's culture-jamming efforts (Figure 16).

The contest between pinkwashing and Palestine-focused cinematic activism at LGBTQ+ film festivals brings some important points about the pros and cons of mainstreaming to the fore. Frameline, the BPFF, and Outside the Frame all share one thing in common: They all practice cinematic activism as part of larger social movements. However, they operate from radically different ideological standpoints and have enjoyed varying degrees of success in terms of attaining increased visibility and inclusion of their respective social movements within mainstream US cultural and political discourses. For example, the Frameline Film Festival, also known as the San Francisco International LGBTQ+ Film Festival, was established as the Gay Film Festival

Figure 16. A second version of the Street Cred/BAAQUP culture-jammed Out in Israel poster, this time targeting the Frameline Film Festival. N.d.

of Super-8 Films in 1977. Identity-based film festivals of the 1970s emerged from social movements that centered marginalized identities and sought to make "interventions into hegemonic representational regimes."[43] Frameline's emergence must therefore be situated within the historical context of the homophile movement of the 1960s, a relatively socially conservative gay men's social movement, and the more radical, leftist gay liberation movement that emerged in the aftermath of the Stonewall riots of 1969. The LGBTQ+ rights movement of the twenty-first century thus far—with its emphasis on topics such as marriage equality, the ability to serve openly in the US military, and increased representation in entertainment media—traffics in a discourse of homonationalism that seeks to attain rights and inclusion through appeals to "equality" and "inclusion" within the dominant cultures of the nation—whiteness, patriarchy, ableness, wealth, etc. Just as the homonationalist LGBTQ+ rights movement became the most commonplace and normalized iteration of the LGBTQ+ movement within mainstream US culture and politics, so too did Frameline take on a more centrist political ethos in terms of the festival's turn toward professionalization, integration with the film industry, and subsequent corporatization in terms of both how the organization is structured and its fiscal sponsorship. For example, some of the festival's biggest corporate sponsors include Bank of America, Showtime, and Gilead, the pharmaceutical company that manufactures several HIV drugs and that many activists have accused of profiteering off of the HIV and AIDS crisis, which disproportionately affects the LGBTQ+ community. Frameline therefore offers a clear example of how the politics of visibility actually hinder the goals of radical leftist social movements.

Despite its dubious financial relationship to corporations and governments that are known for exacerbating the inequalities, inequities, and violence that leftist, anticapitalist, and anti-imperialist LGBTQ+ activists in the United States oppose and are organizing to remedy, Frameline is readily recognized among the activist film festival circuit and film festival studies alike as the premier example of how film festivals function as the cultural arm of larger political and social justice movements.[44] In this sense, the history of Frameline's origin as part of the gay liberation movement of the 1970s and its development into its current iteration as a corporate institution is indicative of the larger transition within the LGBTQ+ rights movement from social justice activism to rainbow capitalism.

The history of cinematic activism within the LGBTQ+ social movement in the United States offers a comparative example of how mainstreaming, not unlike the politics of visibility, necessitates the concession of certain (often leftist) goals and ideals for the sake of increased representation and inclusion within dominant US culture and politics. That same mainstreaming trajectory of LGBTQ+ cinematic activism should also serve as a cautionary tale for Palestine-related cinematic activism. Put another way, Frameline and the BPFF, with their emphasis on visibility and mainstreaming, have more in common with each other than either one has with the radical queer, feminist, anti-imperialist film festival Outside the Frame. Although seemingly in opposition to one another in that the former has a history of pinkwashing and the latter has showcased antipinkwashing films, both Frameline and BPFF share similar motivations to increase visibility for their respective movements and incorporate those movements within more mainstream cultural and political realms. For Frameline, visibility is a means to an end: inclusion. For Outside the Frame, the allure of visibility is bait and mainstreaming is a trap that not only separates the representation of social justice issues from their material realities but also falsely compartmentalizes Palestinian liberation and queer liberation as if they are separate and unrelated movements. In this sense, the visibility politics projected through things such as cinema, film festivals, and exhibition in elite institutions functions to alienate the image from the people, things, and causes it purports to represent. Such a separation creates a disconnect between the *appearance* of progress toward equity and equality and the reality of continued (and even worsening) inequity and inequality. BPFF certainly falls somewhere in the middle, but the ambition to "mainstream Palestine" places the festival farther into the realm of visibility politics within the larger spectrum of representational politics and cinematic activism.

It is worthwhile highlighting some key differences between the Boston and San Francisco examples of cinematic activism for Palestine, BPFF and Outside the Frame, respectively. Where organizers in Boston are reluctant to endorse any particular stand or ideology, the Bay Area activists are transparent in their political and ideological leanings and endorsement of BDS. Where Boston emphasizes visibility, San Francisco emphasizes disruption. Where Boston emphasizes humanization and education, San Francisco emphasizes solidarity and direct action. Where Boston has become a site wherein Palestinian identity and cultural authenticity are at times objectified and contested, San Francisco fosters unity and collectivity through shared cultural politics of anti-imperialism, decolonial feminism, and queer liberation. I point out these differences between the two festivals not to cast judgement or delineate one as "better" than the other. The social and cultural contexts of these festivals are substantially different, and they each succeed in the practice of cinematic activism for Palestine in ways that are necessarily variable and important.

While it would be easy to critique Outside the Frame for the dearth of Palestinian films exhibited at its festival, it's worthwhile noting that Outside the Frame never purported to be a "Palestine Film Festival" or a "Palestinian Film Festival." While BPFF has Palestinian culture and community baked into its mission statement, Outside the Frame was designed for a particular radical queer leftist audience, and all of the Palestinian, Jewish, and other SWANA and Black, Indigenous, and/or People of Color (BIPOC) folks who align themselves (whether identifying as queer or not) with radical queer leftist liberatory politics.

## Spectatorial Potentiality

The cultural contexts of Boston and San Francisco are indeed quite dissimilar. Indeed, the previous chapters in this book have highlighted in various ways how Boston has historically been a particularly hostile place for the representation of Palestinian liberation and solidarity politics. That said, just as the public transit advertisements draw audience members who otherwise may not have been aware of the festival, or Palestine in general, the festival's overall emphasis on visual culture and performing arts draws people to participate in the festival's production itself. As Suhail notes:

> Many of them [volunteers] came from nonactivist backgrounds. They were just interested in film and cinema and cared about Palestine enough to do it. . . . Many of them were drawn to this because this was the least political—at least on the surface—initiative. It was something that was cultural and engaging and exciting. But it clearly had a political undertone.[45]

Many of the festival participants who were interviewed for this project reiterated the importance of film's visual elements in making the topic of Palestine more accessible to US viewers and bringing people into awareness about Zionism and Israeli apartheid. Since the 1990s, a great body of scholarship has emerged dealing with the primacy of visuality, visibility, and visual representations in the formation of culture, knowledge, and power relations. Scholars such as W. J. T. Mitchell, Nicholas Mirzoeff, Susan Sontag, Ella Shohat, Robert Stam, and Martin Jay have debated virtues of "the visual turn," including visual culture's capacity to stir empathy and mobilize people to action, and as a tool for both democratization and domination. The concept of "visual literacy" has also served as a useful means through which scholars have explored the primacy of the visual, from understanding the import of painting in fifteenth-century Italy as a means of documenting social history, to the emphasis on visual pedagogy in progressive education.[46] While certainly not unique to the contemporary moment nor the North American context, visual literacy in the United States has taken on new meaning in the new millennium and amplified significantly during the Covid-19 pandemic, as screen culture has dominated many aspects of people's social lives. In a moment marked by the primacy of the visual, Palestinian visual culture has served both to make the topic of Palestine intelligible to a wider audience and to lend legitimacy to the issue of Palestine, as Suhail commented in 2013: "Palestinian cinema on any mainstream venue is nearly impossible. But now it's considered a very current and important vehicle for expression. . . . People have begun to accept cinema as a genuine vehicle for speaking about these issues. People are becoming more sophisticated in terms of watching documentaries."[47]

Audience member Alma reiterated this point, stating, "I've noticed that people give legitimacy to film in ways that they wouldn't necessarily always give to a personal narrative as told by a person."[48] In her efforts to form closer social bonds with new friends and coworkers, Alma attempts to educate her peers about Palestine by sharing her own personal experiences of life under Israeli occupation. However, in the face of her US peers' microaggressive disbelief of her accounts and their denials of the validity of her experiences, Alma turned to film to corroborate her experience and do that pedagogical work on her behalf. Not unlike how the AAUG filmstrips functioned to alleviate the burden of narrativizing the Palestinian condition, Palestinian cinema has become, in Alma's words, "a way for me to tell my story without me telling it." Alma made particular note of the psychological dimensions of visual culture and its capacity to evoke empathy within an otherwise uninformed or even hostile spectator:

> Whatever images have been in their brain from their childhood or adulthood, that's what they connect it [Palestine] to. . . . Maybe it's cliché, maybe it's sad that I'm hoping that people will identify it [Palestine] with some other image of horror that they've seen, but I find that those are the moments where people are like, "Oh my god, this is horrible."[49]

The process of identification that Alma describes enables a spectator to affectively learn about the Palestinian people by recalling their own experiences with or knowledge of trauma or state violence. Alexandra Juhasz, in her study on video within AIDS activism of the 1990s, highlights the process of identification promulgated through AIDS media in the service of the larger AIDS activism movement. Identification is not contingent on a spectator's *identity,* but rather functions as a "psychoanalytic mechanism" through which a spectator can and does empathetically *identify with* a person or subject. It is through this process of identification with that the work of "communication—and politics—begin."[50]

Identification is therefore not simply about spectatorship, but it is about *experience.* Miriam Hansen describes a public sphere as a "social horizon of experience," and experience is "that which mediates individual perceptions with social meaning; conscious with unconscious processes, loss of self with self-reflexivity; experience as the capacity to see connections and relations."[51] This process of identification is produced through the experience of the festival and is the thrust behind many of the festival's goals, such as education and humanization. The spatial and social dynamics of the festival are in many ways the structure behind the festival's experience. Palestinian American spectator Georgina described the tenor of the festival:

> There's a tremendous amount of excitement. There are people who haven't seen one another, old friends reconnecting at this event. People who come back every year. . . . So there's this very strong sense of identification, of energy around being together. There's this real sense of community in the foyer of the MFA where people are milling around. There's almost an electric energy in the air as people come together before the film.[52]

The importance of the social connectivity produced through the festival's culture is not to be discounted, especially in the wake of Oslo's divisiveness and the post–September 11 political climate of the United States. Similar to Georgina, Ruba said, "The festival was creating that community where we who share the same politics can just be together, celebrating, and feeling like, you know, we're not isolated, we're not freaks for what we think."[53]

While cultural connectivity works to build a sense of community around Palestinian cinema, it is the coherence of this connectivity through visual and artistic means that serves the festival's other major goal of education. Seven of my interlocutors were active visual or performing arts practitioners, several of whom have in one way or another contributed their creative skills or products toward the festival's production. In the words of Jewish American filmmaker Rachel: "I really see myself as using storytelling as a way to humanize people that are demonized. Also, I find so much commonality between Jewish and Palestinian culture that I feel like if people only opened their eyes, they would actually see it."[54] Rachel's documentary screened at the festival during one of the years I attended. She ascribed what I interpret as the compulsory Zionism she experienced within her family and extended community as a symptom of what she referred to as "cultural PTSD [post-traumatic stress disorder]" regarding the Holocaust.

Rachel had a specifically Jewish audience in mind and made it a point to use her own family's experiences with the Holocaust as the framing device for her film: "I don't want to make a film for people who already agree with me. I want to make a film for people who don't know anything or who disagree with me. So they need a familiar face to invite them in."[55] By drawing on her own personal experience and juxtaposing her own family photos of her European Jewish relatives who relocated to the United States with those of displaced Palestinians living in the United States whom she interviewed for the film, Rachel leveraged the process of identification to foment a form of what she called "visual learning" for her viewers.

The humanization of the Palestinian people through this visual process of identification is at the crux of both the festival's pedagogical aims *and* spectators' reception of the festival as a whole. Lamia, another Palestinian audience member, reiterated the importance of "the visual" in affecting a viewer and conjuring in them a conscious comparison between a more familiar historical tragedy and the contemporary reality in Palestine.[56] As an early childhood educator who values progressive education, Lamia believes in a universal human desire to produce and consume art and culture as a way to make sense of the human condition. Lamia referenced the short film *Ismail* (2012), which screened at the seventh annual BPFF in October 2013, as an example of how a film does not necessarily have to refer directly to "politics" in order to represent the political plight of the Palestinian people. Lamia was especially moved by this film, commenting to me on the role such a film plays in humanizing the Palestinian people: "It's important to bring the awareness that the Palestinians are humans, the Palestinians are artists, they're musicians and producers, they're singers, they're actors, [and] they're politically in a place [situation] where they shouldn't be."[57]

Indeed, this sentiment is represented through the film's narrative, but *Ismail* and the history of its protagonist perform the work of cinematic activism that extends far beyond the liberal humanist narrative of "humanization." A period piece by Nora Alsharif set in a refugee camp in 1948, *Ismail* is a short narrative film based on the true story of a day in the life of Palestinian painter and filmmaker Ismail Shammout (1930–2006). Despite being set in the immediate aftermath of the Nakba, the film begins from a place of optimism as nineteen-year-old Shammout and his younger brother, Jamal, attempt to make the most of their relocation to the Khan Younis refugee camp in Gaza. In an effort to financially support the family, the brothers venture to a local train station to sell their homemade sweets, equipped with nothing but a large wooden tray and a small foldable stand, which when viewed from the distance of a long shot, mimic the shape of an oil painter's supply box and easel (Figure 17). Bolstered by a sense of hope after selling all the sweets, the pair head into town to buy supplies for the family, Jamal asking before setting out, "Do you know the way?" Partially unfamiliar with the area and partially distracted by telling his brother a story about how Michelangelo reached the ceiling of the Sistine Chapel, the pair unwittingly take a wrong turn and, alerted by a shepherd on the other side of a barbed wire fence, find themselves in the middle of a mine field. The once optimistic coming-of-age tale morphs into a suspenseful thriller as Shammout walks slowly across the sand, instructing his brother to carefully follow in his footsteps. One close call and an exploded goat later, the two make it across the minefield intact, and the film ends with the two walking off into the sunset, Jamal asking for the end of the story of how Michelangelo reached the Sistine Chapel's ceiling.

As a Palestinian film about a Palestinian artist navigating the colonial violence of dispossession, *Ismail* offers a metanarrative about the overwhelming odds Palestinians must overcome to survive, let alone produce art. Shammout trained as a painter in Cairo and Rome, and in 1965 the PLO appointed him director of arts and national culture.[58] By the early 1970s Shammout began producing short films, including the short documentary *The Urgent Call for Palestine* (1973), which

Figure 17. Poster for Nora Alsharif's short narrative film, *Ismail* (2012).

featured Palestinian Egyptian singer-songwriter Zeinab Shaath singing her English-language protest song of the same title (which, notably, was also used as soundtrack for the AAUG filmstrip *Palestinians: Holding On*).

This exegesis of Shammout's history and Alsharif's fictionalized representation of his life begs the question: What if Shammout had met his end in that minefield in 1948 instead of becoming one of Palestine's most celebrated artists? Scholars of Palestinian cinema have written extensively of the aesthetic of traumatic repetition within Palestinian films of the third and fourth periods (of which Shammout was a part of the former). I take Alsharif's rendering of Shammout's traumatic history as a representation of how Shammout's life constitutes its own archive of traumatic repetition. From his direct involvement with the PLO's arts and culture projects in the 1960s and 1970s and the repurposed audio track of Zeinab Shaath's protest song in the AAUG's filmstrip in the 1970s, to the fictionalization of his life's events in 2013 within the context of a Palestine-themed film festival, the repetition of Shammout's influence within Palestinian cinema speaks to the enduring possibilities of Palestinian cinematic activism to buoy the discourse on Palestinian liberation across decades and historical contexts.

While the majority of my interlocutors (fourteen) referenced Palestinian cinema's capacity to humanize, personalize, or otherwise make the plight of the Palestinian people relatable to American audiences, one festival organizer offered a critique of the humanization discourse. Former festival organizer Ruba expressed the sense of discomfort she feels in needing to prove Palestinian humanity: "In order for you to actually make a difference, you have to touch these people in a place where they can relate to you as a human being. I mean, it's very demeaning for me to actually think in those terms. That I have to, you know, do *this* in order for them to see me as an equal human being and to see Palestinians as worthy of their attention. There's a little bit of resentment there." While she acknowledged the importance of humanization and relatability in the process of changing people's attitudes toward and opinions about Palestine, Ruba's discomfort speaks to the extent to which visibility politics delimit the festival's transformative potential to change the discourse on Palestine by depoliticizing Palestinian cinema in favor of a more palatable goal of "humanization."

While most of my interlocutors agreed that the festival and the films showcased therein serve an educational purpose, some of the festival organizers whom I interviewed were resistant to the use of the word *political* in describing the festival. Many were wary of the relationships between film as an educational tool and the festival as a political entity. Eileen, a festival organizer, stated that she thinks the work done through arts organizing such as is done through the festival lies "somewhere between educational and political activism. It's more than educational. I think educational is too soft [of a word] and political activism is too strong [of a word]. . . . I think it's somewhere in between the two."[59] However, Eileen clarified that the work performed through the films and the film festival constituted a form of "cultural resistance," which she defined as "opposing oppression through culture. Fighting back against oppression through art, through poetry and film and literature and the power of the pen. . . . I think it's very powerful and it's just less direct, but it's no less effective."

Palestinian American festival organizer John further distinguished between the role of the festival and the kinds of political or representational work performed through the films: "As a festival entity, we definitely don't take any political stances. We basically say, 'These films speak for themselves.' We serve as a vehicle to enable their showing and viewing, but the festival itself doesn't make any political statements. The films do."[60] The perception of a film as political, therefore, rests in the eye of the beholder. The BPFF does not itself endorse any specific political parties or platforms, but many of the films showcased in the festival represent a multitude of implicit and explicit political stances. Audience members are therefore left to their own devices to infer political messages from the films they see. For example, during the festival's ninth annual run in October 2015, the BPFF screened a set of films at the Cambridge Public Library under the thematic heading "Palestine Through an LGBT Lens." The evening's screening consisted of *Mondial 2010* (2013), a short dramatic film about two gay Lebanese men on a road trip to Ramallah, followed by *Pinkwashing Exposed: Seattle Fights Back!* A feature-length documentary directed by legal scholar and transgender activist Dean Spade and produced by Basil Shahid, *Pinkwashing Exposed* chronicles the story of how a local LGBTQ+-Palestine solidarity activist group successfully lobbied the City of Seattle's LGBT Commission to cancel an Israeli-government-sponsored pinkwashing event. In addition to explaining what pinkwashing is, the film expressly advocates support for the BDS movement while modeling how to execute a successful boycott on a local level. By drawing on interviews with local LGBTQ+ activists, Palestinian identified and otherwise, the film also illustrates why queer cultural politics are indelibly linked to Palestinian cultural politics, once again exemplifying why the process of identification is so important to the educational mission of the festival's practice of cinematic activism. While the BPFF abstains from taking a stance on BDS, the screening of *Pinkwashing Exposed* clarifies the relationship between the festival and the films, as described by Palestinian American volunteer Suha: "Being involved in the festival is a form of community, whereas the actual films themselves are a form of activism."[61]

However, the placement of a film like *Pinkwashing Exposed,* which more explicitly addresses BDS activism, in a satellite venue outside of the MFA is an example of the problems and limitations of the festival's mainstreaming aims. On the one hand, hosting a free screening in a public library makes these films more accessible to audiences who may be prohibited from attending MFA screenings due to cost or outright racial discrimination within the museum.[62] On the other hand, the marginalization of such films outside of the main venue implies that the identity and cultural politics represented in this particular set of films is somehow unworthy of the primary venue. To screen these particular films at a satellite location serves as a way to include a variety of political discourses and identities within the festival program while simultaneously distancing the festival—and its high-profile venue—from the perceived controversial set of politics represented in the films.

There is an overall understanding of the role of festival organizing as a softer method of or vehicle for political activism, one that performs the work of representation, education, and humanization. In fact, the BPFF was recognized early on as an important venue for Arab American activism, when in 2008 the American Arab Anti-Discrimination Committee (ADC) Massachusetts Chapter honored the BPFF with its Dedication to Activism Through Arts Award.[63] But the festival also performs a different kind of work, that of legitimization through institutionalization, or, in the words of Suhail, "the delicate approach of institutional [*sic*] building and working behind the scenes" to dismantle the compulsory Zionism within American culture and cultural institutions.[64]

As discussed throughout this book, Boston is a city where compulsory Zionism had demonstrated its institutional power through previous attempts to censor Palestinian cinema. One of the points of contention during the *Uprising* controversy in 1991 revolved around the question of the ICA's abuse of its institutional power in defining the legitimacy and limits of freedom of expression of artists hailing from underrepresented groups. In the case of the BPFF, the venues that host and cosponsor the festival—primarily the MFA as cosponsor and satellite venues such as Massachusetts College of Art, Emerson College, Harvard Law School, the Harvard Film Archive, and the Cambridge Public Library—provide a kind of institutional cover that is key to undertaking the work of cinematic activism. The MFA serves as the BPFF's co-presenter, meaning that it is the festival's largest sponsor and venue, and BPFF organizers, volunteers, and audience members alike remarked on the importance of the MFA's institutional status in making the festival's enduring success possible. As Suha remarked, the MFA's support of the festival is critical in "giving it [Palestine] a platform, creating a space where these things can be said."[65] Just as Alma felt that rendering the Palestinian experience cinematically lends legitimacy to the Palestinian cause, so too do participants feel that the festival's placement at the MFA lends legitimacy to the festival and its overarching educational and representational goals. In Mary's words: "Showing our films in the Museum of Fine Arts in Boston lends a certain level of legitimacy to what we're doing. . . . We hear from our community that the legitimacy of being in the MFA is something they are very proud of."[66]

One of the ways in which the MFA lends this legitimacy is through visual means. The MFA's signature logo figures prominently on all of the BPFF's print materials—programs, posters, banners—as well as online through the festival's website and social media posts, serving as, in the words of Eileen, the "stamp of legitimacy" necessary for the festival's success.[67] In addition, the MFA's film department publishes its own monthly film program, which is distributed by mail to the MFA's members and featured on the film department's website. This inclusion in the film department's programming schedule both gives the BPFF a major publicity boost and functions to normalize and—to paraphrase the words of my interlocutors—legitimize Palestinian cinema and Palestine films within a mainstream cultural institution.

The placement of the festival within the MFA not only lends institutional legitimacy to Palestinian cinema and Palestine films; in doing so, Palestinian cinema in particular is—once again—insulated by its elevated status as "art."[68] Suha comments: "In the MFA you have some of the greatest pieces of art and history. So putting something like the Boston Palestine Film Festival right next to these things kind of equalizes the importance and shows how important it [the festival] is."[69] The BPFF's presence at the MFA also raises the festival and all that it represents to a comparable level with other, more established festivals, as explained by John: "All of a sudden, you have a Palestine Film Festival that is on the same footing as a Turkish Film Festival or a Jewish Film Festival or a French Film Festival. It's such a reaffirmation of its presence, the Palestinian presence."[70] As such, part of the work performed through this institutional normalization concerns the representation and validation of Palestinian identity, culture, and experience. In the words of Georgina, the MFA

> is a cultural icon within the City of Boston, so it gives a kind of legitimacy and a kind of recognition of the importance of Palestinian film and the Palestinian experience and Palestinian identity, that couldn't be had elsewhere. There is no other institution

> that could house this festival that would give this community the same level of cultural recognition and affirmation of their existence. This is so important in light of the fact that so many Americans don't even know where Palestine is.[71]

The tensions around cultural validation and institutional legitimacy go beyond the local social or cultural realm of the festival and its immediate participants. Indeed, the exhibition of Palestinian cinema at the BPFF is often just one stop in the rapidly growing Palestine-themed film festival circuit. But exhibition at the BPFF is unique in this circuit, in part due to the festival's relationship with the MFA. Suhail, who has worked with several Palestine film festivals in the United States and Canada, notes that these festivals have also raised the aesthetic bar for Palestinian cinema:

> One thing that Palestinian festivals have also done is given filmmakers an important venue to show their films, and put a thrust behind them to make more cinema—not just make *films,* but make *cinema.* Many filmmakers were making films, but they were not very cinematic. We're saying, "Look, we're doing this in mainstream venues, in museums. Please make films of that caliber because we're tired of seeing the same old cinema verité dark shot of Bil'in."[72]

I do not necessarily agree that the Palestine-themed film festival circuit is a primary reason for the increased production quality of Palestinian cinema. However, I do think it is likely that the competitiveness of global film festival circuits (whether A-level such as Cannes or grassroots such as the BPFF) and their attendant cultures of elitism, in conjunction with the kind of Hollywood attention addressed in the previous chapter, has increased a sense of competition among Palestinian filmmakers trying to get their work seen by wider audiences. This competition in turn has, I contend, pushed Palestinian cinema farther into the realm of what Adorno and Horkheimer refer to as "the culture industry." What I mean by this is that in an attempt to be competitive in these circuits (and markets), many Palestinian films and solidarity films have become increasingly standardized, adhering to what Marxist media studies scholars refer to as a "logic of safety." While the logic of safety is typically useful in understanding Hollywood's formulaic approach to filmmaking and the resultant, never-ending slew of remakes and film franchises, it remains a useful concept for understanding how Palestinian cinema itself reacts to the pressures of global cinema's political economy. Indeed, the best examples of how the logic of safety operates on Palestinian cinema are found in the best-known Palestinian filmmakers within the US context. For example, after his Oscar nod and Golden Globe win in 2006, Hany Abu-Assad has attempted to replicate that success through a succession of political thriller films, including *Omar* (2013), which indeed garnered another Oscar nod, and *Huda's Salon* (2021). Similarly, Elia Suleiman's trilogy of films, *Chronicle of a Disappearance* (1996), *Divine Intervention* (2002), and *The Time That Remains* (2009), adheres strictly to Suleiman's absurdist aesthetics and narratives, at times making each film so similar to the other that it is sometimes hard to decipher among the three. (This is especially true for the first two in the series. The last one, *The Time That Remains,* follows another kind of logic of safety, in that it is far more legible to the plot conventions of European and American narrative cinema.)

The festival program is composed of films selected through a competitive process. As a competitive festival showcased within one of the nation's premier art institutions, the festival lends legitimacy to emerging Palestinian filmmakers who struggle to place their films in other competitive festivals.[73] Organizer Mary commented, "I think the filmmakers are also very proud of the fact that they get a theatrical venue from there, rather than having it just at a university or in some smaller screen somewhere."[74] And while the festival's placement at the MFA benefits burgeoning filmmakers who seek legitimacy within global cinema's creative economy by offering a prestigious venue to list on their curricula vitae, filmmakers must also grapple with the ways in which the proliferation of Palestine film festivals has also contributed to the isolation of Palestinian cinema. Mary pointed out: "The rise of Palestinian film festivals is a good thing, because otherwise their films wouldn't be shown in a mainstream venue in America. But on the flip side, we've also become a sort of ghetto for Palestinian films. So I see it at a crux at this particular moment of our development as a festival. . . . There is this dichotomy here."[75]

"Legitimacy" and "mainstream" are themselves racialized categories, and the BPFF exists within Metro Boston's historically racialized social and cultural landscape, which begs the questions: What characterizes "the mainstream"? "Legitimacy" for and in the eyes of whom? Mary acknowledged the tension inherent in the festival's aspirations for legitimacy through its placement at the MFA: "[It] excludes, in some ways, communities that we want to reach out to because the museum is not a place where all communities actually feel welcome. We try to address that in different ways—by having our free screenings, by having [them at] libraries, acting with other festivals in Roxbury and different communities. Boston itself is segregated in a lot of ways, too."[76] In referencing "Roxbury" and "segregation," Mary alludes to Boston's history of racism and the racial violence enacted on the city's Black and Brown communities.[77] As an organizer, Mary was cognizant of how the festival's placement at the MFA could potentially limit participation by more socioeconomically and racially diverse audiences, thus hindering the festival's goal of disseminating Palestinian cinema to a truly wider—and not simply whiter—audience. And of course, if the goal is for Palestinian cinema to reach a wider audience, that too is in tension with the intention to gain broader cultural connectivity, wherein "mainstream" means being taken up with dominant norms of whiteness, masculinity, and heteronormativity.

What does it mean to mainstream Palestine? And is such an aim possible or even desirable? What is gained and what is lost through such a process? These interrelated intentions to mainstream representations of Palestine and gain legitimacy in order to educate a wider US audience reveal the uneasy tensions inherent to the politics of visibility. While scholars and activists alike may bristle at the word *mainstream,* it would be difficult to argue *against* Palestine's visibility without crossing into the realm of compulsory Zionism. Although the intention to mainstream Palestine is laden with problematic notions of inclusion and is suggestive of aspirations to normativity in very racialized ways, I want to stress the fact that these words come directly from my interlocutors: festival organizers, volunteers, and audience members alike. As problematic as a mainstreaming discourse may be, we as scholars are obligated to sincerely listen to our archives and represent our findings in transparent ways. A critique of the BPFF's mainstreaming discourse must also be reconciled with the relative success of Palestine film festivals across the country, as measured by the proliferation, longevity, and placement of festivals within powerful cultural institutions—such as the BPFF at the MFA, the Chicago Palestine Film Festival at the Gene Siskel Film Center in Chicago, and the Houston Palestine Film Festival at the Houston Museum of Art—at a time when scholars and think tanks alike are publishing study after study that document the suppression and censorship of Palestine activism throughout the United States. While a critique of the mainstreaming discourse can certainly coexist with support for the project of visibility, it is important to recognize that by their very nature, "film festivals incorporate contradictory impulses in their texts, audiences, and discussions."[78] Film festivals therefore offer rich sites wherein a social movement's intellectual, political, and ethical tensions are negotiated.

# Conclusion

*Brand Palestine and the Exception to "the Palestine Exception"*

In mid-January 2024, a South African legal team argued its case before the International Court of Justice (ICJ) charging Israel with genocide against the Palestinians of Gaza, situating the charge within the larger context of what the South African team referred to as a seventy-five-year apartheid regime. The ICJ hearings were broadcast and live streamed through various news media outlets worldwide, including the *Associated Press, PBS News Hour, Al Jazeera, The Times of India,* and many more. The South African legal team was supported by two external counsel members, including Irish attorney Blinne Ní Ghrálaigh, who had previously litigated a genocide case at the ICJ on behalf of Croatia. In her remarks to the court, Ní Ghrálaigh accused the international community, despite its obligations under the Geneva Conventions, of failing to act on behalf of the Palestinian people in the face of abundant visual evidence of genocide "being livestreamed from Gaza to our mobile phones, computers, and television screens." Ní Ghrálaigh went on to stress the uniquely horrifying nature of this atrocity as "the first genocide in history where its victims are broadcasting their own destruction in real time, in the desperate so far vain hope that the world might do something."[1]

The ICJ example makes clear the ways in which new media practices have changed the logics and outcomes of cinematic activism. The question of Palestine has so often been discussed in terms of erasure that sometimes we cannot recognize the proliferation of Palestine's hypervisibility right before our eyes. That hypervisibility has taken shape both through spectacular displays of violence as referenced by Ní Ghrálaigh, as well as through more mundane and curated ways such as in social media influencer content. The events of October 7, 2023, and the ongoing genocide in Gaza have made it abundantly clear just how critical cinematic activism has been to the representation and mobilization of Palestinian liberation and solidarity politics. Yet the genocide demands of us extreme caution before celebrating whatever victories may be associated with the mainstreaming of Palestine. In the era of new media, the mechanisms that make the genocide visible and mobilize people into action are the very same mechanisms that threaten to uphold the status quo of compulsory Zionism. To illustrate this point, allow me to interrogate the proliferation of the social media phenomenon that I refer to as *Brand Palestine.*

In 2022, deep in the weeds of revising this book, I started receiving slick targeted ads interspersed within my Instagram stories advertising black, white, red, and green–themed apparel from "the Censorship Collection" (Figure 18). In the ad, a young, stereotypically Levantine-looking, presumably Palestinian woman models a white sweatshirt adorned with an abstract portrait by Chicago-based collage artist Shahzaad Raja. The collaged figure is a pastiche of Dadaist portraiture, constructed of images symbolic of Palestine. The keffiyeh pattern, a deconstructed version of the Palestinian flag, the apartheid wall and its accompanying graffiti, a dove's shadow, Al-Aqsa Mosque (the Dome of the Rock), and *tatreez* (traditional Palestinian embroidery) patterns come together to create a portrait of a figure from the shoulders up. The subject's eyes and nose are the only visible facial features; their mouth is concealed by the words "free Palestine." The number "48" graces the upper left background of the portrait in handwritten script in a scale and style reminiscent of graffiti, while tally markers frame the figure on the lower left and upper right, implying a kind of morbid scorekeeping. Given the arguments and evidence presented in this book, I cannot help but wonder: In this tally, is Palestine winning or losing?

The back of the shirt contains a list of words and phrases. They appear in the same handwriting-style font as the front of the shirt, yet this time with a strike-through: ~~exile~~, ~~occupation~~, ~~oppression~~, ~~ethnic cleansing~~, ~~apartheid~~, ~~silence~~. The woman models the shirt, along with a brief peek at a silver necklace with the word *Palestine,* as well as a graphic sticker with the brand's logo. Interspersed within the ad's featuring of these two smaller items is a quick shot of the model standing, no longer fluidly modeling the apparel, gazing in stillness at us spectators, the word *censored* superimposed over her mouth. The

Figure 18. Screenshots from the @PaliRoots Instagram story advertising the Censorship Collection. 2022.

ad then proceeds to a series of still snapshots set to the beat of English indie pop band Glass Animals' summer slow jam "Heat Waves," which serves as the ad's soundtrack. The slideshow offers stock imagery of Palestinian civilian resistance: protesters with flags, children with flags, children confronting Israeli soldiers (with flags), keys, cliff jumping in Acre, the Al-Aqsa Mosque, and keffiyeh after keffiyeh after keffiyeh.

The ad in question is for the online store and Instagram influencer account PaliRoots, and it offers a telling example of the current state of cinematic activism for Palestine, albeit on a microcosmic scale. Having finally settled on the title for this book, I was at once pleased and vexed to see a culmination of all the historicizing and argumentative threads synthesized in this book flash before my eyes in a glossy, fifteen-second Instagram story sandwiched between friends' stories about their dogs, their gardens, their Covid-era baking experiments, and memes, oh so many memes. In many ways, this ad mimics the style and form (and in a reductive, entirely visual way, the narrative) of the AAUG filmstrips analyzed in chapter 1. The PaliRoots ad brings the filmstrip format into the twenty-first century, which includes accommodating a twenty-first-century attention span. In the 1970s, the AAUG's filmstrips required a laborious sixty-some minutes to outline basic facts of the Palestinian struggle. Today, the gist of that same information is condensed into fifteen seconds. When I say that Palestine has entered the mainstream, this is in part what I am referring to: The ways in which the criteria of what is considered intelligible, permissible, and even *normal* within a vast representational field of knowledge have shifted to accommodate the topic of Palestine within US mass media, whether in news and entertainment media, in film and television, or through online social media platforms such as Instagram and TikTok.

What struck me about this ad, as well as several others that now populate my stories and Instagram feed, is how precisely it deploys several of the cinematic activism strategies outlined in this book. To begin, this ad, as well as many of PaliRoots' other stories and reels, is itself cinematic in the filmic sense: It is a highly aestheticized miniature music video designed to captivate a spectator with its mimetic representation, not to mention its coolness factor. It is a fleeting moment of cinematic form, complete with narrative arc and soundtrack. It leverages the power of social media for the purposes of exhibition and circulation, on an intimate, micro scale more akin to that of the AAUG filmstrips than, say, a PBS broadcast or a film festival. It is geared to an imagined community of Third Cinema spectators—those already in solidarity with the Palestinian cause—and entices those spectators to take philanthro-spectatorial action for the good of a shared cause: Put your money where your [censored] is.

PaliRoots is one of numerous Palestinian apparel start-up companies that leverage the power of social media–based cinematic activism to promote what I consider to be *Brand Palestine*: the Palestinian cause refashioned for the mainstream through commodification, commercialization, and consumerism. Other examples of Brand Palestine include PaliPower, Palestinian Hustle, West Bank Apparel, and Project Palestine. These brands jockey for viewer attention on social media alongside better-established Palestinian manufacturers such as Hirbawi, as well as kuvrd, which produces keffiyehs from their exilic family-owned factory in Jordan.[2]

A closer look at the PaliRoots Instagram account (which boasts over 400,000 followers) and website reveals a brand whose mission is to "bring awareness to the world about the Palestinian culture by crafting specialty products inspired by its people and identity." The brand, which has been featured in *Forbes* and *Jezebel,* "was created to explore, celebrate, and share Palestinian culture in a modern and positive way." Similarly, several of the brands above, such as Project Palestine, tout themselves as organizations composed of both Palestinians and allies who are "deeply committed to advocating for the rights and liberation of Palestine" through the representation of Palestinian cultural heritage and claim to provide "philanthropy and gratitude . . . to help those who currently live in such horrific situations."[3]

PaliRoots in particular touts itself as philanthropic in nature, advancing the movement through the marketing of boutique Palestinian-made goods and the production and circulation of infotainment through Instagram, as well as the promotion of philanthro-spectatorship and socially responsible conspicuous consumption. To date, PaliRoots has donated over US$3 million to support Palestinians living under apartheid through partnerships with various charities and agencies, including the Middle East Children's Alliance (MECA), through which PaliRoots runs its meal donation program.[4] Altogether, PaliRoots has donated over two million meals through MECA. Like PaliRoots, the majority of the brands mentioned above purport philanthropic aims, each with greater or lesser degrees of transparency about their philanthropic practices.

Earlier on in PaliRoots' brand development, the company exhibited a practice of cinematic activism not only through its philanthropy but through its content as well. As recently as 2022, the social media accounts for this brand also distributed educational media and infotainment focused on Palestinian cultural politics. For example, interspersed between PaliRoots' marketing of its own products (apparel, olive oil soap, stickers, jewelry, and accessories such as caps, socks, and pins) were educational videos on a wide range of topics, ranging from the history of the Nakba to how to make *knafeh* (the classic Palestinian dessert, a sad replica of which used to be mass produced through the chain grocery store Trader Joe's, but has since been discontinued). One particular Instagram reel exemplary of PaliRoots' infotainment is titled "Five Ways to Support the Liberation of Palestine." The post lists five strategies a viewer should employ to support the Palestinian liberation cause:

1. Buy from Palestinian brands.
2. Show up to Palestinian-led protests.
3. Donate to grassroots Palestinian organizations.
4. Educate yourself on Palestinian history and our struggle.
5. Elevate Palestinian voices.

The social media posts of Brand Palestine influencers such as PaliRoots exemplify both the aesthetics and form of Palestinian liberation and solidarity politics, as well as how the methods and goals of cinematic activism can so easily transfer to various new media platforms and formats, including social media apps. The PaliRoots ads incorporate the formal qualities of the Palestine solidarity cinema examined in this book (such as slideshows and rhetorical queries), along with the narratives and plots of both documentary and narrative cinema, while also including the philanthro-spectatorship directives of Palestine film festivals. Not unlike film festivals, PaliRoots provides opportunity for Palestinians in diaspora to fortify their identities through a polyvalent process of conspicuous consumption of media texts and commodities, as well as the opportunity to re-present one's identity through PaliRoots apparel and circulate PaliRoots' infotainment through one's own social media accounts. The PaliRoots Instagram account of merely a few years ago offered an example of how Palestinian liberation and solidarity cinematic activism practices developed and fine-tuned throughout the twentieth century get re/produced, circulated, and received in the context of twenty-first-century new media. However, as the PaliRoots brand expanded and professionalized, especially in the wake of October 7, the infotainment and political directives that made the brand so popular to begin with have been significantly reduced. While PaliRoots does continue to repost more overtly politicized content about Palestine by other creators, the PaliRoots-branded Boycott, Divestment, and Sanctions (BDS) content of yore is no more. In its stead: highly stylized content celebrating PaliRoots' philanthropic achievements. Cinematic activism, true, but the activism has itself become cinema.

What began as a start-up apparel brand that fashioned itself as a *movement*[5] has rapidly transformed into a glossy social media influencer account producing content that is in many ways antithetical to the Palestinian liberation cause. Over the span of three years, from 2022 to 2025, the PaliRoots Instagram account has gone from infotainment content promoting BDS to purveyor of glossy Brand Palestine content largely sanitized of political directives. This removal of BDS references and content from the PaliRoots brand indicates how the very process of mainstreaming traffics uncomfortably close to compulsory Zionism. The 2025 PaliRoots April Fool's Day post illustrates this point succinctly.

April Fool's Day affords an opportunity for brands and influencers to prank their followers with content that is typically so outrageously "off brand" that it is readily apparent as a joke. On April 1, 2025, PaliRoots engaged in this seemingly innocent practice of online folly with a slide deck announcing the latest product available for preorder: PaliRoots Action Figures™. The post consisted of nine images depicting the PaliRoots creative and marketing team stylized as plastic action figures—complete with accessories like Apple laptops, coffee mugs, and glasses—encased in clear plastic toy packaging. Several commenters were quick to point out the thoughtlessness of this particular prank, pointing out how the use of artificial intelligence (a technology deployed by the Israeli military to target Palestinians in Gaza) to generate these images is antithetical to the Palestinian liberation movement. Other commenters critiqued the promotion of Apple products in these images, pointing out the tech company's role in perpetrating violence and exploitation in the Democratic Republic of the Congo. PaliRoots never responded to these critical comments but did engage with various influencers, including Palestinian filmmakers and other cultural producers, who bolstered the prank through their own comments praising the product.

All of this exemplifies and contributes to the mainstreaming of Palestine in the US context on multiple levels. We need not go much farther beyond a simple explanation of social media targeted-advertising algorithms to understand how the media texts of influencer accounts and brands travel beyond individual accounts to build networks in order to reach wider audiences. Spectatorial reach aside, Brand Palestine social media accounts encapsulate both the potentials and the pitfalls of the larger project of mainstreaming Palestinian liberation and solidarity politics. Returning to the philanthropic vagueness and lack of transparency mentioned above, spectators must be wary about navigating this already crowded Brand Palestine market, as several of the purported pro-Palestine brands circulating through social media are either vague about their philanthropic projects or make no claims to philanthropy whatsoever.

In many ways, the surge in Brand Palestine perhaps best encapsules how in today's cultural marketplace there is a very real possibility of reducing the Palestine liberation movement to a simulation of solidarity. Through the mass production and consumption of Palestine solidarity media and commodities, the representation of the Palestinian liberation struggle veers further into the debased territory of Debordian spectacle and teeters on the precipice of Baudrillard's fourth stage of representation, the simulacrum, or the ways in which representation becomes wholly divorced from its reality. That simulacral malaise is accompanied by an almost crass directive to put one's money where one's mouth is: Free Palestine, shop the Censored Collection. The PaliRoots April Fool's Day prank makes abundantly clear how, despite attempts at promoting philanthro-spectatorship and socially conscious conspicuous consumption, the mainstreaming of Palestine within the context of neoliberal capitalism unwittingly upholds compulsory Zionism. Through this discouraging realization, another critical point becomes clear: Palestine's liberation, and the liberation of all oppressed people, requires the abolition of capitalism.

Is it possible to free Palestine through cinematic activism? The answer to this question depends on how we define "free." If by "free" we mean abolishing the apartheid regime and establishing either an independent Palestinian nation-state or a single democratic binational nation-state, I'm afraid the answer is a resounding no. However, if by "free" we mean supporting the Palestinian cinematic movement, diversifying and expanding the Palestinian film and commodities industries, directing mutual aid to Palestinians and financial resources toward the Palestinian economy, and providing financial support for philanthropic projects that work toward improving material conditions of Palestinian lives in an effort to support Palestinian agency and self-determination outside of the parameters of the nation-state, then perhaps the answer is . . . maybe? Whatever discomfort you are feeling, dear reader, as I present these two vastly different visions of Palestinian liberation, I share it wholeheartedly with you.

Some of the answers to the above question lie in the answer to a series of other questions lurking throughout this entire book: What do we mean by Palestinian liberation? What are the available liberatory possibilities within the context of global neoliberal capitalism? And what compromises must we be willing to entertain in order to achieve variations of liberation? These latter two questions are an especially bitter pill to swallow because they originate not from a place of optimism, but from a place of pessimism.[6] Which leads to a final and perhaps most important question: Regardless of what we conceive liberation to be, *how* must we go about accomplishing it? Palestinian civil society and liberation activists have been clear about the "how" since 2005: The optimal modus operandi for abolishing Israel's apartheid regime is through the BDS movement.[7]

What responsibility, if any, does Brand Palestine have to the Palestinian liberation movement? Must all Palestinian cinema and media have specific directives or be in league with movement goals? In what ways do Palestine films and solidarity cinema and media confound or collude with compulsory Zionism? In the US context, does cinematic activism succeed in subverting the hegemony of compulsory Zionism? Do all Palestine films and solidarity cinema and media operate in the service of cinematic activism? Does cinematic activism advance Palestine solidarity politics in the United States? Do Palestine solidarity politics advance the Palestinian liberation movement? This last question is beyond the purview of this book. Yet all of these are important queries to keep in mind for anyone—artists, filmmakers, scholars, students, activists—who is participating, or even merely interested, in any kind of Palestinian liberation and solidarity work, myself included.

Creative forms and practices of communication are necessary for social movements to distribute their messaging, demands, and goals to wider audiences. But art and media are also critical to developing a social movement's *culture,* that which coheres diverse peoples together and which builds and maintains morale in the face of grueling, unsexy, thankless labor and devastating political setbacks. As Sa'ed Atshan has argued, a kind of "purity politics" exists among the left, especially with regard to Palestine solidarity politics within queer activism.[8] These purity politics have resulted in a kind of self-cannibalizing critique.

That said, it is important for any social movement to evaluate its creative communications and its media texts and practices with a critical eye toward the movement's ethics and goals. It actually came as a great shock to me to realize that, of the breadth of Palestine-focused cinematic activism texts or practices analyzed in this book, *only two examples*—Street Cred's culture jamming and the Outside the Frame Film Festival—advocate for BDS. This is not a coincidence, but rather reflective of a larger strategy inherent to cinematic activism for Palestine in the US context. As Elia Suleiman insisted on the right of Palestinian art and cinema to be considered on its own accord *as art and cinema* and *not* as an object associated with a political movement (see chapters 3 and 4), so too do much of Palestine films and cinematic activism practices in the United States rely on the privileged status of artistic freedom of expression as a constitutionally protected right. Given the profoundly organized and pervasive attempts to criminalize BDS in the United States, it makes sense now more than ever to amplify a kind of strategic naivete of playing up the constitutionally protected status of artistic freedom of expression (despite the fact that such a strategy reifies the legitimacy of the settler-colonial state and its statutes). Put another way: Art, film, and creative media have afforded an exception to "the Palestine exception" to free speech. It makes perfect sense that many activists and artists would choose the soft power of cinema and cinematic activism to counter compulsory Zionism. Cultural hegemony, after all, is all about soft power, and in order for a counterpublic to indeed do the work of countering, it must operate on the same register. This is why it is called a "culture war."

Organizations such as Palestine Legal and Visualizing Palestine have documented the well-organized efforts to delegitimize Palestinian speech and Palestine solidarity speech through spurious accusations of antisemitism, as well as efforts to outright criminalize BDS at various state and local government levels in the United States. These attempts to delegitimize and criminalize the Palestinian liberation discourse in the United States have risen exponentially over the last decade alongside the equally exponential increase in representations of Palestinian cinema and Palestine films in mainstream US media platforms and popular culture. Given the prior precedent of succeeding through a "freedom of expression" argument, I believe that Palestinian cinema and Palestine solidarity cinematic activism have great potential to strategically advance Palestinian liberation movement goals, including advocating for BDS. That said, as demonstrated throughout this book, Palestine solidarity cinematic activism—even without BDS directives—has been perceived as such a threat to compulsory Zionism that, at various times, the institutions and activists of compulsory Zionism have waged intense campaigns to waylay, control, and even outright censor Palestinian cinema and solidarity cinema. Those attempts have, somewhat ironically, produced the controversies that I have historicized in this book and that have in many ways helped to propel Palestinian liberation and solidarity politics further into the US public sphere.

That is all to say, even without express advocacy for the preferred modus operandi (BDS) of the Palestinian liberation movement, Palestine solidarity cinematic activism has successfully produced a counterhegemony in the context of the United States. We see this evidenced beyond the typical Palestine solidarity activism circles and now manifesting in more mainstream realms, such as Palestinian film and television content on streaming platforms, social media, and references in popular culture. We also see it in newer and emerging Palestinian liberation and solidarity cinematic activism projects, such as the establishment of No Evil Eye Cinema in 2019 and its Cinematic Interventions to Freeing Palestine and the Global South symposia series and syllabus, and the founding of Watermelon Pictures in April 2024. Projects such as No Evil Eye Cinema and Watermelon Pictures indicate a new wave of cinematic activism for Palestine. The work organizations like these do to produce, exhibit, and distribute Palestinian cinema and Palestine films helps to enable Palestinian and solidarity cinematic activists to continue the longer history of cinematic activism for Palestine as described in this book, and it will undoubtedly change and expand that cinematic activism in ways that seemed unimaginable in the 1970s. Indeed, my great hope is that the Palestinian liberation and solidarity cinematic activism of today will revolutionize cinematic activism for Palestine in ways that even seem unimaginable now.

I am not so naive to conflate the increased representation of Palestine and Palestinian cultural productions in the US context with achievements of liberation. Indeed, there will certainly be those who perceive the argument of this book as a betrayal of the cause.[9] But I feel it is important to acknowledge the massive cultural shift that has taken place in the United States over the past fifty years and the role of cinematic activism in producing that shift. Palestine, as a legitimate, self-determined people, nation, and culture, *exists* in the US cultural imagination and field of representation, a fact that was actively and forcefully denied a mere fifty years ago. There is much work still to do, both within the Palestine solidarity movement in the United States and within the Palestinian liberation movement at large. But one thing is for sure: None of that work can get done without the uses of cinema and media. Palestinian cinema, Palestine films, and cinematic activism are necessary components of the movement, whether simply to serve as a medium for the movement's communication or to produce the cultural fabric of the cause.

# Acknowledgments

This book began as a dissertation during my time as a doctoral student in the Department of American Studies and Ethnicity at the University of Southern California (USC). At USC I had the support of a tremendous dissertation committee. I am grateful to Evelyn Alsultany, Sarah Gualtieri, Jack Halberstam, Olivia Harrison, and Kara Keeling for helping to shape this project's intellectual foundations and mentoring me through the doctoral process. Special thanks to Sarah and Evelyn for always believing in this project and encouraging me to trust my scholarly instincts. I am also grateful to the numerous other faculty members at USC with whom I worked and interacted along the way: Sarah Banet-Weiser, Macarena Gomez-Barris, Karen Halttunen, Lanita Jacobs, Neetu Khanna, Virginia Kuhn, Viet Nguyen, Panivong Norindr, Laura Pulido, Vanessa Schwartz, Nayan Shah, Karen Tongson, and Ruth Wilson Gilmore. Special thanks to Kitty Lai and Jujuana Preston.

This project was made possible through countless grants and numerous fellowships. Special thanks to the University of Michigan College of Literature, Science and the Arts, and the University of Michigan Office of Research for providing research and publication funds. I am also grateful for financial support for my doctoral research from the USC Department of American Studies and Ethnicity, the USC Department of Middle East Studies, the USC Visual Studies Research Institute, and the Center for Arab American Philanthropy. I am also grateful for the two-year Mellon Postdoctoral Fellowship in the Asian American Studies and Middle East and North African Studies Programs at Northwestern University (NU), as well as for additional grant funding from the NU Graduate School and the NU Office of Undergraduate Research. The two years I spent at NU provided critical time, resources, and mentorship that resulted in the expansion and development of this book project. Thanks to Brian Edwards and Hamid

Naficy for your insights and your humor. Thanks to the crew of other emerging scholars who traveled through NU alongside me and who provided feedback, commiseration, and community: Sarah Dees, Nell Haynes, Hi'ilei Hobart, Kaneesha Parsard, Elizabeth Schwall, Mitali Thakor, and Emrah Yıldız. Thanks also to Danielle Dougé, who helped me with research as an undergraduate student.

I am also thankful for the semester I spent as a faculty fellow at the Charles Warren Center for Studies in American History at Harvard University. While there I was extremely lucky to workshop a chapter of this book with an outstanding group of ethnic studies faculty, postdoctoral fellows, and graduate students, including Genevieve Clutario, Robert Diaz, Jason Ferreira, Lorgia García Peña, Nicole Guidotti-Hernández, Allen Isaac, Denise Khor, Ju Yon Kim, Marisol Lebron, Anjali Nath, Takeo Rivera; Warren Center postdocs Christina Davidson, Courtney Sato, Kristina Shull, and Hannah Waits; and graduate students Keish Kim, Keisha Knight, and Christopher Rodelo. Although our time together was cut short by the hard lockdown of the Covid-19 pandemic, I will always cherish the time we spent in workshop, talking over lunch, and eventually holding space for each other over Zoom.

I am eternally grateful to have the mentorship and comradery of a network of scholars and writers who helped pave the way forward for folks like me to do the kind of work I wanted to do and to be the scholar and teacher I wanted to be. Massive gratitude to Evelyn Alsultany, Sa'ed Atshan, Louise Cainkar, Carol Fadda, Keith Feldman, Sarah Gualtieri, Elaine Hagopian, Pauline Homsi Vinson, Amira Jarmakani, Suad Joseph, Joe Kadi, Alex Lubin, Saree Makdisi, Melani McAlister, Nadine Naber, Therí Pickens, Junaid Rana, Stephen Sheehi, and Ella Shohat. I would also like to send a shout-out to my undergraduate mentors who, although they may not know it, helped germinate the seeds of my scholarly inquiries. Thank you to Darcy Buerkle, Kevin Rozario, Meridel Rubenstein, and Frazer Ward. Thanks also to several of my high school teachers, especially Rhona Carlton-Foss, Tom Evans, Tad Lawrence, Orlando Leyba, Alice McMahon, Anne Rearick, and Lori Taylor. Thanks also to my second-grade teacher, Marina Seevak, and my childhood piano teacher, Ada Park Snider. Thanks also to Barbara Post, who was never officially my teacher, but who helped me learn many things nonetheless.

I owe special gratitude to numerous librarians and archivists who helped me locate some truly spectacular materials for this project. Many thanks to Alexis Braun Marks, Amber Davis, Kat Hacanyan, and the rest of the folks at the Eastern Michigan University Archive. Thanks also to the folks at the Northwestern University Archive. I am hugely thankful for Caroline Jorgenson and Kristine Krueger at the Margaret Herrick Library in Los Angeles. Also, big thanks to Fred Beldin, Phill Hallman, and Evyn Kropf at the University of Michigan. Thanks also to Chelsea Sellin at the Western Neighborhoods Project/Outsidelands.org and Tricia Gesner at the Associated Press. I am also thankful to all the folks behind the scenes at various film festivals, including the Boston Palestine Film Festival, the Chicago Palestine Film Festival, the Outside the Frame Film Festival, and the Mizna Arab Film Festival. Special thanks to Michelle Baroudi, Deeg Gold, Michael Maria, Kate Raphael, and Nina Shoman-Dajani. Extra special thanks to Street Cred/Bay Area Art Queers Unleashing Power, Queers Undermining Israeli Terrorism!, and everyone behind the scenes of Outside the Frame: Queers for Palestine Film Festival.

I have made many dear friends and colleagues along this wild ride. Thank you to George Abraham, Cas Adair, Dunya Alwan, Kaveh Askari, Sophia Azeb, M. Aziz, Crystal Baik, Lisa Bhungalia, Layla Bin Nasr, Lara Bradshaw, Jordan T. Camp, micha cárdenas, Genevieve Carpio, Jolie Chea, Jih-Fei Cheng, Amy Chu, Sony Coráñez Bolton, Jennifer DeClue, Adrian De Leon, Josen Diaz, Treva Ellison, Kate Fortmueller, Colby Gordon, Maryam Griffin, Christina Heatherton, Feng-Mei Heberer, Emily Hobson, Emily Hue, Ren-Yo Hwang, Happy Hyder, Huda Jadallah, Maryam Kashani, Sarah Kessler, Jina Kim, Alison Kozberg, Viola Lasmana, Sharon Luk, Luci Marzola, Najwa Mayer, Jeff Melnick, Celeste Menchaca, Joshua Mitchell, Anjali Nath, Rachel Norman, Dana Olwan, Nathan Pogar, Kareem Rabie, Nic John Ramos, Emily Raymundo, Jed Samer, Lila Sharif, Rana Sharif, Lara Sheehi, Stephen Sheehi, Sriya Shrestha, and Tasneem Siddiqui. Special thanks to my fellow Palestinian media studies comrade, Sulafa Zidani.

There are certain folks who will forever be a part of me. My gratitude for my chosen family cannot be contained in the words on this page. I am nourished by your love and friendship, and I cannot imagine being who I am today without you in my life. Charlotte Karem Albrecht: I am eternally thankful for your surreptitious side-eye and loving me despite my inability to fix my face. Mejdulene Shomali: My brother in chaos, you have kept me from the void more times than you will ever know. Tahereh Aghdasifar: Your bombastic laughter truly makes me feel like it is all going to be OK. Lamise Shawahin: I know that you would have my back in a street fight and that is one of the greatest honors to have in this world. *Falastin hurra*! T. Hammidi: My desert sibling, thank you for always welcoming me back to Joshua Tree and indulging in collaborative SWANA creativity. Jih-Fei Cheng: My fellow Capricorn sibling, your love and kindness helped me trust myself in graduate school, and I will always be thankful that you saw me for who I really am. Meiver De La Cruz: Your humor is medicine to my soul. Thank you for always showing up and being a steadfast comrade through all this bullshit. Lara Bitar: We love each other harder than we fight each other. You're a hero, don't ever forget it. Jennifer Lynn Kelly: Your loyalty, love, and care made getting through the viper's den of certain fields bearable. Marisol LeBron: *Bayan, bayan*! Thank you to my fellow Smith College American Studies bandits: Jacqui Shine and Katy Haas. Thank you to Devon Wilson-Hill for always being ready to pick up where we leave off. Thank you to my fellow Cambridge SWANA comrade, Derya Hanife Altan, for commiserating through possum memes.

I have had the esteemed privilege of having a number of brilliant people read and provide feedback on this work. Thank you to Evelyn Alsultany, Blake Atwood, Sara Awartani, Amira Jarmakani, Charlotte Karem Albrecht, Alex Lubin, Najwa Mayer, and Ella Shohat. Special thanks to all those who attended my manuscript workshop at the University of Michigan, especially Caryl Flinn, Colin Gunckel, and Melani McAlister. I have had the joy and privilege of working with a fantastic editor at the University of Minnesota Press, Leah Pennywark. Leah, thank you for believing in this project (and in me!) at a time of immense precarity and uncertainty for Palestinian writers and those writing about Palestinian liberation politics in the United States. Thanks also to Anne Carter, William John Brown, Wendy Holdman, Kristine Hunt, Alena Rivas, Carla Valadez, and all the folks at the University of Minnesota Press. Thanks to Shelby Brewster for indexing. I would also like to thank Jim Burr at the University of Texas Press: Although this book did not land there, I am grateful for your support of this project.

Thank you to my anonymous peer reviewers for your incisive comments, constructive feedback, and enthusiastic encouragement. I am also grateful to have worked with several excellent developmental editors: Kemi Adeyemi, Liz DeWolf, and Laura Portwood-Stacer.

Thank you to all of my University of Michigan (UM) colleagues in the departments of American Culture and Film, Television, and Media and in the Arab and Muslim American Studies Program. Thanks especially to Su'ad Abdul Khabeer, Juan Cole, Greg Dowd, Larry LaFountain-Stokes, Yeidy Rivero, and Magdalena Zaborowska, for your leadership in what feels like never-ending crises within the academy and the world at large. Many thanks to Judy Gray, Hayley North, Mary Freiman, Stephanie Hart, Katia Kitchen, and Spencer Wright. I am also hugely grateful to Jason Young, Asma Baban, and the 2024–2025 cohort of fellows at the UM Institute for the Humanities. I am lucky to be surrounded by an incredible community of folks in Michigan: Retikha Adikhari, Sigrid Anderson, Marc Arthur, Sara Awartani, Stephen Berrey, Melissa Borja, William Calvo-Quirós, John Cheney-Lippold, Anne Cong-Huyen, Sascha Crasnow, Clare Croft, Cameron Cross, Manan Desai, Caryl Flinn, Yvette Granata, Hollis Griffin, Kaitlin Guidarelli, Colin Gunckel, Sandra Gunning, Kelli Hanson, Kristin Hass, Annie Heffernan, Dan Herbert, Jennifer Hsieh, Bethany Hughs, Kei and Stephanie Kai-Ro, Charlotte Karem Albrecht, Yarden Katz, Nancy Khalil, Aliyah Khan, Lydia Kelow-Bennet, Mark Kligerman, Alexander Knysh, Kriss Lare, Scott Larson, Kate Livingston, Christopher McNamara, Yasmin Moll, Sarah Murray, Susan Najita, Lisa Nakamura, Matthew Noble-Olson, Devin O'Hara, Alyssa Paredes, Doo Jae Park, Melissa Phruksachart, Ess Pokornowski, Ava Purkiss, Swapnil Rai, Niloofar Sarlati, Ian Shin, Amy Stillman, SaraEllen Strongman, Johannes Von Moltke, Jessica Kenyatta Walker, Anna Watkins Fisher, and Emilia Yang. Shout out also to some awesome graduate students (and former graduate students): Tanite Chahwan, Henry Chen, Sena Duran, Belquis Elhadi, and Alice Mishkin.

I could not have made it this far in life without the love and support of my mom, Layla, and my sister, Thuraya. Life has not been easy on our family. Thank you to my mom, Layla, a.k.a. *jabal al-nar*: From you I learned *sumud* and how to stand tall when speaking truth to power. Thuraya: Thank you for teaching me old-school street smarts. Thanks also to my extended family members, especially the Basils, Raif Hijab, Rami Hijab, and Manal Mitri.

I would be remiss not to thank my domesticated canine and feline companions. Jasper Ferdinand Baby: My soulmate, my ride or die. You are the ur-dog, the bubba against which all bubbas will be measured. Pirate Kitty Boyfriend: You drool, which is fine. I am grateful for your ragtag ding-dong survivalist presence in my life. Thank you for continually reminding me to lighten up.

Thank you to all the filmmakers of the world—past, present, future, known, and unknown—for memorializing our world and envisioning new ones.

Lastly, أميرة, there are no words, only the ر (*ra*), in both its presence and its absence.

# Notes

## Introduction

1. For studies on the Palestinian experience through the framework of genocide, see Nur Masalha, *The Palestine Nakba: Decolonising History, Narrating the Subaltern, Reclaiming Memory* (Zed Books, 2012); Haifa Rashed and Damien Short, "Genocide and Settler Colonialism: Can a Lemkin-inspired Genocide Perspective Aid Our Understanding of the Palestinian Situation?," in *New Directions in the Sociology of Human Rights*, ed. Patricia Hynes, Michele Lamb, Damien Short, and Matthew Waites (Routledge, 2016), 20–47; Rosemary Sayigh, "On the Burial of the Palestinian Nakba 1," in *Routledge International Handbook of Ignorance Studies*, ed. Matthew Gross and Linsey McGoey (Routledge, 2023), 279–89.

2. Jonathan Glazer, "Academy Award Acceptance Speech," March 10, 2024, Dolby Theatre, Los Angeles, accessed April 18, 2024, https://aaspeechesdb.oscars.org/link/096-12/.

3. Southwest Asia and North Africa, abbreviated to the acronym SWANA, functions as a decolonial way to refer to what is commonly referred to by the Eurocentric phrase "the Middle East."

4. I use the phrase "Palestinian liberation and solidarity politics" to refer to a range of opinions and beliefs that take as their starting point the recognition and condemnation of Zionist colonization of Palestine, Zionist ethnic cleansing of Palestinians from their land, and Zionist apartheid rule over Palestinians. Additional opinions and beliefs include but are not limited to the belief that Palestinians have the right to self-determination, that Palestinians are entitled to universal human rights and protections under international law (in accordance with the Geneva Conventions), that colonized people have a right to resist colonization through armed struggle, and that the oppression and exploitation of the Palestinian people is imbricated with the oppression and exploitation of numerous and diverse peoples, including but not limited to BIPOC people, LGBTQ+ people, women, people with disabilities, and other minoritized peoples around the globe. The phrase "Palestinian liberation and solidarity politics" does not refer to an endorsement of any political parties or governmental organizations. Finally, the core

of Palestinian liberation and solidarity politics can be summarized in the words of the Boycott, Divestment, and Sanctions (BDS) movement's call to the international community from Palestinian civil society in 2005, which states that "non-violent punitive measures" such as consumer boycotts, financial divestment, and state and government sanctions "should be maintained until Israel meets its obligation to recognize the Palestinian people's inalienable right to self-determination and fully complies with the precepts of international law by: 1. Ending its occupation and colonization of all Arab lands and dismantling the Wall, 2. Recognizing the fundamental rights of the Arab-Palestinian citizens of Israel to full equality; and 3. Respecting, protecting and promoting the rights of Palestinian refugees to return to their homes and properties as stipulated in UN resolution 194." Stanley L. Cohen, "Palestinians Have a Legal Right to Armed Struggle," *Al Jazeera,* July 20, 2017, https://www.aljazeera.com/opinions/2017/7/20/palestinians-have-a-legal-right-to-armed-struggle; "Palestinian Civil Society Call for BDS," BDS, July 9, 2005, https://bdsmovement.net/call.

5. "Student intifada" is a bilingual portmanteau phrase of English and Arabic. *Intifada* means "shaking off" in Arabic and refers to two distinct Palestinian uprisings against the Israeli military occupation in the West Bank and Gaza Strip: the First Intifada (1987–1993) and the Second Intifada (2001–2005).

6. Alexander Fabino, "Starbucks Loses $11 Billion in Value amid Boycotts," *Newsweek,* December 5, 2023, https://www.newsweek.com/starbucks-market-loss-boycotts-strikes-red-cup-day-1849713; "Pro-Palestinian Protesters Block Seattle Freeway for Several Hours," *Associated Press,* January 6, 2024, https://apnews.com/article/seattle-protest-israel-hamas-b7f8988e5139089633072322e79cbcd3; Kelly O'Mara and Caroline Smith, "Protesters Briefly Block Highway 101 in SF, Call for End to War in Gaza," *KQED,* February 19, 2024, https://www.kqed.org/news/11976328/protesters-briefly-block-highway-101-in-sf-call-for-end-to-war-in-gaza; Tony Kurzweil, "Protesters Block L.A. Freeway Demanding Cease-Fire in Gaza" *KTLA,* December 13, 2023, https://ktla.com/news/local-news/protesters-block-110-freeway-demanding-israel-palestine-ceasefire/; John Antczak, "Pro-Palestinian Protesters Block Airport Access Roads in New York and Los Angeles," *PBS News Hour*, December 27, 2023, https://www.pbs.org/newshour/politics/pro-palestinian-protesters-block-airport-access-roads-in-new-york-and-los-angeles.

7. For details, see Tal Axelrod, "How US Attitudes on Israel and Palestinians Had Been Shifting Before Hamas Attack," *ABC News,* October 11, 2023, https://abcnews.go.com/Politics/hamas-attack-us-attitudes-israel-palestinians-shifted-party/story?id=103892349; Audie Cornish, "Liberal American Attitudes Are Starting to Shift on Israelis and Palestinians," *All Things Considered,* NPR, May 21, 2021, https://www.npr.org/2021/05/21

/999241551/liberal-american-attitudes-are-starting-to-shift-on-israelis-and-palestinians; Elliot Davis Jr., "How American Views of the Israeli-Palestinian Conflict Have Evolved," *US News & World Report,* October 12, 2023, https://www.usnews.com/news/best-countries/articles/2023-10-12/how-american-views-of-the-israeli-palestinian-conflict-have-evolved; David Ingram, "Is It TikTok? Here's Why Some Young Americans Sympathize with Palestinians," *NBC News,* November 19, 2023, https://www.nbcnews.com/tech/internet/tiktok-s-young-americans-sympathize-palestinians-rcna124476; Travis Mitchell, "Modest Warming in U.S. Views on Israel and Palestinians," *Pew Research Center's Religion & Public Life Project* (blog), May 26, 2022, https://www.pewresearch.org/religion/2022/05/26/modest-warming-in-u-s-views-on-israel-and-palestinians/; Lydia Saad, "Democrats' Sympathies in Middle East Shift to Palestinians," Gallup, March 16, 2023, https://news.gallup.com/poll/472070/democrats-sympathies-middle-east-shift-palestinians.aspx.

8. "The Palestine Exception to Free Speech: A Movement Under Attack in the US," Palestine Legal and Center for Constitutional Rights, September 2015, https://palestinelegal.org/the-palestine-exception.

9. The phrase "Palestinian liberation and solidarity movement within the United States" refers to a broad network of transnational organizations that includes (in alphabetical order) the Boycott, Divestment, and Sanctions movement; Faculty and Staff for Justice in Palestine; Film Workers for Palestine; the Gaza Freedom Flotilla coalition; If Not Now; the International Jewish Anti-Zionist Network; Jewish Voice for Peace; the Palestinian Feminist Collective; the Palestinian Youth Movement; Queers Undermining Israeli Terrorism!; Screen Actors Guild–American Federation of Television and Radio Artists (SAG-AFTRA) Members for a Ceasefire; Students for Justice in Palestine; the US Campaign for the Academic and Cultural Boycott of Israel; and Within Our Lifetime, just to name a few.

10. Yara Hawari, "Arab Normalization and the Palestinian Struggle for Liberation," *Al-Shabka* (blog), October 18, 2022, https://al-shabaka.org/commentaries/arab-normalization-and-the-palestinian-struggle-for-liberation/.

11. Hawari, "Arab Normalization and the Palestinian Struggle for Liberation."

12. "Samsung Next Leaves Israel as Economy Suffers from Gaza War," *The New Arab,* April 12, 2024, https://www.newarab.com/news/samsung-next-leaves-israel-economy-suffers-gaza-war; "UAE's ADNOC, BP Suspend Gas Deal with Israel amid Gaza Anger," *The New Arab,* March 14, 2024, https://www.newarab.com/news/uaes-adnoc-bp-suspend-gas-deal-israel-amid-gaza-anger.

13. Cherien Dabis (@cheriendabis), "MO is a global sensation!! Making us one step closer to 'rebranding' Palestine! So grateful to all of you for showing up and proving that audiences everywhere are hungry for authentic

representation of our community. Thank you @netflix and @a24 for believing," Instagram, August 30, 2022, https://www.instagram.com/p/Ch4nK_QAY41/.

14. See Evelyn Alsultany, *Broken: The Failed Promise of Muslim Inclusion* (New York University Press, 2022); Sarah Banet-Weiser, *Authentic TM: The Politics of Ambivalence in a Brand Culture* (New York University Press, 2012); Roderick Ferguson, *The Reorder of Things: The University and Its Pedagogies of Minority Difference* (University of Minnesota Press, 2012); Roopali Mukherjee and Sarah Banet-Weiser, "Introduction: Commodity Activism in Neoliberal Times," in *Commodity Activism: Cultural Resistance in Neoliberal Times* (New York University Press, 2012).

15. Banet-Weiser, *Authentic TM,* 4.

16. Adrienne Rich, "Compulsory Heterosexuality and Lesbian Existence," *Signs: Journal of Women in Culture and Society* 5, no. 4 (July 1980): 635.

17. Erella Shadmi, "Women, Palestinians, Zionism: A Personal View," *News from Within* 8, no. 10–11 (1992): 13.

18. Ella Shohat, "Sephardim in Israel: Zionism from the Standpoint of Its Jewish Victims," *Social Text,* no. 19/20 (1988): 1–35.

19. Cathy J. Cohen, "Punks, Bulldaggers, and Welfare Queens: The Radical Potential of Queer Politics?," *GLQ: A Journal of Lesbian and Gay Studies* 3, no. 4 (1997): 442,

20. Gil Z. Hochberg, "Introduction: Israelis, Palestinians, Queers: Points of Departure," *GLQ: A Journal of Lesbian and Gay Studies* 16, no. 4 (2010): 497.

21. Charlotte Karem Albrecht, *Possible Histories: Arab Americans and the Queer Ecology of Peddling* (University of California Press, 2023), 9.

22. C. Heike Schotten, *Queer Terror: Life, Death, and Desire in the Settler Colony* (Columbia University Press, 2018), xvi.

23. Schotten, *Queer Terror,* 167.

24. Nadine Naber, Eman Desouky, and Lina Baroudi, "The Forgotten -ism: An Arab American Women's Perspective on Zionism, Racism, and Sexism," in *Color of Violence: The INCITE! Anthology,* edited by INCITE! Women of Color Against Violence (Duke University Press, 2016), 103.

25. Michael Omi and Howard Winant, *Racial Formation in the United States* (Routledge, 2014), 125.

26. Umayyah Cable, "Compulsory Zionism and Palestinian Existence: A Genealogy," *Journal of Palestine Studies* 51, no. 2 (2022): 66–71, https://doi.org/10.1080/0377919X.2022.2040324.

27. See Melani McAlister, *Epic Encounters: Culture, Media, and U.S. Interests in the Middle East Since 1945* (University of California Press, 2005); Luke Peterson, *Palestine-Israel in the Print News Media: Contending Discourses* (Routledge, 2015); Jack G. Shaheen, *Reel Bad Arabs: How Hollywood Vilifies a People* (Olive Branch, 2009); Ronald R. Stockton, "Ethnic Archetypes and the Arab Image," in *The Development of Arab American Identity,* edited by Ernest McCarus (University of Michigan Press, 1994).

28. Michael W. Suleiman, "Development of Public Opinion on the Palestine Question," *Journal of Palestine Studies* 13, no. 3 (1984): 109.

29. Edward W. Said, *Orientalism* (Vintage, 1979), 3.

30. Stuart Hall uses the phrase "regime of representation" to describe the work that racial stereotyping performs in the constructions of "otherness" and the hegemonic power such representations wield for the purpose of social exclusion. Stuart Hall, Jessica Evans, and Sean Nixon, eds., *Representation: Cultural Representations and Signifying Practices* (Sage, 2013), 70.

31. Robert Allen Warrior, "Canaanites, Cowboys, and Indians: Deliverance, Conquest, and Liberation Theology Today," in *Native and Christian,* edited by James Treat (Routledge, 1996), 99.

32. Steven Salaita, "Inter/Nationalism from the Holy Land to the New World: Encountering Palestine in American Indian Studies," *Native American and Indigenous Studies* 1, no. 2 (2014): 129–30.

33. McAlister, *Epic Encounters,* 161–63.

34. Ramon Lobato, *Shadow Economies of Cinema: Mapping Informal Film Distribution* (British Film Institute, 2012).

35. Lobato, *Shadow Economies of Cinema,* 10.

36. Issam Nassar, Stephen Sheehi, and Salim Tamari, *Camera Palaestina: Photography and Displaced Histories of Palestine* (University of California Press, 2022), 115.

37. Jacques Rancière and Gabriel Rockhill, *The Politics of Aesthetics* (Bloomsbury Academic, 2006), xiv.

38. Hollis Griffin, "Triggers, Traumas, and Other Useful Things, or Gender and Sexuality Studies Out in the World," Sally G. McMillen Lecture in Gender and Sexuality Studies, Davidson College, N.C., March 20, 2024.

39. Jamie Dunn, "How Cinema for Gaza Channels Cinephilia into Activism," *The Skinny,* April 8, 2024, https://www.theskinny.co.uk/film/news/how-cinema-for-gaza-channels-cinephilia-into-activism.

40. Nassar, Sheehi, and Tamari, *Camera Palaestina,* 123.

41. Edward W. Said, *Reflections on Exile and Other Essays* (Harvard University Press, 2000), 562–63.

42. Rashid Bashshur, "Unfulfilled Expectations: The Genesis and Demise of the AAUG," *Arab Studies Quarterly* 29, no. 3/4 (2007): 8.

43. Nadia Yaqub, *Palestinian Cinema in the Days of Revolution* (University of Texas Press, 2021), 12.

44. Terri Ginsberg, *Visualizing the Palestinian Struggle: Towards a Critical Analytic of Palestine Solidarity Film* (Palgrave Macmillan, 2016), 3.

45. Brian L. Ott and Robert L. Mack, *Critical Media Studies: An Introduction* (Wiley-Blackwell, 2020). 119.

46. "U.S. House Votes in Favor of TikTok Ban Bill Amid First Amendment and Other Questions," *Democracy Now!,* March 14, 2024, https://www.democracynow.org/2024/3/14/headlines/us_house_votes_in_favor_of_tiktok_ban_bill_amid_first_amendment_and_other_questions.

47. James McMahon, *The Political Economy of Hollywood: Capitalist Power and Cultural Production* (Routledge, 2022), 2.

48. McMahon, *The Political Economy of Hollywood,* 3.

49. McMahon, *The Political Economy of Hollywood,* 2–3.

50. Guy Debord, *Society of the Spectacle,* ed. Fredy Perlman (Black & Red, 2000).

51. Many thanks to Amira Jarmakani for suggesting the phrase "strategic naivete."

52. Umayyah Cable, "A Film By Any Other Name? Palestinian Cultural Authenticity and the Politics of Categorization," *Palestine in America* 1, no. 14 (February 2023); Umayyah Cable, "'Farha' and the Claustrophobic State of Palestinian Cinema," Institute for Palestine Studies blog, January 12, 2023, https://www.palestine-studies.org/en/node/1653553.

53. Randy Nichols and Gabriela Martinez, eds., *Political Economy of Media Industries: Global Transformations and Challenges* (Routledge, 2020), 2; Vincent Mosco, *The Political Economy of Communication* (Sage, 2009).

54. Mishuana Goeman, "Introduction to Indigenous Performances: Upsetting the Terrains of Settler Colonialism," *American Indian Culture and Research Journal* 35, no. 4 (2011): 1–18.

## 1. Producing Education, Distributing Solidarity

1. For more on the history of film and filmstrips as educational tools and for the promotion of "global citizenship" ideology, see Michael Dimmick, "Maria Varela's Flickering Light: Literacy, Filmstrips, and the Work of Adult Literacy Education in the Civil Rights Movement," *Community Literacy Journal* 14, no. 2 (2020): 49–71; Regina Longo, "Palimpsests of Power: UNESCO-'Sponsored' Film Production and the Construction of a 'Global Village,' 1948–1953," *The Velvet Light Trap* 75 (Spring 2015): 88–106.

2. See Melani McAlister, *Epic Encounters: Culture, Media, and U.S. Interests in the Middle East Since 1945* (University of California Press, 2001); Luke Peterson, *Palestine-Israel in the Print News Media* (Routledge, 2014); Luke Peterson, "Discourse, Palestine, and the Authoritative News Media," in *Practicing Transnationalism: American Studies in the Middle East,* ed. Eileen T. Lundy and Edward J. Lundy (University of Texas Press, 2016), 94–114; Jack G. Shaheen, *The TV Arab* (Popular Press, 1984); Jack G. Shaheen, *Reel Bad Arabs: How Hollywood Vilifies a People* (Olive Branch, 2009); Ronald R. Stockton, "Ethnic Archetypes and the Arab Image," in *The Development of Arab American Identity,* ed. Ernest McCarus (University of Michigan Press, 1994).

3. Amahl Bishara's ethnography of US news media production in Palestine poses an intervention with this regard by privileging the labor and agency of local Palestinians working for US news outlets. Her work reframes our understanding of mainstream US news representations of Palestinian

politics. Amahl Bishara, *Back Stories: US News Production and Palestinian Politics* (Stanford University Press, 2013).

4. Some examples of the scholarship on Palestinian cinema include, but are not limited to Greg Burris, *The Palestinian Idea: Film, Media, and the Radical Imagination* (Temple University Press, 2019); Nurith Gertz and George Khleifi, *Palestinian Cinema: Landscape, Trauma, and Memory* (Indiana University Press, 2008); Terri Ginsberg, *Visualizing the Palestinian Struggle: Towards a Critical Analytic of Palestine Solidarity Film* (Palgrave Macmillan, 2016); Hamid Naficy, *An Accented Cinema: Exilic and Diasporic Filmmaking* (Princeton University Press, 2001); Helga Tawil-Souri, "Where Is the Political in Cultural Studies? In Palestine," *International Journal of Cultural Studies* 14, no. 5 (September 2011), 467–82; Nadia Yaqub, *Palestinian Cinema in the Days of Revolution* (University of Texas Press, 2018).

5. Keith Feldman and Pamela Pennock briefly reference these filmstrips in their respective monographs. Keith Feldman, *A Shadow over Palestine: The Imperial Life of Race in America* (University of Minnesota Press, 2015), 167; Pamela Pennock, *The Rise of the Arab American Left: Activists, Allies, and Their Fight Against Imperialism and Racism, 1960s–1980s* (University of North Carolina Press, 2017), 31.

6. *Pro-Arab Propaganda in America: Vehicles and Voices, a Handbook* (Anti-Defamation League of B'nai B'rith, 1983), ii.

7. *Pro-Arab Propaganda in America,* i.

8. Film screenings are mentioned several times in *The AIPAC College Guide.* See Jonathan S. Kessler and Jeff Schwaber, *The AIPAC College Guide: Exposing the Anti-Israel Campaign on Campus* (American Israel Public Affairs Committee, 1984).

9. Kessler and Schwaber, *The AIPAC College Guide,* v.

10. Feldman, *A Shadow over Palestine*; Pennock, *The Rise of the Arab American Left*; Janice J. Terry, "Community and Political Activism Among Arab Americans in Detroit," in *Arabs in America: Building a New Future,* ed. Michael W. Suleiman (Temple University Press, 1999), 241–54.

11. Edward Said, 'The Arab Portrayed,' in *The Arab-Israeli Confrontation of June 1967: An Arab Perspective,* ed. Ibrahim Abu-Lughod (Northwestern University Press, 1970), 1–9; Michael W. Suleiman, "American Mass Media and the June Conflict," in *The Arab-Israeli Confrontation of June 1967: An Arab Perspective*, ed. Ibrahim Abu-Lughod (Northwestern University Press, 1970), 138–54; Janice Terry and Gordon Mendenhall, "1973 US Press Coverage on the Middle East," in *Arabs in America: Building a New Future,* ed. Michael W. Suleiman (Temple University Press, 1999); Robert H. Trice, "The American Elite Press and the Arab-Israeli Conflict," *Middle East Journal* 33, no. 3 (1979): 304–25.

12. Rashid Bashshur, "Unfulfilled Expectations: The Genesis and Demise of the AAUG," *Arab Studies Quarterly* 29, no. 3/4 (2007); Sarah M. A. Gualtieri,

"Genealogies of a Field Less Traveled," *Journal of American Ethnic History* 37, no. 3 (2018): 69–76; Sarah M. A. Gualtieri, "Edward Said, the AAUG, and Arab American Archival Methods," *Comparative Studies of South Asia, Africa and the Middle East* 38, no. 1 (2018): 21–29; Pennock, *The Rise of the Arab American Left.*

13. Suleiman, "American Mass Media and the June Conflict."

14. Edward Said, *After the Last Sky: Palestinian Lives* (Columbia University Press, 1999); Edward Said, "Invention, Memory, and Place," *Critical Inquiry* 26, no. 2 (2000): 175–92.

15. Pennock, *The Rise of the Arab American Left,* 29.

16. AAUG Member Directory, 1974, Box 5, Ibrahim Abu-Lughod Papers, Northwestern University Archive, Evanston, Ill.

17. Thomas G. Smith, foreword to *Learning with the Lights Off: Educational Film in the United States,* ed. Devin Orgeron, Marsha Orgeron, and Dan Streible (Oxford University Press, 2012), x.

18. Devin Orgeron, Marsha Orgeron, and Dan Streible, "A History of Learning with the Lights Off," in *Learning with the Lights Off: Educational Film in the United States,* ed. Devin Orgeron, Marsha Orgeron, and Dan Streible (Oxford University Press, 2012), 64.

19. Terry, "Community and Political Activism Among Arab Americans in Detroit," 246–47.

20. Pennock, *The Rise of the Arab American Left,* 208–9.

21. For an oral history and autoethnographic analysis of the AAUG as told from the perspective of its former leaders, see Bashshur, "Unfulfilled Expectations"; Elaine C. Hagopian, "Reversing Injustice: On Utopian Activism," *Arab Studies Quarterly* 29, no. 3/4 (2007): 57–73.; Michael W. Suleiman, "'I Come to Bury Caesar, Not to Praise Him': An Assessment of the AAUG as an Example of an Activist Arab-American Organization," *Arab Studies Quarterly* 29, no. 3/4 (2007): 75–95.

22. In an archival clip within Mohanad Yaqubi's documentary film *Off Frame aka Revolution Until Victory,* Palestinian *fida'i* (resistance fighter) and prominent Fateh Party leader within the PLO Saleh Ta'amari articulates the motives behind the Palestinian liberation struggle, stating that "Our great love to our country is greater than our hatred to our enemy. Love is our motive, not hatred. That's why we shall win." Mohanad Yaqubi, email message to author, April 22, 2025; Mohanad Yaqubi et al., *Off Frame aka Revolution Until Victory* (Torch Films, 2016).

23. For a more detailed history of the Palestinian resistance movement of the late 1960s through the 1970s and its consolidation into the PLO coalition, see Loubna Qutami, "Reborn as *Fida'i*: The Palestinian Revolution and the (Re)Making of an Icon," *International Journal of Communication* 16 (2022): 4659–83.

24. Melissa Johnson, "How Ethnic Are US Ethnic Media: The Case of Latina Magazines," *Mass Communication and Society* 3, no. 2–3 (2000): 223.

25. Jeanne Carr's letters to the editor of the *Chicago Tribune,* Ibrahum Abu-Lughod papers, Northwestern University Archive, Evanston, Ill.

26. Allen Carr's photographic slides, Ibrahim Abu-Lughod papers, Northwestern University Archive, Evanston, Ill.

27. Amy McCormac (daughter of Allen and Jeanne Carr), email message to author, October 30, 2016.

28. Haidee Wasson and Charles R. Acland, eds., *Useful Cinema* (Duke University Press, 2011), 4.

29. Yaqub, *Palestinian Cinema in the Days of Revolution,* 50.

30. Yaqub, *Palestinian Cinema in the Days of Revolution,* 50.

31. Yaqub, *Palestinian Cinema in the Days of Revolution,* 50.

32. Another way to think about the purpose of AAUG filmstrips is through Foucault's conception of "governmentality." Laurie Ouellette describes governmentality with regard to educational media as an effort to "shape, guide, and reform the conduct of others . . . in order to accommodate certain 'principles and goals' that often intersect with democratic ideals." Relatedly, Lori Kido Lopez discusses how racially marginalized groups utilize media activism to produce a sense of cultural citizenship within US society. The concepts of cultural citizenship and governmentality, then, offer a useful alternate lens through which to understand how Arab American media activists have expressly sought to reform the attitudes and behaviors of a diverse array of US media audiences by appealing to discourses on global citizenship and liberal democratic ideals such as academic freedom and freedom of expression. For more on governmentality, cultural citizenship, and media activism, see Laurie Ouellette, *Viewers Like You: How Public TV Failed the People* (Columbia University Press, 2002); Lori Kido Lopez, *Asian American Media Activism: Fighting for Cultural Citizenship* (New York University Press, 2016).

33. Informational pamphlet and order form for *Palestinians: Holding On,* 1976. Collection identifier 018.AAUG, box 5, folder 13, Association of Arab American University Graduates collection, Eastern Michigan University Archive, Ypsilanti.

34. Edward Said, *The Question of Palestine* (Vintage, 1992).

35. Gualtieri, "Edward Said, the AAUG, and Arab American Archival Methods," 27.

36. Informational pamphlet and order form for *Palestinians: Holding On,* 1976. Collection identifier 018.AAUG, box 5, folder 13, Association of Arab American University Graduates collection, Eastern Michigan University Archive, Ypsilanti.

37. Charles R. Acland, "Celluloid Classrooms and Everyday Projectionists: Post–World War II Consolidation of Community Film Activism," in *Learning with the Lights Off: Educational Film in the United States,* ed. Devin Orgeron, Marsha Orgeron, and Dan Streible (Oxford University Press, 2012), 379.

38. Acland, "Celluloid Classrooms and Everyday Projectionists," 379.

39. Acland, "Celluloid Classrooms and Everyday Projectionists," 380.

40. Marshall McLuhan coined the phrase "global village" in 1962 in order to theorize electronic media's utopian potential and capacity to democratize knowledge. However, as Ginger Nolan points out, McLuhan's notions about the global village are rooted in British colonial strategies of discipline and control, particularly in the Kenyan colonial context of the 1950s. See Marshall McLuhan, *The Gutenberg Galaxy: The Making of Typographic Man* (University of Toronto Press, 1962); Ginger Nolan, *The Neocolonialism of the Global Village* (University of Minnesota Press, 2018).

41. "Speaking of Films," radio script, FAY 2, qtd. in Acland, "Celluloid Classrooms and Everyday Projectionists," 384.

42. Report to the President by the Public Affairs Chairperson, April 1, 1976. Collection identifier 018.AAUG, box 39, folder 1, Association of Arab American University Graduates collection, Eastern Michigan University Archive, Ypsilanti.

43. Letter to AAUG membership from the Public Affairs Committee, March 10, 1977. Collection identifier 018.AAUG, box 39, folder 1, Association of Arab American University Graduates collection, Eastern Michigan University Archive, Ypsilanti.

44. Letter to AAUG membership from the Public Affairs Committee, March 10, 1977. Collection identifier 018.AAUG, box 39, folder 1, Association of Arab American University Graduates collection, Eastern Michigan University Archive, Ypsilanti.

45. "Projects and Programs: New and Continuing, A Set of Proposals," March 25, 1976. Collection identifier 018.AAUG, box 45, folder 13, Association of Arab American University Graduates collection, Eastern Michigan University Archive, Ypsilanti.

46. Letter to AAUG president Elaine Hagopian from Bernice Espy Hicks, cochairperson of the Public Affairs Committee. March 25, 1976. Collection identifier 018.AAUG, box 39, folder 1, Association of Arab American University Graduates collection, Eastern Michigan University Archive, Ypsilanti.

47. Letter to AAUG president Elaine Hagopian from Bernice Espy Hicks, cochairperson of the Public Affairs Committee, March 25, 1976. Collection identifier 018.AAUG, box 39, folder 1, Association of Arab American University Graduates collection, Eastern Michigan University Archive, Ypsilanti.

Letter to AAUG membership from the Public Affairs Committee, March 10, 1977. Collection identifier 018.AAUG, box 39, folder 1, Association of Arab American University Graduates collection, Eastern Michigan University Archive, Ypsilanti.

48. Letter to Robert E. Bentley from May Seikaly, December 13, 1978. Collection identifier 018.AAUG, box 6, folder 4, Association of Arab American University Graduates collection, Eastern Michigan University Archive, Ypsilanti.

49. Letter to David H. Blackburn from Nabeel Abraham, June 14, 1979. Collection identifier 018.AAUG, box 6, folder 4, Association of Arab American University Graduates collection, Eastern Michigan University Archive, Ypsilanti.

50. AAUG Press Catalogue of Publications, January, 1983. Collection identifier 018.AAUG, box 46, folder 4, Association of Arab American University Graduates collection, Eastern Michigan University Archive, Ypsilanti.

51. Letter the AAUG from David H. Blackburn, June 6, 1979. Collection identifier 018.AAUG, box 6, folder 4, Association of Arab American University Graduates collection, Eastern Michigan University Archive, Ypsilanti.

52. Letter the AAUG from David H. Blackburn, June 6, 1979. Collection identifier 018.AAUG, box 6, folder 4, Association of Arab American University Graduates collection, Eastern Michigan University Archive, Ypsilanti.

53. Letter the AAUG from David H. Blackburn, June 6, 1979. Collection identifier 018.AAUG, box 6, folder 4, Association of Arab American University Graduates collection, Eastern Michigan University Archive, Ypsilanti.

54. Pennock, *The Rise of the Arab American Left.*

55. One interesting thing about how AAUG acquired *Occupied Palestine* is that the sale was facilitated by, and ownership of the film passed through, Emile Durzi. Durzi was an AAUG member and owner of Algiers, a popular Arabic coffeehouse located in Harvard Square, Cambridge. The AAUG materials suggest that Durzi was the initial contact point between AAUG and the Redgrave team; however, it is unclear how Durzi was connected to the Redgrave team. Either way, the transaction of passing the film from Redgrave to the AAUG was handled via Durzi. Memo certifying transfer of ownership of *Occupied Palestine* from Algiers Corporation to the AAUG, August 1982. Collection identifier 018.AAUG, box 5, folder 14, Association of Arab American University Graduates collection, Eastern Michigan University Archive, Ypsilanti; AAUG Press Catalogue of Publications, January, 1983. Collection identifier 018.AAUG, box 46, folder 4, Association of Arab American University Graduates collection, Eastern Michigan University Archive, Ypsilanti; "Confirmation Outgoing Transfer of Funds" for support of Vanessa Redgrave Legal Fund in exchange for *Occupied Palestine.* Collection identifier 018.AAUG, box 49, folder 4, Association of Arab American University Graduates collection, Eastern Michigan University Archive, Ypsilanti.

56. Nat Hentoff, "Vanessa Redgrave Versus the Boston Symphony Orchestra," *The Washington Post*, November 21, 1987, A31.

57. Letter to Larry Ekin from Elaine C. Hagopian, September 25, 1983. Collection identifier 018.AAUG, box 49, folder 4, Association of Arab American University Graduates collection, Eastern Michigan University Archive, Ypsilanti.

58. Similarly, Gualtieri argues that Boston is a primary origination point and locus of transnational Arab American studies scholarship and

activism. Gualtieri, "Edward Said, the AAUG, and Arab American Archival Methods," 23.

59. Umayyah Cable, "Forging Her Own Path: An Interview with Scholar-Activist Elaine Hagopian," in *Arab American Women: Representation and Refusal,* ed. Michael W. Suleiman, Suad Joseph, and Louise Cainkar (Syracuse University Press, 2021), 321.

60. Fundraising request to the AAUG New England Chapter membership. May 17, 1982. Collection identifier 018.AAUG, box 5, folder 14, Association of Arab American University Graduates collection, Eastern Michigan University Archive, Ypsilanti.

61. Memo to Samir Nakib from Eileen Tahmoush, May 5, 1982. Collection identifier 018.AAUG, box 5, folder 14, Association of Arab American University Graduates collection, Eastern Michigan University Archive, Ypsilanti.

62. AAUG Press Catalogue of Publications, January, 1983. Collection identifier 018.AAUG, box 46, folder 4, Association of Arab American University Graduates collection, Eastern Michigan University Archive, Ypsilanti.

63. AAUG film rental agreements, 1982–1983. Collection identifier 018. AAUG, box 5, folder 13, Association of Arab American University Graduates collection, Eastern Michigan University Archive, Ypsilanti; "Occupied Palestine" rental dates log, 1982–1983. Collection identifier 018.AAUG, box 5, folder 13, Association of Arab American University Graduates collection, Eastern Michigan University Archive, Ypsilanti.

64. Memo relaying phone conversation with Samaa El Ibyari about *Occupied Palestine,* March 23, 1983. Collection identifier 018.AAUG, box 5, folder 13, Association of Arab American University Graduates collection, Eastern Michigan University Archive, Ypsilanti.

65. Memo relaying phone conversation with Samaa El Ibyari about *Occupied Palestine,* March 23, 1983. Collection identifier 018.AAUG, box 5, folder 13, Association of Arab American University Graduates collection, Eastern Michigan University Archive, Ypsilanti.

66. Memo relaying phone conversation with Samaa El Ibyari about *Occupied Palestine,* March 23, 1983. Collection identifier 018.AAUG, box 5, folder 13, Association of Arab American University Graduates collection, Eastern Michigan University Archive, Ypsilanti.

67. Letter to AAUG president Naseer Aruri from AAUG New York Chapter executive committee, August 1, 1983. Collection identifier 018.AAUG, box 5, folder 13, Association of Arab American University Graduates collection, Eastern Michigan University Archive, Ypsilanti.

68. Since the AAUG owned this building, it would have been feasible to customize the space to meet these needs. "Arab Media Center: Proposal for an Audiovisual Resource, Distribution, and Production Center," January 1984. Collection identifier 018.AAUG, box 46, folder 2, Association of Arab

American University Graduates collection, Eastern Michigan University Archive, Ypsilanti.

69. "Arab Media Center: Proposal for an Audiovisual Resource, Distribution, and Production Center," January 1984. Collection identifier 018.AAUG, box 46, folder 2, Association of Arab American University Graduates collection, Eastern Michigan University Archive, Ypsilanti.

70. "Arab Media Center: Proposal for an Audiovisual Resource, Distribution, and Production Center." January 1984. Collection identifier 018.AAUG, box 46, folder 2, Association of Arab American University Graduates collection, Eastern Michigan University Archive, Ypsilanti.

71. Noah Elias Habeeb, "The Arabic Hour: Understanding Arab-American Media Activism and Community-Based Media" (master's thesis, Tufts University, 2018), 83–84.

72. Cable, "Forging Her Own Path."

73. Acland et al., *Useful Cinema,* 4.

74. Charles A. O'Reilly III and Michael L. Tushman, "Ambidexterity as a Dynamic Capability: Resolving the Innovator's Dilemma," *Research in Organizational Behavior* 28 (2008): 185–206.

## 2. From Grassroots to Mass Media

1. Duncan Campbell, "Film-Maker David Koff on His Radical Documentary Occupied Palestine," *The Guardian,* May 1, 2013, https://www.theguardian.com/film/2013/may/01/david-koff-documentary-occupied-palestine; John Stanley, "'Occupied Palestine' / The Arab Point of View of the Israeli Occupation," *San Francisco Chronicle,* April 6, 1986.

2. Herb, "Film Reviews: Reviewed at Frisco Fest—Occupied Palestine," *Variety,* November 4, 1981, 26.

3. For more on the debates over the categorization of Palestinian films, see Umayyah Cable, "A Film By Any Other Name? Palestinian Cultural Authenticity and the Politics of Categorization," *Palestine in America* 1, no. 14 (February 2023); Umayyah Cable, "Projections of Palestine: Negotiating Diasporic Palestinian Identity in the United States Through Film Festival Participation," in *Sajjilu Arab American: A Reader in SWANA Studies,* ed. Louise Cainkar, Pauline Homsi Vinson, and Amira Jarmakani (Syracuse University Press, 2022).

4. For studies on the televisual, editorial, and filmic representation of Palestine and Palestinians in the United States, see Melani McAlister, *Epic Encounters: Culture, Media, and U.S. Interests in the Middle East Since 1945* (University of California Press, 2005); Luke Mathew Peterson, *Palestine-Israel in the Print News Media: Contending Discourses* (Routledge, 2015); Jack G. Shaheen, *Reel Bad Arabs: How Hollywood Vilifies a People* (Interlink, 2012).

5. Herb, "Film Reviews."

6. For an extensive history of Palestinian revolutionary and solidarity cinema from the 1960s to the 1980s, see Nadia Yaqub, *Palestinian Cinema in the Days of Revolution* (University of Texas Press, 2021).

7. Stuart Hall uses the phrase "racialized regime of representation" to describe the work that racial stereotyping performs in the constructions of "otherness" and the hegemonic power such representations wield for the purpose of social exclusion. Stuart Hall, Jessica Evans, and Sean Nixon, eds., *Representation: Cultural Representations and Signifying Practices* (Sage, 2013).

8. Helen Hatab Samhan, "Not Quite White: Race Classification and the Arab American Experince," in *Arabs in America: Building a New Future,* ed. Michael W. Suleiman (Temple University Press, 1999), 211–12.

9. Nadine Naber, *Arab America: Gender, Cultural Politics, and Activism* (New York University Press, 2012), 30–32.

10. Dale Maharidge, *The Coming White Minority: California's Eruptions and America's Future* (Times Books, 1996); Naber, *Arab America,* 59–60.

11. Sarah M. A. Gualtieri, *Arab Routes: Pathways to Syrian California* (Stanford University Press, 2019).

12. According to the US Census Bureau's 2005–2009 American Community Survey, California has the largest Arab American population in the United States. According to 2000 census data, the national average percentage of people who self-identify as Arab was 0.4%. In the San Francisco Bay Area the percentage of self-identified Arab people ranged from 0.7% to 2.7%. California has the highest Palestinian-identified population; however, the Chicago area has the most concentrated community of Palestinian-identified people. US Census Bureau, "Census 2000 Brief: The Arab Population: 2000," accessed April 20, 2024, https://www.census.gov/library/publications/2003/dec/c2kbr-23.html; "Demographics," Arab American Institute, accessed April 20, 2024, https://www.aaiusa.org/demographics.

13. I thank Denise Khor for providing me with this concept during our time together as faculty fellows at the Charles Warren Center for Studies in American History at Harvard University. For more on "overlapping media publics," see Ronald N. Jacobs, "Media, Culture, and Civil Society," *Questions de communication* 29 (2016): 379–93.

14. Therese Poletti and Tom Paiva, *Art Deco San Francisco: The Architecture of Timothy Pflueger* (Princeton Architectural Press, 2008), 37.

15. Poletti and Paiva, *Art Deco San Francisco,* 37.

16. John Ward Anderson, "FBI Probes Attacks on Arab Group: FBI Probes for Rights Violations in Attacks Against Arab Group," *The Washington Post,* December 6, 1985; Eric Malnic, "Ex-JDL Activist Found Guilty in Bombing Death," *Los Angeles Times,* October 15, 1993.

17. Today, Frameline is the longest-running and largest LGBTQ+-themed film festival in the world, and it promotes a mission to "change the world

through the power of queer cinema." "About Frameline," accessed April 20, 2024, https://www.frameline.org/about/frameline/.

18. Aidin Vaziri, "A History of San Francisco's Castro Theatre," *San Francisco Chronicle,* June 22, 2022, accessed April 20, 2024, https://www.sfchronicle.com/projects/2022/san-francisco-castro-theatre-timeline-history/; Poletti and Paiva, *Art Deco San Francisco,* 37.

19. Fredric Jameson was critiqued for arguing that Third World literature (and by extension, other cultural productions such as cinema) must primarily be understood as an allegory for national struggle and liberation. Fredric Jameson, *The Prison-House of Language: A Critical Account of Structuralism and Russian Formalism* (Princeton University Press, 1974); Fredric Jameson, "Third-World Literature in the Era of Multinational Capitalism," *Social Text,* no. 15 (1986): 65–88.

20. Hamid Naficy, *An Accented Cinema: Exilic and Diasporic Filmmaking* (Princeton University Press, 2001), 10–16.

21. Terri Ginsberg, *Visualizing the Palestinian Struggle: Towards a Critical Analytic of Palestine Solidarity Film* (Springer, 2016); Campbell, "Film-Maker David Koff"; Joumana El Alaoui, "'I Wanted to Make a Film [on] the Conflict between Zionism and the Palestinians': David Koff on His Groundbreaking 1981 Film 'Occupied Palestine' (Updated)," Mondoweiss, June 18, 2013, https://mondoweiss.net/2013/06/palestinians-groundbreaking-palestine/.

22. Ginsberg, *Visualizing the Palestinian Struggle,* 3.

23. Ginsberg makes this claimed based on an interview with Koff in 2013. However, when I reached out to Jabara via email to confirm this, he had no recollection of communications with Koff. Ginsberg, *Visualizing the Palestinian Struggle,* 41.

24. One reason for my critical interrogation of Koff's knowledge of Arab studies and Arab American studies is because of his later contributions to these fields. For example, in the wake of *Occupied Palestine*'s contentious premiere and the aftermath of Israel's invasion of southern Lebanon in 1982, Koff himself contributed to the scholarly discourse on Palestine by publishing an annotated timeline of the Israeli invasion of Lebanon, as well as a review of Noam Chomsky's *The Fateful Triangle.* David Koff, "Chronology of the War in Lebanon and the Palestine-Israel Conflict, March–May 1983," *Journal of Palestine Studies* 12, no. 4 (1983): 102–53; David Koff, "Chronology of the War in Lebanon, June–August 1983," *Journal of Palestine Studies* 13, no. 1 (1983): 137–63; David Koff, "Chronology of the War in Lebanon, September–November, 1983," *Journal of Palestine Studies* 13, no. 2 (1984): 127–57; David Koff, review of *The Fateful Triangle: The United States, Israel and the Palestinians,* by Noam Chomsky, *Journal of Palestine Studies* 13, no. 3 (1984): 120–24.

25. The filmstrip does not provide a citation for this US$113 billion figure. However, this number falls within the range that scholars and experts have put forth when attempting to quantify and estimate the dispossession of

Palestine in financial terms. For example, Brynen notes that in 1962 the United Nations Conciliation Commission for Palestine (UNCCP) drafted a report based on official records from the period of the British Mandate of Palestine, along with reports directly from refugees, to estimate the value of refugee property (land only) at $825 million, which would, in his estimation, be "worth around USD 8.6 billion in 2016, or almost USD 80 billion if UNCCP upper estimates of moveable property are included and a 3 per cent annual real rate of return is applied (after inflation)." In a 2008 study commissioned by the PLO's Negotiations Support Unit, Senechal considered a much wider definition of "property" to include not only land but businesses, holy sites, moveable assets such as financial accounts and personal property, and loss of employment and livelihoods at US$3.3 billion in 1948. That US$3.3 billion figure rises to US$310 billion (in 2008) when inflation and compound interest are applied. While these numbers are wildly disparate, it is reasonable to believe that even the highest estimate in the aforementioned figures reflects a substantial undervalue. According to a United Nations Trade and Development report from 2019, there is an estimated US$524 billion worth of oil and natural gas reservoirs off the coast of the Gaza Strip. While Palestine could not lay claim to the entirety of those reservoirs (as they overlap with other Mediterranean nations), those oil and natural gas resources are not factored in to the previous estimates of the value of Palestinian property losses. Rex Brynen, "Compensation for Palestinian Refugees: Law, Politics and Praxis," *Israel Law Review* 51, no. 1 (March 2018): 29–46. Thierry J Senechal, "Valuation of Palestinian Refugee Losses," Palestine Liberation Organization, 2008, https://web.archive.org/web/20240912220146/http://www.ajtransparency.com/files/2767.pdf; Atif A. Kubursi, "Palestinian Losses in 1948: Calculating Refugee Compensation," accessed September 25, 2024, https://prrn.mcgill.ca/research/papers/kubursi.htm.

26. Kenneth Burke, *Counter-Statement* (University of California Press, 1968), 124.

27. Ginsberg, *Visualizing the Palestinian Struggle*. 43.

28. Edward W. Said, *The Question of Palestine* (Vintage, 1992).

29. Ginsberg, *Visualizing the Palestinian Struggle*, 46, 49.

30. Letter to Nabila Shehadeh from Khalil Jahshan, September 7, 1983. Box 5, file 13, Assocation of Arab American University Graduates Collection, Eastern Michigan University, Ypsilanti.

31. Patricia Aufderheide, "Public Television and the Public Sphere," *Critical Studies in Media Communication* 8, no. 2 (1991): 168–83; Lewis A. Friedland, "Public Television as Public Sphere: The Case of the Wisconsin Collaborative Project," *Journal of Broadcasting & Electronic Media* 39, no. 2 (March 1995): 147–76; William Hoynes, *Public Television for Sale: Media, the Market, and the Public Sphere* (Routledge, 2019).

32. Laurie Ouellette, *Viewers Like You: How Public TV Failed the People*

(Columbia University Press, 2002); Allison Perlman, *Public Interests: Media Advocacy and Struggles over US Television* (Rutgers University Press, 2016).

33. Ouellette, *Viewers Like You,* 105–39.

34. Ouellette, *Viewers Like You,* 107–8.

35. Ouellette, *Viewers Like You,* 111.

36. Jay Sharbutt, "Latest 'Theme Night' on PBS Anathema to Some," *Los Angeles Times,* April 14, 1986.

37. John Corry, "TV View; Balanced Journalism Needn't Preclude a Point of View: [Review]," *The New York Times,* April 20, 1986.

38. The exact number remains contested. Ilan Pappe, *The Ethnic Cleansing of Palestine* (Oneworld, 2007).

39. Although these local debates were mentioned in news coverage over the *Flashpoint* controversy, I have failed to acquire any video documentation of such segments, with one exception. My mother, Layla Hijab Cable, was a participant in the local debate produced by WGBH, Boston's PBS station. My access to that documentation is due entirely to her fastidious use of our home VCR to record any and all things Palestine related that made their way into our living room via both network and public television.

40. Khalidi was not actually a member of the AAUG at the time, but he was personally close with Ibrahim Abu-Lughod. It is my understanding that the AAUG speakers' bureau sometimes functioned less as an official go-to list and more as a scholar-activist phone tree wherein people were tapped for various media engagements based on interpersonal and academic relationships. This is perhaps one of the contributing reasons why the AAUG weathered accusations of elitism.

41. Umayyah Cable, "Forging Her Own Path: An Interview with Scholar-Activist Elaine Hagopian," in *Arab American Women: Representation and Refusal,* ed. Michael W. Suleiman, Suad Joseph, and Louise Cankar (Syracuse University Press, 2021), 311.

42. Sharbutt, "Latest 'Theme Night.'"

43. Corry, "TV View."

44. Corry, "TV View."

45. Corry, "TV View."

46. Scott Blakey, "KQED Mideast Program Sets Off Controversy: [FINAL Edition]," *San Francisco Chronicle,* March 14, 1986; John Carmody, "WNET Forgoes Mideast Program," *Newsday,* March 14, 1986.

47. Steve Daley, "PBS Strikes Balance with 3 Unbalanced Films," *Chicago Tribune,* April 10, 1986.

48. Stanley, "'Occupied Palestine.'"

49. Edward W. Said, "Permission to Narrate," *Journal of Palestine Studies* 13, no. 3 (1984): 27–48.

50. Joan Peters famously argued this in *From Time Immemorial,* which has since been refuted by scholars such as Rashid Khalidi. See Rashid Khalidi,

*Palestinian Identity: The Construction of Modern National Consciousness* (Columbia University Press, 2009).

51. Cable, "A Film By Any Other Name?"; Umayyah Cable, "'Farha' and the Claustrophobic State of Palestinian Cinema," Institute for Palestine Studies, accessed April 15, 2024, https://www.palestine-studies.org/en/node/1653553.

## 3. An *Uprising* at *The Perfect Moment*

1. Patti Hartigan, "Mapplethorpe Show to Open amid Controversy: ICA Founder Raps Selections," *The Boston Globe,* August 1, 1990.

2. Patti Hartigan, "'Censorship' Is Again the Cry in ICA Flap," *The Boston Globe,* April 26, 1991.

3. I use the phrase *gay and lesbian* throughout this chapter in keeping with the nomenclature of the 1990s and use the now more commonplace designation of *LGBTQ+* when referring to contemporary sexual and gender identities.

4. Lisa Lowe, *Immigrant Acts: On Asian American Cultural Politics* (Duke University Press, 1996), 27–30.

5. Jodi Melamed, "The Spirit of Neoliberalism: From Racial Liberalism to Neoliberal Multiculturalism," *Social Text* 24, no. 4 (December 1, 2006): 2.

6. Melamed, "The Spirit of Neoliberalism," 1–3.

7. Evelyn Alsultany, *Arabs and Muslims in the Media: Race and Representation after 9/11* (New York University Press, 2012), 12.

8. Ella Shohat and Robert Stam derive this definition from Michael Denning's discussion of political correctness as "a bizarre kind of superego" that mediates between contentious social movements. Ella Shohat and Robert Stam, *Unthinking Eurocentrism: Multiculturalism and the Media* (Routledge, 2014), 341–42; Michael Denning, "The Academic Left and the Rise of Cultural Studies," *Radical History Review* 1992, no. 54 (October 1, 1992): 21–47.

9. Lisa Duggan, *The Twilight of Equality?: Neoliberalism, Cultural Politics, and the Attack on Democracy* (Beacon, 2012), 50.

10. John Greyson, "Pinkface," *Camera Obscura: Feminism, Culture, and Media Studies* 27, no. 2 (2012): 145–53; Gil Z. Hochberg, "Introduction: Israelis, Palestinians, Queers: Points of Departure," *GLQ: A Journal of Lesbian and Gay Studies* 16, no. 4 (October 1, 2010): 493–516; Michael Connors Jackman and Nishant Upadhyay, "Pinkwatching Israel, Whitewashing Canada: Queer (Settler) Politics and Indigenous Colonization in Canada," *Women's Studies Quarterly* 42, no. 3/4 (2014): 195–210; Colleen Jankovic, "'You Can't Film Here': Queer Political Fantasy and Thin Critique of Israeli Occupation in *The Bubble*," *Canadian Journal of Film Studies* 22, no. 2 (2013): 97–119; Colleen Jankovic and Nadia Awad, "Queer/Palestinian Cinema: A Critical Conversation on Palestinian Queer and Women's Filmmaking," *Camera Obscura: Feminism, Culture, and Media Studies* 27, no. 2 (2012): 135–43; Jasbir K. Puar,

*Terrorist Assemblages: Homonationalism in Queer Times* (Duke University Press, 2018); Jasbir Puar, "Citation and Censorship: The Politics of Talking About the Sexual Politics of Israel," *Feminist Legal Studies* 19, no. 2 (2011): 133–42; Sarah Schulman, "Israel and 'Pinkwashing,'" *The New York Times,* November 22, 2011; Sarah Schulman, *Israel/Palestine and the Queer International* (Duke University Press, 2012); Amalia Ziv, "Performative Politics in Israeli Queer Anti-Occupation Activism," *GLQ: A Journal of Lesbian and Gay Studies* 16, no. 4 (2010): 537–56.

11. For more information on LGBTQ+ Arab American and antipinkwashing activism, see Umayyah Cable, "Coming Out for Community, Coming Out for the Cause: Arab American Lesbian Feminist Activism in the 1990s." *Meridians* 23, no. 2 (October 2024): 465–89.

12. Salim Tamari, "A Farcical Moment? Nabulsi Exceptionalism and the 1908 Ottoman Revolution," *Jerusalem Quarterly* 60 (2014): 92.

13. Ella Shohat, "Post-Third-Worldist Culture: Gender, Nation, and the Cinema," in *Feminist Genealogies, Colonial Legacies, Democratic Futures,* ed. M. Jacqui Alexander and Chandra Talpade Mohanty (Routledge, 1997), 183–209.

14. Hamid Dabashi, ed., "Introduction," *Dreams of a Nation: On Palestinian Cinema* (Verso, 2006), 11.

15. Gil Z. Hochberg, *Visual Occupations: Violence and Visibility in a Conflict Zone* (Duke University Press, 2015), 7.

16. Hartigan, "Mapplethorpe Show," 16.

17. Richard Bolton, *Culture Wars: Documents from the Recent Controversies in the Arts* (New Press, 1992), 344.

18. Patti Hartigan, "Artists Criticize ICA Restriction," *The Boston Globe,* July 11, 1990, 43.

19. Hartigan, "Artists Criticize ICA Restriction," 43.

20. Steven Epstein, "Specificities: AIDS Activism and the Retreat from the 'Genocide' Frame," *Social Identities* 3, no. 3 (October 1, 1997): 415–38.

21. John D. H. Downing, *Radical Media: Rebellious Communication and Social Movements* (Sage, 2000); Alexandra Juhasz, *AIDS TV: Identity, Community, and Alternative Video* (Duke University Press, 1995).

22. Jih-Fei Cheng, "How to Survive: AIDS and Its Afterlives in Popular Media," *Women's Studies Quarterly* 44, no. 1/2 (2016): 74.

23. Marcia Pally, "Cincinnati: City Under Siege," in *War of Words: The Censorship Debate,* ed. George Beahm (Andrews McMeel, 1993), 127.

24. Kobena Mercer, "Just Looking for Trouble: Robert Mapplethorpe and Fantasies of Race," *Cultural Politics* 11 (1997): 240–54; Kobena Mercer and Isaac Julien, "True Confessions," in *Black Male: Representations of Masculinity in Contemporary American Art*, ed. Thelma Golden (Whitney Museum of Art, 1994), 191–200.

25. Jodi Melamed, "Reading Tehran in *Lolita,*" in *Strange Affinities: The*

*Gender and Sexual Politics of Comparative Racialization,* ed. Grace Kyungwon Hong and Roderick A. Ferguson (Duke University Press, 2011), 88.

26. Chandan Reddy, *Freedom with Violence: Race, Sexuality, and the US State* (Duke University Press, 2011), 5.

27. Matthew Gilbert, "Poignant Views at the ICA," *The Boston Globe,* May 1, 1991, 44.

28. Gilbert, "Poignant Views at the ICA," 44.

29. Gilbert, "Poignant Views at the ICA," 44.

30. Elia Suleiman and Jayce Salloum, *Introduction to the End of an Argument,* Canada, 1990.

31. Patti Hartigan, "Grossman Quits ICA Board over Palestinian Films," *The Boston Globe,* April 24, 1991, 48.

32. Hartigan, "Grossman Quits ICA Board," 43.

33. Catherine Willford, "After Boston Censorship Attempts, Palestinian Film Series Rescheduled," *The Washington Report on Middle East Affairs* (American Educational Trust, October 1991), 72.

34. Hartigan, "Grossman Quits ICA Board," 48.

35. Nadine Naber, Eman Desouky, and Lina Baroudi, "The Forgotten -ism: An Arab American Women's Perspective on Zionism, Racism, and Sexism," in *Color of Violence: The INCITE! Anthology,* edited by INCITE! Women of Color Against Violence (Duke University Press, 2016), 102–3.

36. Grossman quoted in Hartigan, "Grossman Quits ICA Board," 48.

37. Naber, Desouky, and Baroudi, "The Forgotten -ism," 10.

38. Sussman quoted in Patti Hartigan, "Panel to Join Palestinian Series at ICA," *The Boston Globe,* April 25, 1991.

39. "Museum Accused of Censorship," *Telegram & Gazette,* May 3, 1991, 8.

40. Willford, "After Boston Censorship Attempts," 72.

41. Patti Hartigan, "Remaining Film Pulled from ICA Series," *The Boston Globe,* May 3, 1991, 47.

42. John Reinstein quoted in Hartigan, "Remaining Film Pulled from ICA Series," 47.

43. Gerald Peary, "Off-Balance at the ICA," letter to the editor, *The Boston Globe,* May 3, 1991.

44. Allan Parachini, "NEA Faces New Controversy in New York Show Art: National Endowment Seeks Voluntary Return of $10,000 to Quiet Criticism," *Los Angeles Times,* November 6, 1989.

45. Susan Wyatt quoted in Patti Hartigan, "Palestinian Film Series Is Withdrawn from ICA," *The Boston Globe,* May 2, 1991, 12.

46. Susan Wyatt quoted in Hartigan, "Panel to Join Palestinian Series at ICA," 69.

47. Suleiman quoted in Hartigan, "'Censorship,'" 76.

48. Suleiman quoted in Hartigan, "Palestinian Film Series Is Withdrawn from ICA," 1.

49. Achille Mbembe, "Necropolitics," trans. Libby Meintjes, *Public Culture* 15, no. 1 (2003): 11–40.

50. Epstein, "Specificities," 415.

51. Richard Arens, review of *Israel in Lebanon: The Report of the International Commission to Enquire into Reported Violations of International Law by Israel During Its Invasion of the Lebanon* by Seán MacBride et al., *Journal of Palestine Studies* 13, no. 1 (October 1, 1983): 102–8; Edward W. Said, "Permission to Narrate," *Journal of Palestine Studies* 13, no. 3 (1984): 27–48; Rosemary Sayigh and Julie Peteet, "Between Two Fires: Palestinian Women in Lebanon," in *Caught Up in Conflict: Women's Responses to Political Strife*, ed. Rosemary Ridd and Helen Callaway (Red Globe, 1986), 106–37.

52. Hartigan, "Palestinian Film Series Is Withdrawn from ICA," 1.

53. Sussman quoted in Hartigan, "Remaining Film Pulled from ICA Series," 47.

54. Hartigan, "Palestinian Film Series Is Withdrawn from ICA," 12.

55. Hartigan, "Remaining Film Pulled from ICA Series," 47.

56. Suleiman and Shohat had been in conversation long before the ICA event and continued to work together after it. Shohat was credited for advising on *Intifada: Introduction to the End of an Argument.* Furthermore, Shohat's essay "Reflections of an Arab-Jew," written during the First Gulf War for the liberal weekly *Village Voice,* was censored. However, Suleiman with Shohat incorporated key segments of that censored piece into another of Suleiman's films, *Homage by Assassination* (1992). See Ella Shohat, *On the Arab-Jew, Palestine, and Other Displacements: Selected Writings of Ella Shohat* (Pluto Press, 2017).

57. Shohat, *On the Arab-Jew, Palestine, and Other Displacements,* 186–88.

58. Ella Shohat, letter to Institute of Contemporary Art, June 11, 1991, private archive of Ella Shohat.

59. Shohat, *On the Arab-Jew, Palestine, and Other Displacements,* 7.

60. Shohat, *On the Arab-Jew, Palestine, and Other Displacements,* 11.

61. Sami Shalom Chetrit, *Intra-Jewish Conflict in Israel: White Jews, Black Jews* (Routledge, 2009); Ella Shohat, "Sephardim in Israel: Zionism from the Standpoint of Its Jewish Victims," *Social Text,* no. 19/20 (1988): 1–35.

62. Shohat quoted in Evelyn Alsultany, "Arab Jews, Diasporas, and Multicultural Feminism: An Interview with Ella Shohat," in *Arab and Arab American Feminisms: Gender, Violence, and Belonging,* ed. Rabab Abdulhadi, Evelyn Alsultany, and Nadine Naber (Syracuse University Press, 2015), 48.

63. Shohat, *On the Arab-Jew, Palestine, and Other Displacements,* 33.

64. Matthew Gilbert, "Israeli Filmmakers View Palestinians with Sympathetic Eye," *The Boston Globe,* June 13, 1991, 85.

65. Shohat quoted in Patti Hartigan, "Curator Withdraws from ICA Series," *The Boston Globe,* June 12, 1991, 76.

66. Shohat quoted in Hartigan, "Curator Withdraws from ICA Series," 76.

67. Patti Hartigan, "ICA Announces That Film Series Will Go On," *The Boston Globe,* June 13, 1991, 85.

68. Hartigan, "Curator Withdraws from ICA Series," 76.

69. Puar, *Terrorist Assemblages,* 204.

70. Emily K. Hobson, *Lavender and Red: Liberation and Solidarity in the Gay and Lesbian Left* (University of California Press, 2016), 195.

71. Akiva Tor quoted in Matthew S. Bajko, "LGBT Israeli Festival Draws Protests," *Bay Area Reporter,* April 14, 2010, https://www.ebar.com/story.php?ch=news&id=240639; Akiva Tor quoted in Tony K. LeTigre, "Protesters Call Out Frameline over Israeli Sponsorship," *Bay Area Reporter,* June 22, 2011, https://www.ebar.com/story.php?ch=news&id=241673.

## 4. It's an Honor Just to Be Nominated

1. That same evening, members of the Jewish Defense League (JDL) picketed outside of the Academy Awards ceremony, complete with burning Vanessa Redgrave in effigy. Bruce Fretts, "Oscars Rewind: The Most Political Ceremony in Academy History," *The New York Times,* January 11, 2019, https://www.nytimes.com/2019/01/11/movies/oscars-1978-politics-vanessa-redgrave.html.

2. Fred Zinnemann Papers, Margaret Herrick Library, Los Angeles, CA.

3. Anthony Shaw and Giora Goodman, *Hollywood and Israel: A History* (Columbia University Press, 2022), 11.

4. In her exhaustive history of the revolutionary period of Palestinian cinema, Nadia Yaqub makes the case that Palestinian cinema of that era "falls squarely within the realm of third cinema . . . as noncommercial endeavors, third cinema would actively avoid any dependence on star actors or directors." The PLO's cozy relationship with Redgrave (a major star of both stage and screen) is an early example of how the Palestinian cinematic movement was not solely devoted to Third Cinema and would indeed embrace stardom and celebrity, especially with the onset of the fourth period of Palestinian cinema and the rise of Palestinian narrative cinema. Nadia Yaqub, *Palestinian Cinema in the Days of Revolution* (University of Texas Press, 2021), 50–51.

5. Evelyn Alsultany, *Broken: The Failed Promise of Muslim Inclusion* (New York University Press, 2022), 15.

6. Nancy Wang Yuen, *Reel Inequality: Hollywood Actors and Racism* (Rutgers University Press, 2016); Robert Boucaut, "'Oscar': An Institutional and Contested Persona Reading of the Academy Awards," *Persona Studies* 7, no. 1 (July 2021): 6–19.

7. James F. English, *The Economy of Prestige: Prizes, Awards, and the Circulation of Cultural Value* (Harvard University Press, 2005); James McMahon, *The Political Economy of Hollywood: Capitalist Power and Cultural Production* (Routledge, 2022); Vincent Mosco, *The Political Economy of Communication:*

*Towards Alternative Worlds* (Sage, 2009); Janet Wasko, "Critiquing Hollywood: The Political Economy of Motion Pictures," in *A Concise Handbook of Movie Industry Economics,* ed. Charles C. Moul (Cambridge University Press, 2005).

8. This argument is informed by the reading of Yuen's work on racism in Hollywood alongside the work of Keith Feldman, who argues that post–World War II anti-Black racism is deeply informed by US imperial politics and commitments to Zionism. Keith P. Feldman, *A Shadow over Palestine: The Imperial Life of Race in America* (University of Minnesota Press, 2015); Yuen, *Reel Inequality.*

9. For more on the relationships between social justice commodification, social media "virtue signaling," and conspicuous consumption, see Elaine Wallace, Isabel Buil, and Leslie de Chernatony, "'Consuming Good' on Social Media: What Can Conspicuous Virtue Signalling on Facebook Tell Us About Prosocial and Unethical Intentions?," *Journal of Business Ethics* 162, no. 3 (March 1, 2020): 577–92; Roopali Mukherjee and Sarah Banet-Weiser, *Commodity Activism: Cultural Resistance in Neoliberal Times* (New York University Press, 2012).

10. Brian Schaefer, "The Epic Battle in Hollywood over the Holy Land," *Moment Magazine* (blog), March 15, 2018, https://momentmag.com/the-epic-battle-in-hollywood-over-the-holy-land/; "'Occupied Palestine' Doc'y Finds New Life 30 Years After a Bombthreat Killed Its Release," *Mondoweiss,* October 16, 2013, https://mondoweiss.net/2013/10/occupied-palestine-bomb threat/; Esmat Elhalaby, "Los Angeles Intifada," *Michigan Quarterly Review* 59, no. 4 (2020): 661–74; Abdeen Jabara and Joe Stork, "Political Violence Against Arab-Americans," *MERIP Middle East Report,* no. 143 (1986): 36–38, https://doi.org/10.2307/3012014.

11. For additional analysis of Redgrave's speech, see Nurith Gertz and George Khleifi, *Palestinian Cinema: Landscape, Trauma, and Memory* (Indiana University Press, 2008); Terri Ginsberg, *Visualizing the Palestinian Struggle: Towards a Critical Analytic of Palestine Solidarity Film* (Springer, 2016); Shaw and Goodman, *Hollywood and Israel.*

12. There were doubts about the authenticity of Lillian Hellman's story. It is now widely believed that Hellman appropriated the story of real-life antifascist activist Muriel Gardiner. Tim Stokes, "Muriel Gardiner: The Heiress Who Saved Countless Lives," *BBC News,* September 18, 2021, https://www.bbc.com/news/uk-england-london-58399839; Katya Cengel, "The American Heiress Who Risked Everything to Resist the Nazis," *Smithsonian Magazine,* March 2023, https://www.smithsonianmag.com/history/american-heiress-risked-everything-resist-nazis-180981554/.

13. Thirty years later, in fall 2009 Jane Fonda would go on to sign an open letter to the Toronto International Film Festival in protest of the festival's normalization of Israel in the wake of Israel's bombing of Gaza during Operation Cast Lead from December 2008 to January 2009. When Fonda became the target of Zionist ire for signing the letter, she withdrew her support,

stating that statement's language was "unnecessarily inflammatory" and that she had "signed the letter without reading it carefully enough, without asking myself if some of the wording wouldn't exacerbate the situation rather than bring about constructive dialogue." Jane Fonda quoted in Chris McGreal, "US Actor Jane Fonda Backs Away from Israel Row at Toronto Film Festival," *The Guardian,* September 16, 2009, https://www.theguardian.com/film/2009/sep/16/toronto-festival-israel-tel-aviv.

14. Fretts, "Oscars Rewind."

15. Elhalaby, "Los Angeles Intifada."

16. Memorandum of meeting between FZ, Vanessa, and Alvin, Fred Zinnemann Papers.

17. Memorandum of meeting between FZ, Vanessa, and Alvin, Fred Zinnemann Papers.

18. Transcription of articles from the *New York Post* and *Daily News,* Fred Zinnemann Papers.

19. "Fox Refuses JDL Demands on 'Julia,' Redgrave Boycott," *Hollywood Reporter,* January 27, 1978, Vanessa Redgrave subject file, Margaret Herrick Library, Los Angeles.

20. "Feedback, Redgrave, 'The Palestinian,' and the Jews," *Los Angeles Times,* January 29, 1978, Vanessa Redgrave subject file, Margaret Herrick Library, Los Angeles.

21. "SAG Supports 20th Century Fox Stance over Redgrave," *Hollywood Reporter,* February 3, 1978, Vanessa Redgrave subject file, Margaret Herrick Library, Los Angeles.

22. Twentieth Century Fox's proposed post-Oscar statement on Redgrave, Fred Zinnemann Papers.

23. "1977 (50th) Academy Awards, Actress in a Supporting Role," Academy Awards Acceptance Speech Database, accessed April 18, 2024, https://aaspeechesdb.oscars.org/link/050-4/.

24. Fretts, "Oscars Rewind."

25. Emphasis mine. "1977 (50th) Academy Awards, Writing (Screenplay—based on material from another medium)," Academy Awards Acceptance Speech Database, accessed April 18, 2024, https://aaspeechesdb.oscars.org/link/050-21/.

26. Memorandum of meeting between FZ, Vanessa, and Alvin, Fred Zinnemann Papers.

27. For a detailed history of how the PFU was established, see Khadijeh Habashneh, *Knights of Cinema: The Story of the Palestine Film Unit,* trans. Nadine Fattaleh (Palgrave Macmillan, 2023).

28. Yaqub, *Palestinian Cinema in the Days of Revolution,* 66.

29. Yaqub, *Palestinian Cinema in the Days of Revolution,* 134–41.

30. For an oral history of the Palestine Film Unit, see Habashneh, *Knights of Cinema.*

31. Edward W. Said, *Dreams of a Nation: On Palestinian Cinema,* ed. Hamid Dabashi (Verso Books, 2006).

32. The PFU archive was later "discovered" in the Israeli military archive. Rona Sela, "Seized in Beirut: The Plundered Archives of the Palestinian Cinema Institution and Cultural Arts Section," *Anthropology of the Middle East* 12, no. 1 (June 2017): 83–114, https://doi.org/10.3167/ame.2017.120107.

33. Edward Said, "Permission to Narrate," *Journal of Palestine Studies* 13, no. 3 (1984): 27–48.

34. Zygmunt Bauman famously argued that the Holocaust was a distinctly modern phenomenon in that it was one of the hallmarks of modernity—bureaucracy—that enabled the mass and efficient extermination of human life. Zygmunt Bauman, *Modernity and the Holocaust* (Cornell University Press, 1989).

35. "Rules, 2002 (75th) Academy Awards," Academy Awards Collection, Margaret Herrick Library Digital Collections, accessed September 12, 2022, https://digitalcollections.oscars.org/digital/collection/p15759coll9/id/625/rec/6.

36. Michael Posner, "Oscar Draws Ire for Snubbing Palestinian Film," *The Globe and Mail,* December 19, 2002; Phinjo Gombu and Rob Salem, "Foreign Films Get a Snub; Works from Three Countries Not Eligible for Award Decision Prompts Outcry over Academy Rules," *Toronto Star,* December 16, 2002.

37. Lorenza Munoz, "Palestinian Film Is Ineligible for Oscar Consideration," *Los Angeles Times,* December 14, 2002.

38. "Rules, 2002 (75th) Academy Awards."

39. Gertz and Khleifi, *Palestinian Cinema,* 36.

40. Geoffrey W. Melada, "The Politics of Art," *Jewish Exponent,* January 9, 2003.

41. Pavlik quoted in Melada, "The Politics of Art."

42. Klein quoted in Melada, "The Politics of Art."

43. Pavlik quoted in Atira Winchester, "Arts in Brief," *Jerusalem Post,* October 23, 2003.

44. Yuen, *Reel Inequality.*

45. Sherri Muzher, "Academy Snubs Fine Palestinian Movie," *USA Today,* January 24, 2003.

46. Edward W. Said, *The Question of Palestine* (Vintage, 1992).

47. McMahon, *The Political Economy of Hollywood,* 3.

48. Such a statement is either true or false depending on how one defines the borders of Palestinian cinema. In 2003 Palestinian German filmmaker Lexi Alexander's *Johnny Flynton* was nominated for an Oscar in the category of Live Action Short. In terms of content and aesthetics, the film is not a Palestine film. However, as a woman and a Palestinian, Alexander's achievement of securing an Oscar nomination is monumental. Alexander's contributions to the larger project of Palestinian cinema is largely absent throughout

the scholarship in Palestinian film studies. This absence tells us a great deal about how the category of Palestinian cinema are constructed and policed.

49. In 2019, the Academy changed the title of this category to Best International Film; however, the eligibility rules remain the same. Alissa Wilkinson, "The Oscars' International Film Category Is Broken," *Vox*, February 4, 2020, https://www.vox.com/culture/2020/2/4/21042912/international-oscars-foreign-film-rules-language.

50. Box office data is no longer an adequate way to measure a film's popularity or success. The advent of streaming technology, direct-to-streaming releases (which became the norm during the early period of the Covid-19 pandemic), and streaming services' refusal to publicize comprehensive, quantitative streaming data under the auspice that it is proprietary data have obfuscated film viewership and revenue data. That said, technically speaking, Palestinian German filmmaker Lexi Alexander's film *Punisher: War Zone* (2008), a Marvel antihero movie from Lionsgate Entertainment, grossed just over $8 million at the US box office, whereas *Paradise Now* grossed only $1.45 million. "Paradise Now," Box Office Mojo, accessed April 20, 2024, https://www.boxofficemojo.com/title/tt0445620/; "Punisher: War Zone," Box Office Mojo, accessed April 20, 2024, https://www.boxofficemojo.com/title/tt0450314/.

51. Hollywood Foreign Press Association, email correspondence with author, February 23, 2024.

52. Parker quoted in Abigail Pogrebin, *Stars of David: Prominent Jews Talk About Being Jewish* (Crown, 2007), 149.

53. Daniel Dayan and Elihu Katz, *Media Events: The Live Broadcasting of History* (Harvard University Press, 1992), 43–53.

54. "Golden Globes U.S. Viewership 2024," Statista, accessed April 18, 2024, https://www.statista.com/statistics/266669/golden-globes--number-of-viewers/; John Koblin, "Golden Globe Viewership Continues Rapid Decline," *The New York Times*, January 11, 2023, https://www.nytimes.com/2023/01/11/business/media/golden-globe-viewership-declines.html.

55. Support for this claim is derived through a comparison of how the term *terrorism* was used in the British and American press prior to 1948. There are several news articles from the 1940s that describe activities of the Zionist paramilitary organizations as "terrorism." As of now, I have yet to find an academic article or book that historicizes this point. "Britain Asks Zionists to Disavow Terror," *The New York Times*, October 11, 1946; Fitzhugh Turner, "Group Portrait of the Stern Gang," *New York Herald Tribune (European Edition)*, October 6, 1948, International Herald Tribune Historical Archive, 1887–2013; Fitzhugh Turner, "Gurion Appeals for an Orderly Change of Rule," *New York Herald Tribune (European Edition)*, October 16, 1947, International Herald Tribune Historical Archive, 1887–2013.

56. Reggie Ugwu, "The Hashtag That Changed the Oscars: An

Oral History," *The New York Times*, February 6, 2020, https://www.nytimes.com/2020/02/06/movies/oscarssowhite-history.html.

57. For more on the history of Black and Palestinian solidarity, see Robin D. G. Kelley, "From the River to the Sea to Every Mountain Top: Solidarity as Worldmaking," *Journal of Palestine Studies* 48, no. 4 (August 1, 2019): 69–91, https://doi.org/10.1525/jps.2019.48.4.69; Michael R. Fischbach, *Black Power and Palestine: Transnational Countries of Color* (Stanford University Press, 2018); Michael R. Fischbach, *The Movement and the Middle East: How the Arab-Israeli Conflict Divided the American Left* (Stanford University Press, 2019); Alex Lubin, *Geographies of Liberation: The Making of an Afro-Arab Imaginary* (University of North Carolina Press, 2013).

58. What started out as a token of appreciation in the tradition of a party favor bag at a child's birthday party has ballooned into such high-value gifts that it has even prompted the Internal Revenue Service to intervene, legally classifying these gift bags as income and therefore taxable. Anosheh Azarmsa, "Award Shows, Gifts, and Taxes: A Criticism of the Tax Treatment of Celebrity Gift Bags," *Loyola of Los Angeles Entertainment Law Review* 28 (2007): 27.

59. Ali Abunimah, "Academy Disavows Oscars Gift Bag Featuring Israel Junket," *The Electronic Intifada* (blog), February 18, 2016, https://electronicintifada.net/blogs/ali-abunimah/academy-disavows-oscars-gift-bag-featuring-israel-junket.

60. Abunimah, "Academy Disavows Oscars Gift Bag."

61. Jennifer Lawrence chose to exercise the offer, but did not herself make the trip. Instead, she regifted the trip to her parents. Abunimah, "Academy Disavows Oscars Gift Bag"; "Israel Trying to 'Bribe' Hollywood Stars with Oscar 'Swag Bag,' BDSers Say," *The Jerusalem Post,* February 10, 2016, https://www.jpost.com/israel-news/israel-trying-to-bribe-hollywood-stars-with-oscar-swag-bag-bdsers-say-444460; Itay Stern, "And the Oscar Goes to . . . BDS? Hollywood Stars Snub Israel Swag Bag Visit," *Haaretz,* February 25, 2017, https://www.haaretz.com/israel-news/2017-02-25/ty-article-magazine/.premium/and-the-oscar-goes-to-bds-hollywood-stars-snub-israel-visit/0000017f-e6b4-df2c-a1ff-fef544bc0000.

62. "Ramy Youssef Calls for a Gaza Cease-Fire on the Red Carpet at the Oscars," *ABC7 Los Angeles,* March 11, 2024, https://abc7.com/ramy-youssef-red-carpet-interview-cease-fire-gaza/14511608/.

63. "2023 (96th) Academy Awards, International Feature Film," Academy Awards Acceptance Speech Database, https://aaspeechesdb.oscars.org/link/096-12/.

64. Barnett R. Rubin, "Jonathan Glazer on Gaza and the Holocaust," *The Nation,* March 19, 2024, https://www.thenation.com/article/world/israel-palestine-holocaust-antisemitism-war/.

65. Jordan Hoffman, "Pro-Israel 'Zone of Interest' Producer Len Blavatnik

Did Not Sign Off on Jonathan Glazer's Oscars Statement," *The Hollywood Reporter* (blog), March 13, 2024, https://www.hollywoodreporter.com/news/general-news/jonathan-glazer-oscars-speech-len-blavatnik-1235851549/.

## 5. Mainstreaming Palestine

1. Though controversy over the festival's placement at the MFA did not play out publicly, there was indeed tension behind the scenes when the festival first started. The MFA's film program is funded predominantly by the Carl and Ruth Shapiro Family Foundation, a prominent Boston-area Jewish philanthropic organization. Bo Smith, the MFA film program's director at the time the festival was founded, was integral to the establishment of the Boston Palestine Film Festival (BPFF) at the MFA, for it was he who agreed to the MFA's cosponsorship of the festival. According to festival organizer Suhail, Smith faced considerable blowback from MFA donors for this decision. Smith, who founded the film program at the MFA in 1987, left his position as head of film and video at the MFA in 2008 one year after the BPFF launched. Leslie Brokaw, "Farewell to a Leading Light of Film," *The Boston Globe,* October 26, 2008; Suhail, Boston Palestine Film Festival former festival organizer, personal interview with the author, October 25, 2013.

2. One caveat: For only the second time in the BPFF's history, the festival canceled its in-person screenings in the aftermath of October 7, 2023. Instead of its typical in-person exhibitions, the BPFF pivoted to streaming films online. The first time the festival pivoted to streaming delivery was in 2020 due to the Covid-19 pandemic. Nik DeCosta-Klipa, "Boston Palestine Film Festival Nixes Live Screenings in Wake of Israel-Hamas Conflict," *WBUR,* October 12, 2024, https://www.wbur.org/news/2023/10/12/boston-palestine-film-festival-israel-hamas-newsletter.

3. Eileen, Boston Palestine Film Festival organizer, telephone interview with the author, July 29, 2014.

4. For readings on small sample sizes, see M. L. Small, "'How Many Cases Do I Need?': On Science and the Logic of Case Selection in Field-Based Research," *Ethnography* 10, no. 1 (2009): 5–38, https://doi.org/10.1177/1466138108099586.

5. Anne Rasmussen, "The Sound of Culture, the Structure of Tradition: Musician's Work in Arab Detroit," in *Arab Detroit: From Margin to Mainstream,* ed. Nabeel Abraham and Andrew Shryock (Wayne State University Press, 2000), 552–53.

6. Evelyn Alsultany uses the term "field of meaning" to describe how government discourses collude with televisual representations of Arabs and Muslims to delimit a "range of acceptable ideas about the War on Terror," as well as ideas about Arabs and Muslim American subjectivity more broadly.

Evelyn Alsultany, *Arabs and Muslims in the Media: Race and Representation after 9/11* (New York University Press, 2012), 14.

7. Edward Said, "The Joan Peters Case," *Journal of Palestine Studies* 15 (1986): 144–50, https://www.jstor.org/stable/2536835.

8. "New Jewish Unit Plans University," *The New York Times,* August 20, 1946, 10.

9. David H. Gellis, "Summers Says Anti-Semitism Lurks Locally," *The Harvard Crimson,* September 19, 2002, http://www.thecrimson.com/article/2002/9/19/summers-says-anti-semitism-lurks-locally-university/.

10. Matt Rocheleau, "MIT's President Opposes Boycott," *The Boston Globe,* December 31, 2013.

11. "District Partnerships," Facing History and Ourselves, accessed March 23, 2014. https://web.archive.org/web/20140413005308/https://www.facinghistory.org/for-educators/school-anddistrict/district-partnerships.

12. Elaine Hagopian, "Reversing Injustice: On Utopian Activism," *Arab Studies Quarterly* 29, no. 3/4 (2007): 57–73.

13. For more on the relationship between the Holocaust, Palestine, and collective memory, see Michael Rothberg, *Multidirectional Memory: Remembering the Holocaust in the Age of Decolonization* (Stanford University Press, 2009).

14. For examples of the FHAO curriculum, see "Discussing the Israel-Palestine Conflict in the Classroom," Facing History and Ourselves, last updated June 16, 2023, accessed September 30, 2024, https://www.facinghistory.org/en-gb/resource-library/discussing-israel-palestine-conflict-classroom.

15. Leonard Zakim was also one of four local partisan activists, along with my mother, Layla Hijab Cable, who squared off in an additional debate segment produced by WGBH (the local Boston PBS station) to accompany the broadcast of *Flashpoint: Israel and the Palestinians*, as discussed in chapter 2.

16. Doug Hanchett and Cara Nissam, "The Boss May Honor Zakim at Dedication of Bridge," *Boston Herald,* October 4, 2002, 3.

17. "The Leonard P. Zakim Bunker Hill Memorial Bridge," https://leonardpzakimbunkerhillbridge.org/.

18. Maryssa Cook-Obregon and Katherine Hanna, "6th Annual Boston Palestine Film Festival Set for October 5–13, 2012," press release, Boston Palestine Film Festival, October, 2012.

19. Nadine Naber, *Arab America: Gender, Cultural Politics, and Activism* (New York University Press, 2012), 53.

20. Mary, Boston Palestine Film Festival organizer, telephone interview with the author, November 23, 2013.

21. Randa A. Kayyali, "How Is the AAUG Remembered? Restrained Nostalgia, Historical Omissions, and My Side of the Story," *Arab Studies Quarterly* 40, no. 1 (2018): 28.

22. Mary, telephone interview.
23. Mary, telephone interview.
24. Buzzy Gordon, "The Lost Lesson of Sabra and Shatilla," *The Forward,* October 5, 2007, A9; John Walcott and David C. Martin McClatchy, "This Summer's Mideast Crisis Feels like . . . An Echo of History. In 1982, Israel Sent Troops into Lebanon to Hunt Militants—and Disaster Followed," *The Sacramento Bee,* August 6, 2006, E1; Joshua Mitnick, "In Lebanon Strife, Memories of Past War for Israel," *The Christian Science Monitor,* July 25, 2006, 1; Scott Wilson, "Calls Mount for Olmert to Step Down; Blistering Critique of Israel's Role in Lebanon War Shakes His Governing Coalition," *The Washington Post,* May 2, 2007, A10.
25. Mary, telephone interview.
26. Luke Peterson, *Palestine-Israel in the Print News Media: Contending Discourses* (Routledge, 2015).
27. Miriam Hansen, *Babel and Babylon: Spectatorship in American Silent Film* (Harvard University Press, 1994), 208.
28. Cindy Hing-Yuk Wong, "Publics and Counterpublics: Rethinking Film Festivals as Public Spheres," in *Film Festivals: History, Theory, Method, Practice,* ed. Marike de Valck, Brendan Kredell, and Skadi Loist (Routledge, 2016), 87.
29. Ruba, Boston Palestine Film Festival former organizer, personal interview with the author, October 25, 2013.
30. Nadine Naber, "Introduction," in *Race and Arab Americans Before and After 9/11,* ed. Amaney Jamal and Nadine Naber (Syracuse University Press, 2008), 2.
31. Naber, "Introduction."
32. Ruba, personal interview.
33. Anton, Boston Palestine Film Festival audience member, personal interview with the author, October 24, 2013.
34. Suhail, personal interview.
35. Suhail, personal interview.
36. Mary, telephone interview.
37. Massachusetts Bay Transportation Authority, "Chapter 1: Introduction," *Ridership and Service Statistics,* July 2014.
38. For more on participatory culture, see Henry Jenkins, *Textual Poachers: Television Fans and Participatory Culture* (Routledge, 2012).
39. Alma, Boston Palestine Film Festival audience member, personal interview with the author, October 26, 2013.
40. Cindy Hing-Yuk Wong, *Film Festivals: Culture, People, and Power on the Global Screen* (Rutgers University Press, 2011), 163.
41. Wong, *Film Festivals,* 188.
42. The website for *Out in Israel* was taken offline shortly after the festival ended. However, the site is preserved through the Internet Archive:

"Welcome to Out in Israel," http://web.archive.org/web/20100401044850 /http://www.outinisraelsf.org/.

43. Skadi Loist and Ger Zielinski, "On the Development of Queer Film Festivals and Their Media Activism," in *Film Festival Yearbook 4: Film Festivals and Activism,* ed. Dina Iordanova and Leshu Torchin (St. Andrews Film Studies, 2012), 49–50.

44. Roya Rastegar, "Seeing Differently: The Curatorial Potential of Film Festival Programming," in *Film Festivals: History, Theory, Method, Practice,* ed. Marike de Valck, Brendan Kredell, and Skadi Loist (Routledge, 2016), 181. An extensive body of literature exists on the role of film festivals in social movements. See Sonia Tascon, *Activist Film Festivals: Towards a Political Subject* (Intellect, 2017); Wong, *Film Festivals*; Marike de Valck, Brendan Kredell, and Skadi Loist, eds., *Film Festivals: History, Theory, Method, Practice* (Routledge, 2016); Dina Iordanova and Leshu Torchin, eds., *Film Festival Yearbook 4: Film Festivals and Activism* (St. Andrews Film Studies, 2012).

45. Suhail, personal interview.

46. Michael Baxandall, *Painting and Experience in Fifteenth-Century Italy: A Primer in the Social History of Pictorial Style* (Oxford University Press, 1988); James Elkins, *Visual Studies: A Skeptical Introduction* (Routledge, 2003).

47. Suhail, personal interview.

48. Alma, personal interview.

49. Alma, personal interview.

50. Alexandra Juhasz, *AIDS TV: Identity, Community, and Alternative Video* (Duke University Press, 1995), 19.

51. Hansen, *Babel and Babylon,* 12–13.

52. Georgina, Boston Palestine Film Festival volunteer, personal interview with the author, October 21, 2013.

53. Ruba, personal interview.

54. Rachel, Jewish American filmmaker, personal interview with the author, October 23, 2013.

55. Rachel, personal interview.

56. Lamia, Boston Palestine Film Festival audience member, personal interview with the author, October 20, 2013.

57. Lamia, personal interview.

58. Rona Sela, "Seized in Beirut: The Plundered Archives of the Palestinian Cinema Institution and Cultural Arts Section," *Anthropology of the Middle East* 12, no. 1 (June 2017): 83–114; Nadia Yaqub, *Palestinian Cinema in the Days of Revolution* (University of Texas Press, 2021).

59. Eileen, telephone interview.

60. John, Boston Palestine Film Festival organizer, personal interview with the author, December 14, 2013.

61. Suha, Boston Palestine Film Festival volunteer, personal interview with the author, October 20, 2013.

62. In 2019 the MFA came under increased scrutiny after a predominantly Black and Brown group of middle school students on a field trip experienced multiple incidents of racism from both staff members and patrons. See Cristela Guerra, "The Boston Kids Who Experienced Racism at the MFA End the Year with a SneakerBall," WBUR, December 27, 2019, https://www.wbur.org/news/2019/12/27/sneakerball-helen-y-davis-mfa-racist-incident.

63. Boston Palestine Film Festival, "About: History," accessed May 23, 2014, https://bostonpalestinefilmfest.org/about/; Valck et al., *Film Festivals*; Iordanova and Torchin, *Film Festivals and Activism.*

64. Suhail, personal interview.

65. Suha, personal interview.

66. Mary, telephone interview.

67. Eileen, telephone interview.

68. See the previous chapter's discussion of Palestinian cinema and the Academy and Golden Globe Awards.

69. Suha, personal interview.

70. John, personal interview.

71. Georgina, personal interview.

72. Suhail, personal interview.

73. Valck et al., *Film Festivals.*

74. Mary, telephone interview.

75. Mary, telephone interview.

76. Mary, telephone interview.

77. "Mapping Segregation." *The New York Times,* July 8, 2015, accessed March 16, 2016, http://www.nytimes.com/interactive/2015/07/08/us/census-race-map.html.

78. Wong, *Film Festivals,* 164.

## Conclusion

1. "World Has Failed Gaza in 'Livestreamed Genocide', South Africa's Delegation Says at ICJ—Video," *The Guardian,* January 11, 2024, https://www.theguardian.com/world/video/2024/jan/11/world-has-failed-gaza-in-livestreamed-genocide-south-africas-delegation-says-at-icj-video.

2. "About Us," kuvrd, access September 30, 2024, https://kuvrd.ca/pages/about-us.

3. When this conclusion was first drafted in September 2023, the Project Palestine website stated that the company aims to "provide aid directly to fellow Palestinian civilians . . . [by] contributing to the livelihood of civilians while simultaneously bettering the local economy." By April 2024, this language was replaced with a vague blurb about "philanthropy and gratitude." "About Us & Our Work," https://projectps.co/pages/about-us, accessed

September 30, 2024; "About Us," https://projectpalestine.co/pages/about-us, accessed April 26, 2025.

4. Previous versions of the PaliRoots website listed several organizations, including the United Nations Relief and Works Agency, Zam Zam Water, the Palestinian Children's Relief Fund, Wafa House, Penny Appeal, and the Arab American Association of New York. As of April 2025, only the Middle East Children's Alliance remains listed as a recipient of PaliRoots philanthropy. "Philanthropy," https://www.paliroots.com/pages/philanthropy, accessed April 26, 2025.

5. When I first accessed the PaliRoots website in 2022, the first section of the brand's "Our Mission" page was titled "The PaliRoots Movement." This "movement" language has since been removed from the website, which itself has undergone a dramatic paring down. See the archived version: "Our Mission," https://web.archive.org/web/20220520125347/https://www.paliroots.com/pages/our-mission.

6. "Pessimism" here is informed by Joshua Foa Dienstag's discussion of cinema and pessimism in *Cinema Pessimism: A Political Theory of Representation and Reciprocity* (Oxford University Press, 2019).

7. Omar Barghouti, *BDS: Boycott, Divestment, Sanctions: The Global Struggle for Palestinian Rights* (Haymarket Books, 2011).

8. Sa'ed Atshan, *Queer Palestine and the Empire of Critique* (Stanford University Press, 2020).

9. An anonymous "anti-Imperialist diaspora media collective" known as Jisr Collective has been waging a series of written attacks and social media smear campaigns against prominent Palestinian activists and scholars. Targets of these attacks include any and all members of the BDS National Committee, especially cofounder Omar Barghouti, as well as lawyer and scholar Noura Erakat. Jisr Collective's primary criticism toward these individuals hinges on the issue of "normalization."

# Index

**Umayyah Cable** is assistant professor of American culture and film, television, and media at the University of Michigan, Ann Arbor.